# 1
# DEVOLUTION IN GREAT BRITAIN

**STUDIES IN HISTORY, ECONOMICS AND PUBLIC LAW**

EDITED BY THE FACULTY OF POLITICAL SCIENCE
OF COLUMBIA UNIVERSITY

Volume CXXIV]                    [Number 1

Whole Number 272

# DEVOLUTION IN GREAT BRITAIN

BY

WAN-HSUAN CHIAO

AMS PRESS
NEW YORK

COLUMBIA UNIVERSITY
STUDIES IN THE
SOCIAL SCIENCES

272

The Series was formerly known as
*Studies in History, Economics and Public Law.*

Reprinted with the permission of Columbia University Press
From the edition of 1926, New York
First AMS EDITION published 1969
Manufactured in the United States of America

Library of Congress Catalogue Card Number: 76-78010

AMS PRESS, INC.
NEW YORK, N. Y. 10003

# PREFACE

THE subject of devolution has been a much mooted question in England for the last quarter of a century, and since the War it has become increasingly important. On March 5, 1919, the subject was debated in the House of Lords, and on June 3 and 4, in the House of Commons which adopted a resolution in favor of the general principles of devolution. Pursuant to that resolution a Speaker's Conference was appointed in October of the same year to devise a practical scheme for the proposed change. In the Spring of 1920 the Conference adjourned and presented to the Prime Minister a Report in the form of a letter, containing certain principles agreed upon and two separate schemes for the organization of subordinate Legislatures. Although no definite action has as yet been taken by the House of Commons, the question is still a live issue and some action is possible when Parliament is forced to reconsider the question.

This being the present status of the problem, it is worthwhile to discuss the merits or demerits of the proposed change and to consider the probabilities of parliamentary action. Aside from the importance that devolution possesses with regard to the British Constitution, the subject also has a value for comparative study. Students of American Government are familiar with recent tendencies towards federal centralization. Devolution represents an opposite tendency in a country which has had a centralized constitution. May not such a study throw some light upon the limits of federal centralization? May we not find in the end that both tendencies are moving towards a better political equilibrium under different constitutional systems and that both are hence subject to limitations?

The writer has, moreover, a special interest in the subject of devolution. Ever since the establishment of the Republic, China has been confronted by the problem of whether she should adopt a unitary or a federal constitution. It has been urged on the one hand that a federal constitution would be the best system for China on account of the vastness of the country and the divergence of economic and social conditions in the various provinces. On the other hand it is said that China has always had a centralized system and there is no reason why it should be changed, especially in view of the fact that there has been a tendency towards centralization in most federal countries of the world. The arguments for and against federalism are not new—the war is for the most part a war of words. We shall find the same confusion and conflict of opinion with regard to devolution. The essential problem in each case is at bottom neither more nor less than the proper allocation of the functions of government. The writer, therefore, sincerely hopes that a critical study of devolution in Great Britain may help to clarify to some extent the constitutional problem of his own country.

A few words should be said about the methods and materials of this study. Devolution is a highly controversial problem, and as such, it has both theoretical and practical aspects. Theories are indeed very important. They enable us to understand the general aspects of things. But, if divorced from a practical purpose or made without reference to actual facts, they often become mere metaphysical quibblings, which tend to confuse rather than to clarify the particular problem. A strictly pragmatic attitude is, therefore, maintained throughout this study. Our methods consist of, first, finding out the facts of the case; second, critical analysis of the arguments pro and con; and finally, drawing tentative conclusions by a comparison of different constitutional systems and by predicting the probable consequences of devolution in Great Britain. The sources of material are divided into two classes, namely, primary sources and secondary sources. The latter consist of such books, periodicals, and newspapers as have some bearing upon the subject, while the former consist of Parliamentary Papers and Debates, which supply us with the facts and arguments for our study as well as the history of the devolutionary movement.

Finally it should be mentioned that the completion of this work is chiefly due to the supervision and assistance of Professor Lindsay Rogers, to whom the writer wishes to acknowledge his deep indebtedness and heartfelt gratitude.

# TABLE OF CONTENTS

## CHAPTER III

### THE CASE FOR DEVOLUTION (CONTINUED)—CONCURRENT AND ALTERNATIVE REMEDIES

## CHAPTER IV

### PARLIAMENTARY RESOLUTIONS AND PROPOSALS FOR DEVOLUTION FROM 1874 TO 1914

## CHAPTER VII

### THE CASE AGAINST DEVOLUTION—CONSTITUTIONAL AND PRACTICAL OBJECTIONS

## CHAPTER VIII

### PUBLIC OPINION ON DEVOLUTION

## CHAPTER IX

### CONCLUSIONS AND COMPARISONS

# INTRODUCTION

THE English Parliament has been on trial for nearly seven hundred years. During this long period of its existence it has enjoyed a relatively peaceful and continuous growth. Starting out principally as a High Court with judicial and financial functions, Parliament gradually assumed most of the legislative powers, and, with the development of the Cabinet in the seventeenth and eighteenth centuries, gathered unto itself all the executive powers as well. Modern parliamentary government in England thus rests upon the unity of powers in a single legislature at Westminster. Parliament has had a long history, a gradual development, full of accidental as well as conscious changes, and has reached a stage of omnipotence which has perhaps never been achieved by any other legislature in the history of the world.

This omnipotence is what is legally called the sovereignty of Parliament, which is said to be a cardinal principle of the English constitution. The nature of parliamentary sovereignty has been defined by various authorities. Blackstone says it is practically unlimited—that Parliament can do anything and everything which is not naturally impossible.[1] Professor A. V. Dicey defines it as neither more nor less than the supreme right to make or unmake any laws whatsoever.[2] Thus Parliament could, as one writer has put it, " pass a law that every red-headed man should be hanged, and the courts would have to carry out its bidding, and hang every man whose hair was proved to be red. It

[1] *Commentaries* (London, 16th edition, 1825), vol. i, bk. 1, p. 161.
[2] *The Law of the Constitution* (8th edition), pp. 37-38.

could pass a law that every man who now had no property should receive the property of those who had some, who henceforth would have none.  It could destroy a whole country by the use of the army and navy, which are under its control.  It could eject great portions of the British Empire and hand them over to other territories, or to govern themselves." [1]

The supposed omnipotence of Parliament is, however, really a fiction of law rather than a statement of fact; for, as we know only too well, Parliament has not been able to do everything.  Its activities are limited by its own capacity. The development of industry and commerce, the expansion of colonies, the increasing demand of the people for legislation resulting from the extension of the franchise—all these and many other economic and political changes have thrust upon Parliament an enormous burden which did not exist during the seventeenth and eighteenth centuries.  It should be remembered also that the position of the English Parliament is unique in that it acts in three different capacities: first, as the supreme legislature for the United Kingdom (now excluding Southern Ireland); second, as the sole law-making body for the several countries within the United Kingdom; and lastly, as the sovereign authority for the British Empire.  The result of such a state of things is that Parliament has, in the last few decades, been in a rather critical situation.  More and more frequently the criticism is made that Parliament is failing to perform its functions effectively.  It has lost some freedom of discussion through the introduction of various forms of closure.  It has been unable to make full provision for the varying needs of a vast growing community.  It has partly lost its control over the executive.  It is rapidly sharing its powers with the electorate.  In short, parliamentary government, in the sense

[1] Masterman, C. F. G., *How England is Governed*, p. 216.

in which it was understood in the eighteenth and nineteenth centuries, is being profoundly modified. All this is mainly due to the simple fact that Parliament has been called upon to assume more duties and functions than it can reasonably discharge.

In view of the difficulties confronting Parliament, proposals have been made for many years that subordinate legislatures should be created for England, Scotland, Ireland, and Wales, so that a part of the functions of Parliament, so far as they relate to purely local interests, may be transfered to local legislatures. Thus Parliament may be enabled to devote its exclusive attention to matters of national and Imperial interest. Such proposals as the above have been known as devolution. Although these proposals have been made with the primary purpose of relieving the congestion of the business of Parliament, they had, until recently, another purpose as well. This was to provide a satisfactory basis for the solution of the Irish Home Rule problem. For many years devolution was closely associated with Home Rule. Before we enter upon the subject of devolution, therefore, it is perhaps not out of place to say a few words about its connection with Irish Home Rule.

The Home Rule movement in Ireland was started by Sir Isaac Butt, who founded the Home Government Association of Ireland in 1870. He was probably the inventor of the term " Home Rule," which had, however, a wider meaning for Butt than the usual meaning that has been conceived by many other so-called Home Rulers. His proposal was really in the nature of devolution. He described his scheme as a " federal arrangement " under which England, Scotland, and Ireland, united under one sovereign, should have a common executive and a common national council for all purposes necessary to constitute them, toward other nations, as one state, while each of them should have its own domestic administration and its own domestic Parliament for its internal affairs.[1] Such a scheme was proposed by Butt with the primary object of securing Home Rule for Ireland, but the ultimate success of the latter, as Butt clearly saw, would necessitate the extension of the same principle of Home Rule to the other countries as well. In this sense, Butt may be justly regarded as the originator not only of the Irish Home Rule movement but also of " Home Rule all round " or devolution.

The details of Butt's scheme are interesting from the point of view of devolution. The system he contemplated would preserve the Imperial Parliament in its present form. It would leave to that Parliament all its present control over everything affecting the Crown—its Dominions, its colonies, and its dependencies—over the foreign relations of the Empire, and all questions of peace and war. It would leave it the power of preventing any tampering with the permanent taxation, which was the security for the payment of the interest on the national debt, and the other charges on the revenue to which the faith of the Crown and Parliament was pledged. It would also leave it the power of providing by Imperial taxation for Imperial necessities, including an army and a navy such as it judged necessary for the safety of the country, either in peace or war—imposing only a guarantee in the nature of the taxation that the levy should be one to which each member of the United Kingdom should contribute in proportion to its ability and its means.[2]

With regard to the Irish Parliament several important principles were laid down. First, the new Irish Parliament must derive its form as well as its authority from an act of the Imperial Parliament. Secondly, members of the

---

[1] Butt, Sir Isaac, *Home Government for Ireland, or Irish Federalism, its Meaning, its Objects, and its Hopes*, pp. 15-16.

[2] *Ibid.*, p. 33.

House of Commons of the Irish Parliament should be chosen by an election perfectly distinct from that of representatives to the Imperial Parliament. Lastly, the Irish House of Commons ought to be numerous enough to constitute a really popular assembly, composed of not less than 250 and not more than 300 members, and the House of Lords should be composed of resident peers of Ireland.[1]

The powers of the Irish Parliament would be: (1) The Irish Parliament would have all the control over Irish affairs which was possessed by the old Irish Parliament —with this difference only, that Ireland would be subject to the taxation which it would be within the power of the Imperial Parliament, for Imperial purposes, to impose. (2) The Irish Parliament would have control over all the rest of the revenue and resources of Ireland—a control to be exercised under that constitutional restriction which obliged all grants of public money to be made only on the recommendation of the Crown. (3) The Irish Parliament would have control over every matter relating to the internal administration of the country—such as railways, post office, public works, courts of justice, education, manufacturing, and commerce. (4) The Lord Lieutenant of Ireland would be appointed under the Imperial Great Seal. He would be personally responsible to the Imperial Parliament. But all his acts of Irish administration would be done through Irish Ministers responsible to the Irish Parliament. Those Ministers would stand in the same relation to the Irish Parliament as the Ministers in Canada or in the Australian Colony stand to the Colonial Parliaments. This would give Ireland a form of parliamentary government she never had before. And (5) every legislative measure should pass both Houses of Parliament and receive the Royal assent before it became law.[2]

[1] Butt, *op. cit.*, pp. 35-36.
[2] *Ibid.*, pp. 37-40.

As to England Butt suggested that the English representatives and peers in the Imperial Parliament might assemble in a separate Parliament for the transaction of all purely English affairs. If Scotland wished for a separate parliament of her own, an arrangement might be made, whereby the sittings of the English and Imperial Parliaments might be held at intervals so timed as to make it possible for the Scotch and Irish representatives to take part in the discussion of Imperial affairs. In other words, the English Parliament might be summoned in one session and the Imperial Parliament in another, at which the Irish and Scotch representatives would be present.[1]

This, in general, was Butt's scheme for Home Rule or for devolution, as we may call it today. Although he did not succeed in carrying out his scheme, it nevertheless had a considerable influence upon subsequent proposals both for Home Rule in Ireland and for devolution in general. Gladstone's two Home Rule Bills embodied some of the principles of Butt, so far as Ireland was concerned. But they did not go as far as Butt proposed, and consequently an insurmountable difficulty arose from the position of the Irish members in the Imperial Parliament. The first Bill of 1886 excluded the Irish members from the Imperial Parliament entirely. This was obviously unfair to Ireland, because for Imperial purposes she would be subject to taxation without representation. The second Bill of 1893 retained a certain number of the Irish members under the so-called " in and out " plan, which was, however, unfair to England and Scotland. because. while Ireland was to manage its own affairs without the interference of England and Scotland, the affairs of the latter would be, on the contrary, subject to the constant interference of Ireland. Because of the dilemma in which Gladstone found himself

---

[1] Butt, *op. cit.*, pp. 40-41.

in trying to solve the Irish problem and out of which there was no satisfactory way, it was insisted by later Home Rulers that the Irish problem should be dealt with, not as an isolated problem, but under a general scheme of " Home Rule all round," along the lines suggested by Butt.

During the twenty years between Gladstone's second Home Rule Bill and the third Home Rule Bill of 1912, the question of Irish Home Rule was held in abeyance in Parliament. When the question was again raised in 1912, it was regarded by many no longer as a purely Irish problem but rather as a step towards a general scheme of devolution. In introducing the third Home Rule Bill Mr. Asquith declared in the House of Commons: " I myself, while recognizing to the full the priority and the paramount urgency of the Irish claim, have always presented the case for Irish Home Rule as the first step, and only the first step, in a larger and more comprehensive policy. I said so with the utmost distinctness in a speech which I made on the second reading of the Bill of 1893, and in the twenty years which have since elapsed there is not one year which has not illustrated and emphasized with ever-growing cogency and clearness the imperative need, in the interests of the United Kingdom and of the Empire as a whole, for the emancipation from local cares and local burdens of the Imperial Parliament." [1]

Nevertheless, the Irish Home Rule problem has always been dealt with on a separate basis precisely because of " the priority and the paramount urgency of the Irish claim," and also because of the further fact that later on Ireland would not be satisfied with a mere scheme of devolution. Just before the Government of Ireland Act of 1920, there were two diametrically opposed demands in Ireland—the demand of Southern Ireland for complete independence and

[1] *Parliamentary Debates,* Commons, 5th ser., vol. 36, p. 1403.

the demand of Northern Ireland to remain in the Union. The Act of 1920 attempted to satisfy both these demands. It provided for two parliaments in Ireland, one for Southern Ireland and one for Northern Ireland. Southern Ireland, however, rejected the Bill, and subsequently a treaty was signed between England and Ireland on December 6, 1921, which granted Southern Ireland a dominion status similar to that of Canada. The Agreement was ratified by an Act of Parliament on March 31, 1922 entitled Irish Free State (Agreement) Act. The Agreement provides:

Ireland shall have the same constitutional status in the Community of Nations known as the British Empire as the Dominion of Canada, the Commonwealth of Australia, the Dominion of New Zealand, and the Union of South Africa, with a Parliament having powers to make laws for the peace, order and good government of Ireland and an Executive responsible to that Parliament, and shall be styled and known as the Irish Free State.

Subject to the provisions hereinafter set out the position of the Irish Free State in relation to the Imperial Parliament and Government and otherwise shall be that of the Dominion of Canada, and the law, practice and constitutional usage governing the relationship of the Crown or the representative of the Crown and of the Imperial Parliament to the Dominion of Canada shall govern their relationship to the Irish Free State.[1]

The Act of 1922 has finally put the Irish question to rest. The question had taxed to the utmost the resources of English statesmanship for more than half a century, and was thus solved, not on the traditional Home Rule basis as embodied in the previous Bills, but on a broader basis of dominion status. This implies practical independence within the British Empire, limited only with regard to defence and warfare by a few exceptions which are justified by the territorial propinquity between England and Ireland.

[1] *Statutes,* 1922, 12 & 13 Geo. 5, ch. 4, arts. i & ii.

Northern Ireland or Ulster, however, stands on a different footing. The failure of the earlier Home Rule Bills
had been due partly to the resistance of Ulster, which had
always wanted to remain in the Union. The Act of 1920,
as we have said, attempted to satisfy both Northern Ireland
and Southern Ireland by providing for two parliaments in
Ireland with the object, however, of ultimate unity by
agreement between the two sections themselves. For that
purpose it was provided that matters concerning the whole
of Ireland should be dealt with by a Common Council consisting of twenty members from the two legislatures of
Ireland. The president of the Council was nominated by
the Lord Lieutenant and had a casting vote. Ireland was
still to be represented at Westminster by 46 members. This
Act went into effect with regard to Northern Ireland, though
it was rejected by Southern Ireland. Thus the Irish Free
State Agreement specially provides: [1]

Until the expiration of one month from the passing of the
Act of Parliament for the ratification of this instrument, the
powers of the Parliament and the Government of the Irish
Free State shall not be exercisable as respects Northern Ireland,
and the provisions of the Government of Ireland Act, 1920,
shall, as far as they relate to Northern Ireland, remain of full
force and effect, and no election shall be held for the return
of members to serve in the Parliament of the Irish Free State
for constituencies in Northern Ireland, unless a resolution is
passed by both Houses of the Parliament of Northern Ireland
in favour of the holding of such elections before the end of the
said month.
If before the expiration of the said month, an address is
presented to His Majesty by both Houses of the Parliament of
Northern Ireland to that effect, the powers of the Parliament
and Government of the Irish Free State shall no longer

---

[1] *Loc. cit.*, arts. xi-xii.

extend to Northern Ireland, and the provisions of the Government of Ireland Act, 1920 (including those relating to the Council of Ireland), shall, so far as they relate to Northern Ireland, continue to be of full force and effect, and this instrument shall have effect subject to the necessary modifications.

So far as Ulster is concerned, then, the Act of 1920 provides for a substantial measure of devolution. The provisions of the Act are very important to our subject, because it may be considered in fact as the first step in a general scheme of devolution. The principal provisions of the Act may be briefly set forth as an introduction to a study of other schemes for devolution.

The legislative powers devolved to Ulster are as follows: [1] " Subject to the provisions of this Act, the Parliament of Northern Ireland shall have power to make laws for the peace, order, and good government of Northern Ireland with the following limitations, namely, that it shall not have power to make laws except in respect of matters exclusively relating to the portion of Ireland within its jurisdiction, or some part thereof, and (without prejudice to that general limitation) that it shall not have power to make laws in respect of the following matters in particular, namely:

(1) The Crown or the succession to the Crown, or a regency, or the property of the Crown (including foreshore vested in the Crown), or the Lord Lieutenant, except as respects the exercise of his executive power in relation to Irish services as defined for the purposes of this Act; or

(2) The making of peace or war, or matters arising from a state of war; or the regulation of the conduct of any portion of His Majesty's subjects during the existence of hostilities between foreign states with which His Majesty is at peace, in relation to those hostilities; or

---

[1] So far as these provisions apply to Northern Ireland only, the singular number is used.

(3) The navy, the army, the air force, the territorial force, or any other naval, military, or air force, or the defence of the realm, or any other naval, military or air force matter (including any pensions and allowances payable to persons who have been members of or in respect of service in any such force or their widows or dependents, and provision for the training, education, employment and assistance for the reinstatement in civil life of persons who have ceased to be members of any such force); or

(4) Treaties, or any relations with foreign states, or relations with other parts of His Majesty's dominions, or matters involving the contravention of treaties or agreements with foreign states or any part of His Majesty's Dominions, or offences connected with any such treaties or relations, or procedure connected with the extradition of criminals under any treaty, or the return of fugitive offenders from or to any part of His Majesty's dominions; or

(5) Dignities or titles of honour; or

(6) Treason, treason felony, alienage, naturalization, or aliens as such, or domicile; or

(7) Trade with any place out of the part of Ireland within its jurisdiction, except so far as trade may be affected by the exercise of the powers of taxation given to the said Parliament, or by regulations made for the sole purpose of preventing contagious disease, or by steps taken by means of inquiries or agencies out of the part of Ireland within its jurisdiction for the improvement of the trade of that part or for the protection of traders of that part from fraud; the granting of bounties on the export of goods; quarantine; navigation, including merchant shipping (except as respects inland waters, the regulation of harbours, and local health regulations); or

(8) Submarine cables; or

(9) Wireless telegraphy; or

(10) Aerial navigation; or

(11) Lighthouses, buoys, or beacons (except so far as they can consistently with any general Act of the Parliament of the United Kingdom be constructed or maintained by a local harbour authority); or

(12) Coinage; legal tender; negotiable instruments (including bank notes) except so far as negotiable instruments may be affected by the exercise of the powers of taxation given to the said Parliament; or any change in the standard of weights and measures; or

(13) Trade marks, designs, merchandise marks, copyright or patent rights; or

(14) Any matter which by this Act is declared to be a reserved matter, so long as it remains reserved.[1]

It is also provided that " the executive power shall continue vested in His Majesty the King, and nothing in this Act shall affect the exercise of that power, except as respects Irish services as defined for the purposes of this Act; "[2] and that, as respects Irish services, the powers may be delegated to the Lord Lieutenant and be exercised " through such departments as may be established by Act of the Parliament of Northern Ireland, or, subject to any alteration by Act of that Parliament, by the Lord Lieutenant."[3]   Irish services are defined as " all public services in connection with the administration of civil government in Northern Ireland, except the administration of matters with respect to which the Parliament of Northern Ireland has under the provisions hereinbefore contained no power to make laws, including in this exception all public services in connection with the administration of matters by this Act declared to be reserved matters so long as they continue to be reserved."[4]   Thus the following services are declared reserved until the date of Irish Union:[5] (1) The administration of the Royal Irish Constabulary for three years;

[1] *Statutes,* 1920, 10 & 11 Geo. 5, ch. 67, sec. iv.
[2] *Ibid.,* sec. viii(1).
[3] *Ibid.,* sec. viii(3)b.
[4] *Ibid.,* sec. viii(8).
[5] *Ibid.,* sec. ix(1), (2), (3).

(2) the postal service; (3) the Post Office Savings Bank and Trustee Savings Banks; (4) designs for stamps, whether for postal or revenue purposes; (5) the registration of deeds; (6) the Public Record Office of Ireland; and (7) the general subject matter of the Acts relating to land purchase in Ireland until changed by Act of Parliament. For the sake of uniform administration of public services connected with railways, fisheries, and the diseases of animals it is declared that "any powers (not being powers relating to reserved matters) exercisable by any department of the Government of the United Kingdom at the appointed day with respect to railways and fisheries and the contagious diseases of animals in Ireland and the power of making laws with respect to railways and fisheries and the contagious diseases of animals shall, as from the appointed day, become powers of the Council of Ireland." [1] The Parliament of Northern Ireland may, however, authorize the construction and conduct the administration of the railways within its territorial limits.

With regard to the financial powers of the Parliament of Northern Ireland, an Exchequer and Consolidated Fund is created in Northern Ireland.[2] The Parliament of Northern Ireland is given power to levy taxes in its jurisdiction except: (1) customs duties, (2) excise duties on articles manufactured and produced, (3) excess profits duties, (4) corporation profits tax, (5) or any other tax on profits, (6) income tax (including super-tax), and (7) capital tax.[3] Northern Ireland is required to make a contribution towards Imperial liabilities and expenditures such as debts, defence, and foreign affairs to be determined by a Joint Exchequer Board.[4]

[1] *Loc. cit.*, sec. x(2).

[2] *Ibid.*, sec. xx(1).

[3] *Ibid.*, sec. xxi(1).

[4] *Ibid.*, sec. xxiii.

As to the judiciary, the Supreme Court of Judicature of Northern Ireland and the High Court of Appeal for Ireland are established.[1]

The net effect of these provisions of the Act is to give Northern Ireland a substantial measure of devolution as respects matters of local interest. In spite of such a delegation of powers to Northern Ireland, the Imperial Parliament, however, still retains its sovereign right and power to make laws, not only with regard to reserved matters, but also with regard to all other matters with which the Parliament of Northern Ireland has power to deal. The Act expressly declares that the Parliament of Northern Ireland shall have no power " to repeal or alter any provision of this Act (except as is specially provided by this Act), or of any Act passed by the Parliament of the United Kingdom after the appointed day and extending to the part of Ireland within its jurisdiction, although that provision deals with a matter with respect to which the parliament has power to make laws." [2] It also declares that " where any Act of the Parliament of Northern Ireland deals with any matter with respect to which that Parliament has power to make laws which is dealt with by any Act of the Parliament of the United Kingdom passed after the appointed day and extending to the part of Ireland within its jurisdiction, the Act of the Parliament of Northern Ireland shall be read subject to the Act of the Parliament of the United Kingdom, and so far as it is repugnant to that Act, but no further, shall be void." [3]

From a brief description of the Act of 1920 as outlined above it is clear that, so far as Northern Ireland is concerned, devolution has already been put into effect. The

[1] *Loc. cit.*, sec. xxxviii.
[2] *Ibid.*, sec. vi(1).
[3] *Ibid.*, sec. vi(2).

Act has been in operation for about five years and the results so far seem to be quite satisfactory. The problem of devolution that we are going to study in the following pages no longer relates to Ireland. It has reference now only to England, Scotland, and Wales. The primary object of devolution in Great Britain as contrasted with that of Home Rule for Ireland is, as viewed by the advocates of the movement, to relieve the congestion of business in the House of Commons. Incidentally, of course, devolution in Great Britain will give England, Scotland, and Wales an opportunity to manage their own domestic affairs according to their respective needs and requirements, as it does Northern Ireland. The argument that the Irish problem may be solved through devolution can no longer be used, and the merits or demerits of the proposed reform, therefore, must be judged chiefly, if not exclusively, from the standpoint of the Imperial Parliament.

While many people look upon devolution as a necessary change in the interest of Parliament and the United Kingdom, others are strongly opposed to it as a dangerous measure that would threaten separation or disruption of the Union. This is the issue in a nutshell. In order to settle this issue we have to consider: first, whether devolution is really imperatively demanded; secondly, whether it can effectively answer such a demand; thirdly, whether it will bring with it any dangers or difficulties of a graver character than those it is intended to remove; and lastly, whether it is practicable. It is the purpose of the following chapters to discuss these questions.

# CHAPTER I

## The Nature and Object of Devolution

Devolution means delegation of powers. Conceivably all kinds of delegation may be called devolution; but, as it has been currently used in England, the term has denoted a specific form of delegation, namely, the delegation of a portion of the powers of the Imperial Parliament to subordinate legislatures for England, Scotland, and Wales. These legislatures are to manage all the domestic affairs of the respective countries, leaving Parliament to deal exclusively with matters of national and Imperial concern. Two important principles are involved in this definition: first, devolution means primarily a delegation of parliamentary powers and functions, and secondly, such a delegation is a delegation to the several countries of Great Britain on the basis of the national differences in law and administration that exist in these countries.

Devolution, thus defined, should be clearly distinguished from so-called federalism. The term has, indeed, been variously interpreted as "Home Rule all round", or "Federal Home Rule", or "Federal Devolution", or simply "Federalism". The underlying idea is, nevertheless, the same. The use of the word federal or federalism in conjunction with devolution has, however, caused a considerable amount of confusion on the subject. It is important for the sake of clear thinking that this confusion of words should be removed so that the specific meaning of devolution may be understood.

28

It is true that federalism has been advocated in England both as a means of bringing about a closer union between England and her self-governing Dominions on the one hand, and as a method of solving the Irish problem on the other. Devolution is a separate and distinct question from the proposal of federalism in either sense. Federalism in the ordinary and popular sense denotes a process of closer union between several separate states whereby they jointly surrender some of their powers to a central government for certain common purposes and retain certain other powers for themselves. This process may be reversed. A central government may create a federal system by assigning certain important powers to existing local units whereby the local governments acquire an exclusive jurisdiction over those powers as against the central government. The distinctive feature of all federal systems is, therefore, the existence of a legal demarcation of spheres of powers between the central and the local governments. This is the true meaning of federalism as it has been used by various writers on the subject.

Thus, the noted historian, Mr. Edward A. Freeman says that federalism is " any union of component members, where the degree of union between the members surpasses that of mere alliance, however intimate, and where the degree of independence possessed by each member surpasses anything which can fairly come under the head of merely municipal freedom." [1] He further says that " there is what may be called a certain Federal Ideal, which has sometimes been realized in its full, or nearly its full, perfection, while other cases have shown only a more or less remote approximation to it." [2] In order to constitute this perfect ideal form of federalism two requirements are said to be indispensable.

[1] *History of Federal Government*, vol. i, 2nd edition (1893), p. 2.
[2] *Ibid.*, p. 2.

" On the one hand, each of the members of the Union must
be wholly independent in those matters which concern each
member only.   On the other hand, all must be subject to a
common power in those matters which concern the whole
body of members collectively.   Thus each member will fix
for itself the laws of its criminal jurisprudence, and even
the details of its political constitution.   And it will do this,
not as a matter of privilege or concession from any higher
power, but as a matter of absolute right, by virtue of its
inherent powers as an independent commonwealth.   But in
all matters which concern the general body, the sovereignty
of the several members will cease.   Each member is perfectly independent within its own sphere; but there is another sphere in which its independence, or rather its separate
existence, vanishes.   It is invested with every right of sovereignty on one class of subjects, but there is another class
of subjects on which it is as incapable of separat political
action as any province or city of a monarchy or of an in-
divisible republic.   The making of peace and war, the send-
ing and receiving of ambassadors, generally all that comes
within the department of International Law, will be reserved
wholly to the central power.   Indeed, the very existence of
the several members of the Union will be diplomatically unknown to foreign nations, which will never be called upon
to deal with any power except the Central Government.
A Federal Union, in short, will form one State in relation
to other powers, but many States as regards its internal administration.   This . complete division of sovereignty we
may look upon as essential to the absolute perfection of the
Federal Ideal." [1]   Thus the complete division of sovereignty
into exclusive spheres of powers between the central government and the local governments is a norm of federalism
which has been realized only in a few instances in the history

[1] *Op. cit.*, pp. 2-3.

of government from the ancient Greek Federations up to the Federation of the German Empire.   Although Freeman wrote many years ago, his analysis still holds true.

A more recent writer defines " a ' federal state ' (Compositive State, *Bundesstaat*) as " a perpetual union of several sovereign states based first upon a treaty between those states or upon some historical status common to them all, and secondly upon a federal constitution accepted by their citizens. The central government acts not only upon the associated states but also directly upon their citizens.   Both the internal and external sovereignty of the states is impaired, and the federal union in most cases alone enters into international relations." [1]   The most satisfactory definition from the standpoint of political science is given by Professor H. L. McBain and Lindsay Rogers as follows:

" Federal government as distinguished from unitary government is usually defined as a system under which a division of powers is made between a central government on the one hand and local units of government on the other, which division of powers is made by the national constitution and may be altered only by amending the constitution." [2]   After alluding to the fact that, although the difference between a federal system and a unitary system may be said to be one of degree, it is nevertheless one of very important degree both in fact and in law, the same writers lay down two essential tests of federalism: " first, the powers that are conferred upon or reserved to the local units must be of some genuine political significance; and second, these powers cannot be withdrawn from the local units at the unrestricted will of the central government." [3]

[1] Newton, A. P., *Federal and Unified Constitutions*, p. 5.

[2] McBain, H. L. and Rogers, Lindsay, *The New Constitutions of Europe*, p. 68.

[3] *Ibid.*, p. 69.

From these definitions we may conclude that every true
federal system requires the existence of mutually exclusive spheres of powers between the central and local governments.   Whether a federal state exists or not is purely
a constitutional question.   In other words, if there is a
written constitution, which provides for a division of powers
between the central government and local governments, and
which is independent of both the central and local governments, then we have a federal system.   This is true of the
three great federal systems that exist among the English-
speaking peoples, namely, the United States, Canada, and
Australia.   In the United States, the central government
was created by the Federal Constitution, which delegated
certain powers to the Federal Government, while all other
powers not so delegated were reserved to the states.   In
Canada the same result was reached except that the principle
of the division of powers was just the reverse: the powers of
the provincial governments were enumerated, and all others
not thus assigned to them were reserved to the central government.   The result in both cases was that a federal system
was created under which the central government and the
state or provincial government was each supreme in its own
sphere and the powers of each could not be changed except
through a formal amendment to the constitution in the one
case or an act of Parliament in the other.   The Australian
federal system was modelled closely after that of the United
States.

Such being the nature of federalism, it is obviously inaccurate and misleading to identify it with devolution.   It
is not the purpose of the latter to create such a system as
exists in any of these countries that now have federal constitutions.   The idea is simply to set up local legislatures
in England, Scotland, and Wales respectively to deal with
certain matters of a local character, leaving Parliament to

deal with other more important matters.   Such local legislatures are to be strictly subordinate to, and not coordinate
with, Parliament.   The sovereign powers of the latter would
still remain intact and unlimited.   Parliament could modify
or even withdraw the powers of the local legislatures at any
time that it deemed expedient.   Such an absolute sovereign
power of Parliament under a system of devolution would
be incompatible with federalism in the legal and constitutional sense of the term.

A strict federal constitution can, indeed, be established in
Great Britain—if such a thing were desired—in only one
of two ways.[1]   In the first place, the existing Parliament
might be disintegrated into its component parts by a repeal
of the Act of Union between England and Scotland; and
the independent Parliaments of Scotland and England,
thus revived, might contract to surrender to some new
Parliament, in which both Kingdoms would be represented,
all control over certain matters, while each would retain
exclusive control over all other matters.   Or, in the second
place, the present Parliament might pass an act which would
create two or more new Parliaments, one central and several
local, and then itself cease to exist.   But nobody has thus
far made any suggestion in connection with devolution that
Parliament should do either of these two things.   It is impossible to create a federal system by a mere delegation of
powers to local legislatures such as is contemplated by
devolution.

Devolution may, however, resemble federalism in one
respect, namely, in its practical operation.   So long as Parliament should, on grounds of policy or expediency, abstain
from interfering with the powers of the local legislatures of
England, Scotland, and Wales, the new system under devolu-

[1] Adapted from an article entitled " Ireland and Federalism," *The Quarterly Review,* October, 1919.

tion would work on federal lines as does the constitution of
South Africa. The local legislatures to be set up would
resemble the Provincial Councils of South Africa. The
latter, as we know, enjoy a considerable measure of local
self-government but do not possess inherent or exclusive
powers as do the state legislatures of the United States or,
in a less degree, the provincial legislatures of Canada.
Not only can the Union Parliament override the legislation of the Provincial Councils, but it can take away
their powers altogether and terminate their existence. Such
a thing would, of course,· be highly improbable; and consequently the result has been that the South African Constitution, though not federal in theory, does appear to work
on federal lines. This is at best a quasi-federal arrangement, that is a half-way house between true federalism and
mere municipal home rule or local self-government. Such
would be the natural and probable consequence of devolution
in Great Britain.

The confusion between devolution and federalism that
is not infrequently found in the literature of the subject
seems to have been due to the fact that, during the earlier
stages of the movement, devolution was proposed by some,
not only as a method of relieving the congestion of Parliament, but primarily as an alternative means to Home Rule
for Ireland. As early as 1870 Sir Isaac Butt, the founder
of the Home Rule Association (later changed into the Irish
Home Rule League), put forth a proposal of Home Rule
for Ireland, which, as we said before, was described as a
" federal arrangement." This term, however, was used in
a rather loose sense. As contrasted with the earlier policies
of a complete repeal of the Act of Union advocated by
Daniel O'Connell and of independence urged by the Fenian
Brotherhood, Butt's idea was that a separate legislature
should be set up for Ireland with the right to legislate for

all matters relating to Ireland, and to control Irish resources and expenditure, subject to the obligation of contributing a just proportion of Imperial expenses.   Butt clearly saw that unless the same right of Home Rule was extended to England and Scotland, the latter would not consent to Home Rule for Ireland.   Hence his scheme, though devised primarily for Ireland, could be equally applied to the other countries.   Later on, after the failure of Gladstone's Home Rule Bills, devolution was proposed by many people as an alternative policy to Home Rule.   This was spoken of sometimes as " Home Rule all round " and sometimes as " federalism."   The primary purpose of this proposal was not so much to relieve the business of Parliament as to solve the Irish problem.   Ever since then, these terms—" Home Rule all round ", " federalism," and " devolution " have been used interchangeably by different people for different purposes. This accounts for the confusion that exists on the subject.

On account of this confusion between devolution and federalism, it was proposed by the advocates of devolution in 1914 that the term " Devolution " should be officially used instead of the term " Federal Devolution " or " Federalism " to designate the movement we have described. For that purpose Lord Hythe published a letter in the *Times* on June 20, 1914, in which he said that he had been chiefly responsible for the use of the word " federal ", but admitted that this was not an accurate description of the policy advocated.   " ' Federal ' implies," continued the letter, " that the powers of the Central Parliament are limited by the Act of Federation.   Under a Federal Constitution, conflicts of authority may arise between the Central Parliament and the Provincial Legislatures.   Under the United States Constitution a Supreme Court is provided to decide which is in the right.   It is not proposed by any one to establish such a system in this country.   No one has insisted more strongly than the Prime Minister that under the present Bill (referring to the Home Rule Bill) or any other scheme of Home Rule, the supremacy of the Imperial Parliament does and must remain unimpaired. This is fully admitted as far as I know by all so-called federalists in the United Kingdom." [1]

Devolution should be distinguished also from administrative decentralization. The congestion of business in the central government is due not only to the increasing demand for legislation but also to the growing complexity of administration. Although it is becoming more and more difficult to differentiate between legislation and administration in recent years when administrative officers are given large powers of making orders and regulations having the force of law, the problems are, nevertheless, somewhat different. A hundred years ago the functions of the state were fewer in number and much more limited in scope than they are today. The development of industry and local government in the last century has added a large number of new functions and duties to the state. This has meant an increasingly larger degree of administrative decentralization inasmuch as the central government in most countries cannot possibly undertake all these duties itself.

In England also there has been a considerable administrative decentralization in recent decades. This has, however, very little to do with devolution. The latter aims at decentralization not only of the administrative machinery but of the legislative functions of Parliament as well. It is necessary, therefore, to distinguish between devolution and administrative decentralization for the reason that the latter has been thought by some of the opponents of devolution as an all sufficient means of relieving the congestion of Parliament. If so, then devolution would be superfluous. But it is not so. Mere administrative decentralization, however extensive, cannot solve the problem of parliamentary congestion.

[1] *Loc. cit.*, p. 10 f.

Furthermore, administrative decentralization has difficulties of its own. There are possibly four forms of administrative decentralization. In the first place, duties and functions may be transferred from the government at London to the existing local authorities. The two most important local authorities are the Borough and the County. The former is the normal type of urban government, while the latter is the normal type of rural government. In each case the governing authority is the elected Council which administers the local functions through committees. Within the County there are subdivisions known as Rural Districts and within the latter again there are further subdivisions known as Rural Parishes. Of all these types of local government the County Borough is the most highly developed and has most of the powers of self-government. Besides these there are certain areas for special purposes. There is already much conflict of authority and overlapping of functions in the present system of local government. Administrative decentralization to these authorities has probably gone as far as it is likely to go. Even if more powers could be given to these local governments, their areas would still be limited—unless other areas are created—and hence matters concerning two or three localities would still remain to be dealt with by the Central Government.

Secondly, duties and functions may be transferred to the subordinate officers of the Central Government. This is, however, not desirable. " The present tendency," says Mr. Cole, " strongly marked in certain recent extensions of Government activity, is towards a decentralization of actual administrative machinery, without any corresponding decentralization of executive control. Instead of dealing with all questions from his Whitehall office, the modern bureaucrat is well content to plant out his officials all over the country; but he usually pursues them with a stream of orders, regulations, and circulars, by means of which almost the whole effective power is retained in the hands of the central Department. Decentralization in such a form, although it may pave the way to a more reasonable system, for the time being serves mainly to aggravate the problem. It enables a still greater overgrowth of the Departments to take place, and facilitates an extension of their interference in matters of detail as well as on broad questions of policy. Reinforced by their provincial staffs, the Minister and Permanent Under-Secretaries gird up their loins for fresh onslaughts on the public, and ' administrative devolution ', in this form, then becomes an excuse for a further real concentration of power." [1] This is a sufficient and not at all unfair indictment of the present tendency of administrative decentralization. Such decentralization cannot be depended upon either to relieve the central departments or to lighten the burdens of Parliament.

Thirdly, there may be a decentralization of the administrative machinery coupled with a real decentralization of executive control. " This seldom occurs in practice," says the same author, " for the ' will to power ' is strong in the political and permanent heads of the Departments of State; but it does take place in some small degree in proportion as discretionary power is conferred on local officials of the Departments. As soon, however, as there is any approach to devolution in this form, a fresh problem at once presents itself. Control is removed one stage further from Parliament, and new possibilities of corruption and undemocratic action present themselves." [2] This form of decentralization is positively undesirable from the point of view either of the public or of Parliament, although it does secure some relief to the central Departments.

[1] Cole, G. D. H., *The Future of Local Government*, pp. 20-21.
[2] *Ibid.*, p. 21.

Lastly, there is still another way of administrative decentralization, and that is called regional decentralization or regional devolution. The powers that are relinquished by the central authority, instead of being conferred upon local officials of the central Departments, might be transferred to regional bodies chosen by the localities themselves. But such regions do not exist at present. They would have to be created. Mr. Cole alleges that the existing system of local government lacks co-ordination and " that the present areas of Local Government are hopelessly inadequate for the effective performance of a considerable number of functions which it is generally agreed that local authorities, of one sort or another, ought to fulfil." [1] The most important of these functions are housing, town-planning, local transport, health, and education. Under the present system these functions are more or less neglected. For these reasons it is proposed that a certain number of regions should be created in England in order to provide a co-ordinating agency for the local government and to secure efficiency in the administration of local affairs. The principle of regionalism is two-fold: first, to make local areas real units of social feeling : and secondly, to render them suitable for economic and social administration. The regional areas have to be considerably larger than the present areas of local government but not so large as the province. They would embrace both urban and rural areas instead of being either purely urban or purely rural as are present areas of local government. [2] They should " be real and realized unities. in the sense that they must be capable of gathering round themselves a living consciousness among those who inhabit them of a common citizenship based on social realities as well as on purely economic and political convenience." [3]    It

[1] Cole, *op. cit.*, pp. 13-14.

[2] *Ibid.*, p. 40.

[3] *Ibid.*, p. 27.

is suggested that England alone be divided into nine regions around certain well-defined centers of population, and that Great Britain as a whole be ultimately divided into twenty or thirty such regions.[1]

The proposal of regionalism has the merit of enabling Parliament to devolve a large number of powers both administrative and legislative to local governments, which cannot be delegated at the present time. But such a scheme, as pointed out by Mr. Cole, is designed primarily as a method for the reorganization of local government with a view of securing a greater degree of local freedom rather than as a scheme of parliamentary devolution. Although regional decentralization may incidentally relieve some pressure of parliamentary business, its chief purpose is to secure administrative and not legislative decentralization. "There is," declares Mr. Cole, " nothing positive in common between the proposals put forward in this book [referring to regionalism] and the suggestion that subordinate Parliaments should be set up for England, Scotland, and Wales. The doing of this, whether or not it is desirable, would not affect the case for regional organization. There is indeed common to the two proposals the negative argument based on the present congestion of Parliament; but it is clear enough that, even if it made this congestion slightly less, parliamentary devolution could in fact do little to remove it. The impossible burden of administrative supervision, and of dealing with all the internal legislation required by the various interests and Departments, would still remain upon the subordinate Parliaments; and before long the position would become again as bad as it is now. I am not concerned to argue the question whether, on national grounds, ' Home Rule ' for Scotland, Wales and England is, or is not, necessary to national self-expression; but the proposal for regional organization must be clearly distinguished from this

---

[1] Cole, *op. cit.*, pp. 70-72.

quite different question." [1]    This opinion may be taken as
an authoritative statement of the distinction between devolution and administrative decentralization in general.

Finally, devolution should be distinguished from functional decentralization.  The legislative functions of Parliament may be divided either horizontally on a territorial
basis or vertically along the cleavage of political and economic functions.  The former is the substance of devolution, while the latter embodies the gist of Guild Socialism.
Both may be able to solve the problem of the congestion of
business in Parliament, but the underlying ideas and motives
of the two proposals are radically different.  The essence
of the Guild Socialist's attitude is said to be " that Society
ought to be so organized as to afford the greatest possible
opportunity for individual and collective self-expression to
all its members, and that this involves and implies the extension of positive self-government through all its parts." [2]
The indictment by the Guild Socialist of the present parliamentary system is not only that it inevitably results in congestion of business at the center, but also that it violates the
principle of democracy in two very important respects: first,
" that the elector retains practically no control over his representative, has only the power to change him at very in-
frequent intervals, and has in fact only a very limited range
of choice;" [3] and second, that the so-called representative
does not in fact represent the elector.  " Parliament," says
Mr. Cole, " professes to represent all the citizens in all
things, and therefore as a rule represents none of them in
anything. . . . There can be only one escape from the
futility of our present methods of parliamentary government; and that is to find an association and method of re-

[1] Cole, *op. cit.,* pp. 36-37.

[2] Cole, *Guild Socialism Restated,* p. 13.

[3] *Ibid.,* p. 31.

presentation for each function, and a function for each association and body of representatives.   In other words, real democracy is to be found, not in a single omnicompetent representative assembly, but in a system of coördinated functional representative bodies." [1]

Two proposals have been made for the reorganization of the present parliamentary system along functional lines. One is by Mr. Cole and the other by the Webbs.   Mr. Cole proposes that government should be based primarily upon self-governing groups of various interests, and that these interest groups should then combine together geographically to form what is called the Town-ship Commune, the Regional Commune, and the National Commune.[2]   Each graduation of commune should be composed, in general, of six groups of organizations: (1) a number of Industrial Guilds united in a Guild Council, (2) a number of Co-operative Societies united in a Co-operative Council, (3) a collective Utility Council, (4) a number of Guilds for Civil Services, (5) a Cultural Council, and (6) a Health Council. The Communal Body in which all these organizations will be represented shall be simply a co-ordinating rather than an administrative agency.   Its functions will be confined to the following: (1) the financial function of allocation of resources, (2) adjudication of disputes upon appeal, (3) to determine the lines of demarcation between the various functional groups, (4) to determine matters concerning the Commune as a whole, and (5) the coercive function or police force.   The National Commune shall likewise be a mere Co-ordinating Agency, in which both the various National Industrial, Agricultural, Civil Councils, and Regional Communes shall be represented.   Its functions will include Foreign Affairs and perhaps defence.[3]

[1] Cole, *Social Theory,* p. 108.

[2] Cole, *Guild Socialism Restated,* ch. vii.

[3] *Ibid.,* pp. 124-128.

Mr. and Mrs. Webb's plan in some respects resembles that of Mr. Cole. They have accepted much of Mr. Cole's analysis but less of his radical suggestions. They say there are two " complexes " in society, the political complex and the social complex which is economic in nature.[1] Hence they propose that there should be two Parliaments, one political and the other social. The functions of the Political Parliament should be mainly justice, defence, and administration of the Empire.[2] The functions of the Social Parliament should be the control over the Nation's economic and social activities, taxation, public services, etc. Its organization should be modelled after the Municipal Councils.[3]

From the foregoing it is seen that functional devolution either according to Mr. Cole's plan or according to the Webb plan would necessitate a fundamental reorganization of the present parliamentary system both in fact and in law. This would be a much more drastic change than devolution. Although there is one argument in common for these proposals—namely, the congestion of business in the House of Commons and the necessity of transferring some of the functions of Parliament to other organs—beyond that they are radically different. The merits or demerits of functional devolution are not within the scope of our inquiry and hence it is not necessary to enter into them. It would seem that functional devolution, however desirable it may be in theory, is something for the distant future. Its ideals are more lofty and its proposals more far-reaching than devolution on a territorial basis. It presents both a theory and a scheme for the reorganization of present society which is not the aim of devolution. De-

[1] Webb, Sidney and Beatrice, *A Constitution for the Socialist Commonwealth of Great Britain*, p. 137.

[2] *Ibid.*, pp. 111-116.

[3] *Ibid.*, p. 119.

volution aims mainly at relieving the congestion of the
House of Commons, and its success or failure must be
judged upon this ground.  As distinguished from administrative decentralization, the subject matter of devolution
is mainly legislative.  It would, of course, involve decentralization of administration to enable the local legislatures
to carry out their local measures.  But, as distinguished
from functional decentralization, the basis of devolution
is territorial according to the existing divisions of England, Scotland, and Wales, and not functional such as contemplated by Mr. Cole or by Mr. and Mrs. Webb.

The case of devolution rests, therefore, upon one single
contention, namely the congestion of business in the House
of Commons.  Whether such a degree of congestion exists
as to warrant the proposed measure of relief is purely a
question of fact to be ascertained.  Suffice it to say, in this
connection, that the congestion has been complained of as
a serious evil for over seventy years.  As early as 1846 Sir
Robert Peel already deplored the congested conditions of
Parliament.[1]  Later on Gladstone observed that Parliament
was overwhelmed.[2]  Since then statesman after statesman
has said the same thing.  Speaking of the Parliament of
1874, Mr. Hugh Childers remarked that he was increasingly
impressed with the hopelessness of getting through the work
of the United Kingdom with one legislative body at Westminster.[3]  Lord Rosebery spoke in 1902 of " our over-
labouring Parliament." [4]  Again, Mr. Balfour, in moving
the resolution for the closure by compartment in the Committee discussion of the Educational Bill on November 2,

[1] Quoted by J. A. Murray Macdonald, *Parliamentay Debates,* Commons, 5th ser., vol. 116, p. 1885.

[2] Quoted by Sidney Low, *The Governance of England,* p. 88.

[3] Quoted in *The Round Table,* vol. viii, 1918, p. 752.

[4] Hythe, Thomas A. B., *Problems of Empire* (1913), p. 183.

1902, observed: " It amounts to an admission that our rules
—great as are the changes effected in those rules since
closure was first proposed by Mr. Gladstone twenty years
ago—that our rules, with all these changes, are not sufficient
to enable this House to deal with the legislative work that is
put before it." [1]   Lord Loreburn said in the same year: "It
was not Irish affairs merely that obstructed the business in
the House of Commons.   It was English and Scottish and
Imperial business that stopped the way." [2]   Still more recently, December 30, 1912, Mr. Bonar Law made the following remark in the House of Commons: " Under the conditions under whcih we are at present working the House of
Commons has ceased to be a Legislative Assembly in any
sense of the term." [3]   As a result of the War, the evil has
become more serious.   It is hardly necessary to multiply
other opinions; these few representative ones will suffice to
indicate the *prima facie* gravity of the situation even before
the War.

The congestion of Parliament is not only an evil in
itself but has produced other evils of a serious nature.
First and foremost is the sharp reduction of the freedom of
discussion of the members in the House of Commons.
Since the introduction of the various forms of " closure ",
the Government has practically had complete control over
the time and business of the House.   The Government
decides in most cases what laws should be passed and in
what form they should be passed.   The role of an ordinary
member is becoming increasingly more and more passive.
This is not necessarily because the members lack interest in
the active participation in legislation, which they are supposed to attempt, but because of the pressure of business

[1] Hythe, *op. cit.*, p. 184.

[2] *Ibid.*, p. 184.

[3] Quoted in Partridge's *T. A. B., 2nd Earl Brassey*, p. 216.

and the necessity of getting through a certain amount of work each session.   Consequently the members are bound to rely more and more upon the Ministers for the direction of the legislative work of the House and hence are unable to exercise their right of free discussion.   Under such circumstances it is not too much to say, as has been frequently alleged, that the House is becoming a mere machine for registering the will of the Cabinet, and that the power of the latter has become more and more uncontrollable save by a formal vote of censure.

That such a condition exists is beyond question.   Before we present further facts on this point—which will be done in the next chapter—we may quote a representative opinion from a member of the House of Commons:

A " Parliament " means a talking place.   Some of the talk will not be of very much value, but in the long run it is useful. It educates the House, and it brings public opinion to bear upon the Ministers.   This point is the more serious and the more important because, unfortunately, at the present time, we are practically living under a system of single-Chamber Government.   This House, given time, has power to put through anything that it likes, and so long as that is the position it is the more important that what it does put through should be thoroughly considered and carefully discussed, and should not be forced through, as I have known it to be the case with Bills again and again, with half of it, and more than half of it, never discussed at all, but passed under the Closure.   It is dangerous when we are practically under single-Chamber Government, and it is a very great departure from the principles upon which our Constitution has been built up.   It is a danger, I believe, to popular Government.[1]

Again, in recent years there has been going on a kind of

[1] Sir T. Whittaker, *Parliamentary Debates*, Commons, 5th ser., vol. 116, p. 2113.

legislative devolution or " delegated legislation " to the Executive Departments on an ever increasing scale. " The action of our Acts of Parliament," says a recent writer, " grows more and more dependent upon subsidiary legislation. More than half our modern Acts are to this extent incomplete statements of law. If any one opens at random a recent annual volume of public general statutes, he will not have to turn many pages before finding a provision that His Majesty may make Orders in Council, or that some public body or officer or department may make rules or regulations, contributing some addition to the substance or the detail or the working of that particular Act. When the King in Parliament, our supreme law-making authority, expressly allows some other authority to undertake this kind of supplementary law-making, the result is what we call " delegated legislation '." [1] The volume of such delegated legislation is enormous. It is estimated that in the year 1920, while 82 Acts of Parliament were passed, more than ten times as many " Statutory Rules and Orders " of a public character were officially registered under the Rules Publication Act (not all delegated legislation is published). The total number of these Rules and Orders for 1920 was 2473. [2]

Delegated legislation is undoubtedly justifiable to a certain extent on the ground of administrative convenience and legislative elasticity. It may be properly argued that Parliamentary Acts should be confined to broad principles of policy, and that the minor details should be filled in by the Departments, which alone are charged with the responsibility of carrying out the legislation of Parliament. But the actual practice goes very much further. In many cases the Acts of Parliament are nothing more than mere " skeleton legislation " and often quite a number of difficult and

---

[1] Carr, C. T., *Delegated Legislation*, pp. 1-2.
[2] *Ibid.*, p. 2.

controversial points are left to the determination of the Departments. Thus the same writer declares: "One cannot quite say that all major matters of permanent legislative importance are dealt with by Parliament itself and that all minor matters of temporary importance are delegated. Many of the matters which are delegated are of first rate importance." [1]

The real justification of such an enormous amount of delegated legislation must be found partly in the fact that Parliament has not time to do all the work itself. This is the opinion of the writer we have just quoted. "The first [speaking of the justifications of delegated legislation] is the plain fact that Parliament has not time to do otherwise. There was leisure in that medieval Parliament of Estates when grievances were submitted and were referred to the appropriate authority. There was leisure in the Tudor and Stuart times when Crown and Parliament fought over privilege and prerogative. There was leisure even in that third period which ran from 1688 to the Reform Act of 1832 when the party system was elaborated and the Cabinet became part of our constitution. . . . From 1832 onwards the leisure began to disappear. . . . The new franchise introduced the middle classes to their share in legislation and administration. Constituencies became more exacting; politicians became more conscious of the importance of being earnest. Speakers increased in number and speeches in length . . . . Administration grew more complex. The State intervened more and more in domestic affairs. Imperial problems exacted attention. Various shifts were devised for economizing parliamentary time. Legislation occupies only a part of that time, but it was possible to diminish its demands. The invention and extension of the 'provisional order' and 'special order' procedure, the birth of the group

[1] Carr, *op. cit.*, p. 15.

of 'clauses Acts' in 1845, the process of substituting a general or permanent Act for a series of particular or periodical Acts—all these have brought some relief.  But as long ago as 1877 Lord Thring, then parliamentary counsel, said that the adoption of a system of confining the attention of Parliament to material provisions only, and leaving details to be settled departmentally, was probably the only way in which parliamentary government could, as respects its legis-- lative functions, be carried on.  And today even when a substantial party majority has facilitated the working of the parliamentary machine, there is less leisure than ever." [1]

Thus under the present conditions of the congestion of business, the practice of delegating legislation to the Departments is not only unavoidable but positively desirable. The success of this practice, however, depends upon certain safeguards.[2]  First, the delegation of legislative power should be delegation to a trustworthy authority which commands the national confidence.  Second, the limits within which the delegated power is to be exercised ought to be definitely laid down, so that the judiciary may furnish a safegard by seeing that these limits are not violated.  Third, if any particular interests are to be affected by delegated legislation, the legislating authority should consult them before making its laws.  Fourth, publicity should be given to all delegated legislation.  Fifth and lastly, there should be some machinery for amending and revoking delegated legislation.  Parliament has provided a safeguard in this respect by requiring that the Rules and Regulations made under an Act should be laid before both Houses as soon as made. Such Rules and Regulations take effect immediately, but if either House should take exception to any of them within a specified number of days, they could be annulled.  Of all

[1] Carr, *op. cit.*, pp. 19-20.

[2] *Ibid.*, pp. 27-30.

these safeguards the two most important are certainty of authority and parliamentary control. These are, however, not easily obtainable; the same cause of the congestion of business, which compels Parliament to delegate legislative authority to the Departments seems to operate also to render impossible any effective control and supervision by Parliament. The members of Parliament can hardly spare the time, not to inquire whether they have the requisite knowledge or not, to scrutinize all the Orders and Regulations that are laid before them. The result has been that few of these Orders and Regulations are ever amended or annulled.

Parliament being unable to control the power that it delegates to the Executive Departments, there has developed in recent years a system of bureaucracy which almost completely escapes the surveillance of Parliament on the one hand and the supervision of the Law Courts on the other. The Departments and officers not only make laws which daily affect the life of the people but also act, in most cases, as their own judges. In general their decisions are not appealable except on the ground that they are *ultra vires* which is, however, not always easy to prove. Thus many cases of the most flagrant violations of plain justice have been committed by the officers.[1] "In all these matters, legislative and judicial," says a recent writer, "what is really happening is that Parliament is getting rid of its own responsibilities. It is a short and easy method of legislation to delegate wide and ill-defined powers to subordinate bodies. Doubtless it saves the time and simplifies the labours of the House of Commons, but the practical result is that the proper jurisdiction of the courts is ousted. A statute is passed in full publicity, under a running fire of analysis, criticism, and amendment in both Houses; the regulations of

---

[1] Allen, C. K., "Bureaucracy Triumphant", *The Quarterly Review*, vol. 240, 1923, pp. 246-261.

departments and local authorities are created by the tortuous
processes of the official mind and curtained from the vulgar
gaze by departmental ' discretion.' "[1]

So much for the evil of delegated legislation.   Another
evil resulting from the congestion of business is the with-
drawal of legislation from the House of Commons to the
Standing Committees.   Before the War there were four
Standing Committees, but after the War they were increased
to six.   The increase of the number of these Committees
together with other changes of procedure that were effected
in 1919 was primarily for the purpose of saving time for
Parliament.   Practically all important Bills are now referred to one or the other of these six Standing Committees
with the exception of a few important Bills of a political
or financial nature.   The result has been a saving of considerable time for Parliament, but such a saving is not
without its drawbacks.   It tends to diminish the responsibility of the House of Commons; it also tends to decrease
the value and opportunity of discussion in the House; and
lastly, it imposes too severe a strain on the members.   A
few quotations from the members themselves may bear
out these objections :

We have set up this Session [said Sir Edward Carson on June
3, 1919 in the House of Commons] this system of Grand Committees working from morning till night, and I believe that as
things are going at present it will ruin this House.  I admit
that I supported it, but I never for a moment thought that
the business we were on would, as I have no doubt it does,
require them to sit there so· long that the whole of their time
would be taken up, and that they would be able to give no
attention whatever to this House.   I think that that is
disastrous.[2]

[1] *Ibid.*, p. 251.
[2] *Parliamentary Debates*, Commons, 5th ser., vol. 116, p. 1896.

We are trying during the present Session [declared Mr. Marriott in the same debate] a very great experiment of devolution on the spot—of devolution to Grand Committees. I sometimes wonder whether the Members of this House realize the extent of that experiment. I asked the Leader of the House a few days ago whether the Government expected Members of this House to be in two, if not three, places at once, and he replied that the Government had no such expectation. If the Government does not expect a physical, if not a psychical, impossibility, the distribution of business clearly contemplates it, for I made a calculation the other day, and found that, out of the 700 members in this House, you cannot count on more than 480 at the outside of what I may call ordinary, private working Members. We have to deduct seventy Members who are elected for Irish Constituencies but do not sit. We have to deduct about 100 Ministers and their satellites or Parliamentary Secretaries. We have to deduct, say, another 10 per cent for unavoidable casualities, and occasions such as today, and that leaves not more than 480 working Members, including all the lawyers, all the business men and the other Members of the House. I had the curiosity the other day to turn up the numbers of these Grand Committees and, making no allowance for duplication, I find that there are no less than 427 Members on those Grand Committees at the present time—427 out of 480. In addition to that, there are 225 Members—again not allowing for duplication—at the present time serving on Select Committees. I say without hesitation, that if these Grand Committees are going to be regularly worked at the pace they have been worked during the first few months of this Session, then the rest of the work of the House cannot possibly be adequately done.[1]

These statements, though made at a time when the new system has been in effect for but a short while, may nevertheless serve to indicate the tendency of its operation; and,

[1] *Parliamentary Debates*, Commons, 5th ser., vol. 116, pp. 2102-2103.

if the facts are such as has been alleged, only one reasonable conclusion can be drawn, namely, that the system of Grand Committees will not only be unable really to save the time of the House but may bring with it other evils of a nature no less serious than congestion itself.

There is still another evil of the congestion of business, and that is the break-down of the collective responsibility of the Cabinet.   Nowadays the business of the Government has increased alike in quantity and in complexity with the result that no Minister, however diligent, can keep himself acquainted with the work of his own Department, and at the same time be well informed of that of the other Departments.   Thus Major Wood declared in the House of Commons:

The Departmental pressure on Ministers today has so grown in intensity that a Minister tends more and more to be immersed in the day-to-day work of his Department.  He is every day faced with the dilemma of either having to neglect his Department or to neglect the House of Commons, and most of them are bound, perforce, as we know only too well, to neglect the House of Commons.  Unless it be possible to devise some means of squeezing forty-eight hours out of twenty-four, I submit . . . that it is almost impossible for a Departmental chief to form an intelligent opinion upon one-half of the subjects that come before him in his capacity as a member of the Cabinet. . . . Instead of the collective co-operation and responsibility of a Cabinet, we have now got to a great extent Government by semi-independent Departments, with an appeal to a Committee of Ministers to settle their differences, or, if not to a Committee of Ministers, to some outstanding personality such as the Prime Minister.  That is a revolution in our system of Government.[1]

The same view has been expressed in the House of Lords. Thus Earl of Selborne was of this opinion (March 5, 1919):

[1] *Parliamentary Debates,* Commons, 5th ser., vol. 116, p. 1875.

A Minister in a Cabinet today has, connected with the proper administration of his own Department, more work than any human being can get through. The consequence is that he does nothing except to attend to the affairs of his own Department; and he is only too content to leave his colleagues alone and not to criticise them if they will leave him alone and not criticise him. There has been a great change since the day when I first became a Cabinet Minister, not so very long ago. Then I think it was true to say that, if a Cabinet Minister circulated a Memorandum to his colleagues, a confidential paper, or some matter affecting his Department, his colleagues were careful to read that paper before the Cabinet when the matter was going to be discussed. I say without hesitation that these Memoranda which now go round in the Cabinet boxes are waste paper, or mainly so; that the other Cabinet Members have no time to read them, and do not read them.[1]

Aside from the congestion of business and the attendant evils we have described, the present system of a single legislature in Great Britain has another disadvantage, and that is the confusion of domestic and national and Imperial issues. This is unsatisfactory from both the Imperial and the domestic points of view. Sometimes a Parliament returned upon an Imperial issue such as defence, foreign relations, war and peace, is expected also to deal with the problems of education, health, industrial and labour conditions. Again, another Parliament elected on domestic issues may be suddenly called upon to deal with grave international and Imperial issues. Such a state of affairs has been deplored by both English and colonial statesmen and has been made one of the strong arguments for devolution. In the debate in the House of Lords on the Resolution on Local Legislatures (March 5, 1919), Earl Brassey said:

Another danger from the Imperial point of view, which I

[1] *Parliamentary Debates*, Lords, 5th ser., vol. xxxiii, p. 514.

have mentioned over and over again in speeches on this subject
in the last ten or twenty years, is the danger which arises from
the fact that Imperial questions and domestic questions are
submitted to the electors in the same confused issue.   At one
time a great Imperial issue may be to the front, as was the case
during the South African War.   A Government is returned
to power on that issue, and then proceeds to use the majority
so obtained to deal with questions, such as the education question, on lines which, as the subsequent Election showed, the
people of this country did not approve.   At another time some
question purely of interest to the people of these Islands may
be to the front, and a Government may be returned to power
on that issue which the country would not trust with the administration of the larger affairs of the Empire.[1]

It is the purpose of devolution, among other things, to
eliminate this confusion of issues.   This is the more important at the present time when international questions loom
large in British politics and the people everywhere are taking more interest in foreign affairs.   Unless Parliament in
some way rids itself of the enormous mass of local legislation, it cannot hope to deal adequately and effectively with
international questions and the important problems of the
Empire.

To sum up this chapter we may briefly recapitulate the
points we have discussed thus far.   In the first place, with
regard to the nature of devolution we pointed out that it is
not federalism as is often supposed.   Devolution is at best
a quasi-federal arrangement, under which the several countries of Great Britain will each have the management of its
domestic affairs by a Local Parliament of its own and an
executive responsible to it.   The principle of devolution is
two-fold: first, it is legislative; and secondly, it is national.
Hence it is distinguishable from other more or less similar

[1] *Parliamentary Debates*, Lords, 5th ser., vol. xxxiii, p. 511.

proposals such as administrative devolution or functional devolution. All these several proposals have indeed one argument in common, and that is the congestion of business in the House of Commons and the necessity of some measure of relief. Administrative devolution alone will not be able to afford such a measure of relief, and besides it is attended by several difficulties of its own. The suggestion of re-gionalism is very much in line with devolution except it does not proceed upon a national basis. Even if the former is desirable, it is a separate problem by itself; its purpose is the reorganization of the present system of local govern-ment rather than a scheme for parliamentary devolution. Functional devolution is a much more ambitious proposal than territorial devolution. It may be able to relieve the congestion of Parliament as would be the case with territorial devolution, but that, however, is not its chief purpose.

In the second place, we pointed out that the main object of devolution is to relieve the congestion in the House of Commons. There seems to be an urgent demand for such relief, because under present conditions the House is failing to discharge its functions promptly and effectively. Not only that, but the congestion of business has brought about many other evils: first, in order to get through the ordinary work of Parliament the freedom of discussion has to be, and has been, progressively reduced; secondly the present congestion necessitates the development of delegated legislation on a far greater scale than is desirable for whole-some legislative and administrative purposes; thirdly, it en-courages the development of bureaucracy; fourthly, it has made it necessary to set up Grand Committees which, as we have mentioned, are not unobjectionable; and lastly though not least, under the present pressure of business the collec-tive responsibility of the Cabinet is breaking down.

It may well be argued that many if not all of these evils

are due to a number of causes and cannot be logically attributed to the congestion of business alone. The force of this argument is conceded. It would indeed be unreasonable and uncritical to insist that the sole cause of the evils of the present system is the congestion of business. In nature as well as in society we can seldom single out the cause of a particular phenomenon, and we may reasonably conclude that the congestion of business is at least one of the factors that have contributed to produce the evils we have described. If this factor can be removed, all these evils will be considerably diminished if not entirely abolished. We pointed out further that the present system of a single legislature for Great Britain is unsatisfactory, in that domestic and Imperial issues are inevitably mixed up. All these are important arguments for devolution. The central contention upon which the whole case of devolution rests is, therefore, the congestion of business in the House of Commons. The advocates of devolution have all alleged the existence of this major evil. But the opponents may well raise the query, whether it really exists and to what extent does it exist. Therefore until these questions are unequivocally answered, the strength of the case for devolution will not be apparent.

# CHAPTER II

## The Case for Devolution—The Congestion of Business in the House of Commons

### I. INTRODUCTION

THAT the business of the House of Commons is congested has been constantly asserted by men both in and out of Parliament. The seriousness of the evil is admitted by most, if not all, observers of the Mother of Parliaments. Mere allegation and admission, however, are not enough to make out a case for devolution. Something more is needed in the way of evidence and proof. The purpose of this chapter and the next, therefore, is two-fold: first, to show that the alleged congestion does exist and that there is urgent necessity for its relief; and secondly to show that such a relief can be effected only through a measure of devolution. First of all, a few words should be said with regard to the nature of parliamentary functions.

Anyone who is acquainted with the work of Parliament knows that the House of Commons is over-burdened, and almost overwhelmed by the multiplicity of its duties, the variety of its functions, and the diversity of its interests. The situation confronting the House of Commons is indeed without parallel in the history of the world. The Imperial Parliament, which means the House of Commons for all practical purposes, is the sovereign authority, not only of the United Kingdom, but of the whole British Empire. Its executive is supposed to manage the public affairs of forty-five millions or more of English, Scotch, Welsh, and Irish peoples in a group of European islands; it is supposed to

rule over hundreds of millions of Asiatics and Africans;
and it is also supposed to direct the international relations of a loose aggregation of self-governing dominions
under the British Crown.  The subjects it deals with include the most trivial as well as the most important.  The
same machinery and the same men are expected to cope with
all the problems of a vast Empire, ranging all the way from
divorce, police, tramways, gas and water to peace and war.
Even in the United Kingdom alone, the House of Commons
has been doing what is done, in other countries, by different
legislatures.  For instance, in Germany there was, before
the War, in round numbers, one government to every 2,500,-
000 people; in Switzerland, one to every 170,000; in the
United States, one to every 2,000,000; in Canada, one to
every 700,000; in South Africa, one to every 1,200,000;
in the United Kingdom, 45,000,000 people are served by a
single legislature and single executive, which has also to
attend to the external affairs of a quarter of mankind.[1]  " It
is asking too much of human nature," says Sir Sidney Low,
" to suppose that a single set of officials should cope with
all these duties, or that a single ' big public meeting ' should
see that they are adequately performed." [2]

The inevitable result of such a state of affairs is the congestion of business at the center and the neglect of much of
the business of the localities.  The pressure of business was
felt as early as 1837, when the House appointed a committee
to inquire into the ways and means by which the business of
the House might be expedited.  More than eighty-five years
have elapsed since then, and, in spite of the many changes
of procedure that have been adopted, the pressure of business, instead of being abated, has become each year more
and more accentuated.

[1] *The Round Table,* vol. viii, 1918, p. 753.
[2] *The Governance of England* (1920), p. 291.

## II. CAUSES OF THE CONGESTION OF BUSINESS

The ever increasing congestion of business in the House of Commons is due to two causes. The first is the growth of the Empire during the eighteenth and the nineteenth centuries. Historians are fond of comparing the British Empire with the Roman Empire. The former is vastly more extensive than the latter, and while the Roman Empire consisted of contiguous territories around the Mediterranean, the British possessions are scattered all over the world. The five most important possessions, Canada, Australia, New Zealand, the Union of South Africa, and British India, lie in four different continents. The population of the Empire is no less diverse than its geography. The British Dominions, including Egypt (now an independent state) and the Sudan, contain a total population of about 420,000,000, of which the people of European descent number about 54,-000,000; the natives of India over 295,000,000; African races of all kinds about 62,000,000; the rest being Chinese, Malays and so on.[1]

According to the form of government, the colonies may be divided into three groups, namely, the self-governing dominions, the Crown colonies and the protectorates. The self-governing dominions are practically independent; each of them has a legislature and an executive responsible to it. They are subject to the control of the United Kingdom only in their international relations. The Crown colonies are under the direct control of the Colonial Office. India is an empire by itself, and is under the control of the Indian Office. Egypt was not officially classified as a colony, but it was nevertheless under British Suzerainty. The development of such a heterogeneous empire as this has imposed an enormous burden upon Parliament—a burden no other legislature

[1] Lowell, A. L., *The Government of England,* new edition (1920), vol. ii, p. 387.

in the world has ever been called upon to shoulder. The adequate discharge of such a burden alone would require all the time and energy that Parliament could afford.

The second and the chief cause of congestion is the development of modern legislation in the United Kingdom itself. During the Middle Ages, legislation was not the main function of Parliament. Its functions were chiefly financial and judicial in nature. The idea of making law in the modern sense was alien to the medieval mode of thought; whatever legislation was passed was done by way of declaring existing customs or by way of correcting defects in the machinery of administration. Parliament in the Middle Ages was a law-declaring rather than a law-making body. Laws were in the feudal times, as Mr. McIlwain says, " in the main declarations of existing custom "; [1] or they were, as Mr. Jenks says, " not enactments but records." [2]

As to the exact time when Parliament began to assume a preëminently legislative function, it is hard to say. Mr. McIlwain points out that, at any rate, the date cannot be pushed back beyond that Long Parliament when extraordinary acts were done and unusual powers assumed.[3] After the Restoration, the legislative activities of Parliament were accelerated; but nevertheless not many acts were passed in the eighteenth century. Thus Maitland has pointed out that " Notwithstanding the bulk of the Statute Book in the eighteenth century, comparatively few acts of real legislation were passed before the first Reform Act, which produced radical and sweeping changes in the laws, such, for example, as the Poor Law Reform Act of 1834." [4]

[1] McIlwain, C. H., *The High Court of Parliament and Its Supremacy*, p. 42.

[2] Quoted in McIlwain, p. 42.

[3] *Ibid.,* pp. 103-105, note B.

[4] *Constitutional History of England*, pp. 382-384; quoted in McIlwain, p. 103.

Modern legislation developed as a result of three distinct forces during the last century.   Of these the most important was the Industrial Revolution, which brought with it a variety of new problems and difficulties.   The process was greatly accelerated by the extension of the franchise.   The first Reform Bill extended it to the middle class in the cities. The subsequent Reform Bills of 1867 and 1884 further extended it to the farmers and wage earners.   The successive democratization of the franchise brought about another force in the development of legislation, and this was, the changed conception of the function of government.   There has been an ever increasing demand for legislation for the promotion, regulation, and amelioration of social and economic conditions.   Professor Dicey points out three main currents of public opinion in England during the nineteenth century, which determined, to a large extent, the legislation of England.[1]   The first was the old Toryism or legislative quiescence from 1800 to 1830.   The second was Benthamism or Individualism from 1825 to 1870, which was a period of Utilitarian reforms.   The third was Collectivism from 1865 to 1900, which was a period of socialistic legislation.   " From the beginning of the eighteenth century," says Professor Dicey, " till pretty nearly the time of the Reform Bill, the chief duty of the Ministry was not the passing of laws, but the guidance of national policy. . . . All this is now changed. Every speech from the Throne on the opening of Parliament has, for some seventy years and more, contained a legislative programme.   Amendment of the law is supposed to be the chief duty of a Ministry." [2]

The law with which Parliament is chiefly concerned is, however, not the lawyer's law, but what is called on the continent administrative law.   " The substantial business,"

[1] Dicey, *Law and Public Opinion* (2nd edition, 1914), pp. 62-69.
[2] *Ibid.*, p. 85.

says Ilbert, " of Parliament as a legislature is to keep
the machinery of the State in working order, And the laws
which are required for this purpose belong to the domain,
not of private or of commercial law, but of what is called
on the Continent administrative law." [1]  Parliament has
never undertaken to codify the common law of England,
and, in the nature of the case, it is an impossible task.  Furthermore, the development of Parliamentary legislation has
centered chiefly on what is called private legislation as distinguished from public legislation.  Private legislation takes
the form of a private bill which is for the interest of some
person or class of persons, whether an individual, a corporation, or the inhabitants of a county, town, parish, or other
localities, and which originates on the petition of the person
or persons interested.  Public legislation, on the other hand,
takes the form of a public bill which is introduced as a
measure of public policy in which the whole community is
interested, and which originates on the motion of some
member of the House in which the bill is introduced.[2]  These
two kinds of bills are to be distinguished from what are
called Government bills and Private members' bills.  A government bill is one introduced by the government, while a
private member's bill is one introduced by a private member.
Both may be public in nature.  Theoretically every member
has the right to initiate legislation, but, in practice, since the
development of cabinet responsibility, public legislation has
devolved mainly upon the government, although public bills
are still introduced by the cabinet members, not in the capacity of government officers but in the capacity of members
of the House.

The great period of Private Bill legislation resulting in
local and private acts was from 1745 to 1845.[3]  It was esti-

[1] Ilbert, C., *Legislative Methods and Forms*, p. 210.

[2] *Ibid.*, p. 28.

[3] Spencer, F. H., *Municipal Origins*, p. 2.

mated that 11,000 local and private acts were passed during the eighteenth century, and about 21,000, in the nineteenth century — an increase of nearly a hundred percent.[1]  The relative proportion between local acts and public acts also increased during the same period.  It was estimated that, in 1750, 40 public acts were passed, of which 19 were local acts.[2]  In 1751, 29 out of 59 were local acts; in 1752, 34 out of 60; in 1770, 65 out of 114; in 1771, 63 out of 110.[3]  Since then, local acts have formed a majority of the acts placed upon the Statute Book.  Appendix A shows that, of the total number of 28,053 acts passed from 1801 to 1884, 14,774 or more than 50 per cent were local acts;

[1] Ilbert, *op. cit.,* p. 35.

[2] The acts of Parliament are classified as follows:

(1) **Before** 1798:
  (a) Public Acts—including local Acts with special clause that the act should "be judicially taken notice of as such by all judges, justices, and others without being specially pleaded.
  (b) Private acts.

(2) From 1798-1814:
  (a) Public General Acts.
  (b) Local and Personal Acts declared public and to be judicially noticed.
  (c) Private and Personal Acts.

(3) From 1814-1868:
  (a) Public General Acts.
  (b) Local and Personal Acts declared public and to be judicially noticed.
  (c) Private Acts printed by the Queen's printer, copies of which may be given in evidence.
  (d) Private Acts not so printed.

(4) Present Classification since 1868:
  (a) Public General Acts—including acts applying to England, or Scotland, or Ireland, or Wales, and Metropolitan Bills.
  (b) Local Acts, (including acts for Confirming Provisional Orders).
  (c) Private Acts, (Clifford, History of Private Bill Legislation, vol. i, pp. 267-270).

[3] Spencer, *op. cit.,* pp. 311-312.

9,556 or about 30 per cent were public acts, the rest being private acts.  The same appendix shows that, out of the total number of 8,265 acts passed from 1884 to 1914, 6,441 or more than 75 per cent were local acts including public acts of a local character, while only 1,728 or about 20 per cent were public acts.  The figures during the War are not trustworthy for comparison and hence may be left out.

Most of the private legislation in the nineteenth century dealt with the problems of local governmnent.  The urbanization of the country, the rapid growth of population, the development of transportation, manufacturing, etc., rendered the old system of local government inefficient and inadequate. The parish constable could no longer keep order in the town; the unwilling and unpaid overseer of the poor could no longer administer the poor law in a rapidly growing population.  Lighting became necessary when the village street had developed into the tortuous ill-planned ramifications of a rising manufacturing town or a populous suburb. Paving, street cleaning, and street improvement urgently claimed attention.  For each of these functions a new and separate authority had to be created. and this could be done only by an act of Parliament.  Hence the development of local acts, creating separate watch boards, lighting boards, paving commissioners, improvement commissioners, governors or guardians of the poor, inclosure commissioners and so on.  " Take up a volume of the eighteenth century statutes," said Sir Courtenay Ilbert, " and compare it with a volume of the Victorian period, and you will find yourself in a new world.  In the eighteenth century there was no Local Government Board, no Board of Education, no Board of Agriculture, and the duties of the Board of Trade were almost nominal.  Nor were there county councils, district councils, or parish councils.  The municipalities were close, corrupt, irresponsible corporations, existing for the benefit of their members, and not of the local public. The functions, both of the central and of the local authorities, were comparatively few and simple. There were no railways, and no limited companies. Gas and electricity had not been utilized. Parliament concerned itself little or not at all with educational or sanitary questions, and factory legislation was a thing of the future. Industry was indeed regulated, but mainly in a paternal fashion by justices of the peace. In a great part of the country such local administration as was required was exercised by justices, and the numerous laws which were passed in the eighteenth century for conferring on them additional powers, though often intolerably prolix, were comparatively simple.

" The shifting of the center of political gravity after the Reform Act of 1832, the enormous strides of scientific discovery, commercial enterprise and industrial activity, the new problems presented by the massing of great numbers in towns and factories under artificial conditions, the awakened interest in the moral, mental, and material welfare of the working classes, involving demands for enlargement of the functions both of the central and of the local government— all these causes have materially altered the character and increased the volume of Victorian legislation. . . . The net result of the legislative activity which has characterized, though with different degrees of intensity, the period since 1832, has been the building up piecemeal of an administrative machine of great complexity, which stands in as constant need of repair, renewal, reconstruction, and adaptation to new requirements as the plaint of a modern factory. The legislation required for this purpose is enough, and more than enough, to absorb the whole legislative time of the House of Commons, and the problem of finding the requisite time for this class of legislation increases in difficulty each year, and taxes to the utmost, if it does not baffle, the in-

genuity of those who are responsible for the arrangement
of Parliamentary business." [1]

Appendix A shows that, on the whole, discounting certain
years, there has been a constant increase of the number of
local acts passed each year from 1800 to the eve of the Great
War, and that there has been a relative decrease of public
acts during the same period.  It must be remembered too,
that many of the so-called public acts deal with only one or
the other countries of the United Kingdom.  This indicates
but one thing, namely that either Parliament has had to
spend a great portion of its time in the passing of local acts
to the neglect of other duties, or that local matters were not
adequately dealt with by Parliament.  Both results are
undoubtedly true to some extent.  If all this amount of
private legislation had been delegated to some subordinate
legislatures, much of the time of Parliament would have
been saved.  In absence of subordinate legislatures, administrative departments have been empowered to issue subordinate legislation, and this practice is increasing each year.
Under the present system, this is certainly advantageous in
that it saves the time of Parliament and thus facilitates discussion on matters of policy.  It also secures administrative efficiency to some extent by making the administrative
machinery so elastic that individual cases may be dealt with
on the spot.  But, on the other hand, this is at best but a
partial relief, a relief fraught with difficulties.  For Parliament still retains and should retain the control of subordinate legislation by requiring statutory rules and orders
to be laid before both Houses of Parliament.[2]  Since 1890
statutory rules are published under the name of " the Statutory Rules and Orders Revised."  The volume of 1890
runs to 1,100 pages.  It contains bankruptcy rules, rules

---

[1] Ilbert, *op. cit.*, pp. 211-213.

[2] *Ibid.*, p. 41.

for civil bill court in Ireland, rules for winding-up of companies, the revised code under the Elementary Education Act, important Orders in Council under the Foreign Jurisdiction Acts, a long set of rules under the Lunacy Act, the others rules under the Patent Act and the Merchant Shipping Act.[1]  Since 1867, the bills for confirming Provisional Orders are listed under the Local Acts, being public acts of a local character.  Appendix A shows the number of such acts confirmed each year from 1884 to 1914.  The number of these Acts has on the whole increased from year to year. It is true that the purpose of delegated legislation is to fill up details pursuant to some broad general principles laid down by Parliament, but, as a matter of practice it is often difficult, if not impossible, to draw a sharp line between general principles and details, between what is important and what is not important.  Sometimes important changes are made in the law by Provisional Orders without the slightest discussion in Parliament, and most of the Orders are invariably confirmed without opposition.  Such a practice can be justified, as we have already seen, only on the ground that Parliament has not the time to do otherwise.

### III. EVIDENCES OF CONGESTION

In the foregoing section we have discussed the causes of congestion, namely, the growth of the Empire which constantly requires parliamentary supervision and control, and the development of modern legislation in the United Kingdom, especially in the field of private legislation.  These facts in and of themselves do not necessarily show that Parliament is overburdened.  They tend to indicate that it may be overburdened, but not that it is actually overburdened; for in spite of the growth of the Empire and the development of legislation, Parliament might have, never-

[1] Ilbert, *op. cit.*, p. 42.

theless, fulfilled its functions.   There are, however, positive evidences to prove conclusively that it is actually overburdened.   Such evidences are deducible from three sets
of facts; first, changes in parliamentary procedure having as
their main object the checking of the freedom of discussion
in order to facilitate the transaction of more business, which
would otherwise be impossible; second, the failure of legislation, in spite of those changes, on a great many matters
desired by the government and the people; and third, the
neglect of the other functions of Parliament which are
supposed to belong to it.

### 1. *Changes in the Procedure*

Before dealing with the recent changes in the procedure
of the House of Commons, it is, perhaps, desirable to give
some description of its historical development.   In the medieval Parliaments the procedure was much simpler than it
is today.   There is little evidence of this procedure because
the official records were extremely scanty.   What could be
learned about the later parliaments was gathered chiefly
from extra-official sources, such as Hooker's writings and
D'Ewes Journals.[1]   Stubbs has a chapter on the subject
which is perhaps the best authority available.[2]   He tells us
that the Ordinances of 1311 and the acts of parliament in
1330 and 1362 established the rule that parliaments should
be held annually and oftener, if it were found necessary.
Still during the latter part of the fourteenth century, often
two or three years passed without a session.   Under the
Lancastrian Kings the sessions had become much longer
but less frequent.   At the opening of Parliament, there was
usually a speech or a sermon by the chancellor, or the Arch-

---

[1] Porritt, E., *The Unreformed House of Commons*, vol. i, ch. xxvii,
p. 529.

[2] Stubbs, W., *Constitutional History*, vol. iii, ch. xx, pp. 388-517.

bishop of Canterbury, or the lord chief justice. The King was usually present in person. After that the Commons withdrew and met separately. The first duty of the House was to choose a Speaker. Then they began to consider the matters laid before them in the opening speech. As we have seen, the business of Parliament in the earlier times was chiefly financial and judicial, namely, to vote grants for the King and to redress certain grievances of the subjects. On important matters, the Commons sometimes asked the Lords to appoint a committee to deliberate with them. The sittings were held in the morning from eight o'clock.[1]

The King, Lords, and Commons all had the right to initiate legislation, but most of which was founded on the petition of the Commons. A proposition for the change of law, or the redress of a grievance, might originate either in a private petition of an individual aggrieved, or in a proposition by a particular member, or in a general petition of the House. Private petitions were the origin of Private Bill legislation; the other two forms laid the foundation of Public Bill legislation. The procedure in private legislation was half legislative and half judicial. It did not result in statutes but in acts established and notified by letters patent under the great seal. The common petitions of the House were much more important than private petitions, and towards the close of the fourteenth century, they began to be drawn in the form of bills. The procedure on these bills was rather simple. At first, money bills were read three times, and toward the end of the fourteenth century, the practice became quite general. All bills, after their adoption by the Commons, were sent up to the Lords, who could either reject or accept them. The same procedure was followed in the House of Lords. After they were adopted by both Houses, they were sent up to the King and his

---

[1] Stubbs, *op. cit.*, pp. 393-394, 441-444, 473-474.

Council.   The bills assented to by the King thus became the acts of the King.   There was also the practice that a member could not speak twice on the same bill on the same day.[1]

From the time of Elizabeth to the eve of the First Reform Bill, few changes were effected in the procedure of the House.   Committees came into more frequent use.   After the second reading of a bill, it was usually referred to a committee, which meant always a select committee, for there was in the earlier period no practice of referring bills to the Committee of the Whole House.   The latter came to be used only in the reign of James I.   Since 1640, the practice had been for the Speaker to leave the chair when the Committee of the Whole is in session.   Before 1800 whenever the House went into a Committee of the Whole House, the question had to be moved, debated, and put. A chairman had to be nominated and elected each time, accompanied by debates and divisions.   All this was changed in 1800 when a permanent chairman was created, thus saving much time for the House.[2]

During the eighteenth century, Private Bill Committees were loosely organized.   Members sat and voted as they pleased, and there was much lobbying and corruption.   In the nineteenth century, some changes were made in this respect.   During the eighteenth century also, election cases occupied a great part of the time of Parliament.   There were sometimes as many as 60 or 70 disputed election cases at the opening of a new Parliament.   They obstructed public business and caused much expense and trouble to the parties concerned.   In 1770 the hearing and determination of these cases was transferred to a committee, called the Grenville Committee, composed of fifteen members.   It lasted until 1868 when the House at last relinquished its

---

[1] Stubbs, *op. cit.*, vol. iii, ch. xx, pp. 477-480.
[2] Porritt, *op. cit.*, vol. i, ch. xxvii, pp. 531-533, 535.

right to hear and determine these cases and an act of Parliament transferred them to the courts. Thus again time was saved for the House.[1]

The practice of divisions was probably used as early as 1593, but no machinery had as yet been devised. During the reign of Charles II, tellers were appointed, two of the affirmative and two of the negative. Division lobbies were not introduced until after 1834. In the first decade of the eighteenth century, voting by ballot was introduced in the Committees on election cases, but it was discontinued after a few years. Mr. Porritt is of the opinion that the short-lived experiment with the ballot and the Grenville Commitee were the only marked innovations in the procedure from James 1 to 1832.[2]

All the important changes have been brought about since 1832, during the period of modern legislative development. More than fifteen Committees[3] on Parliamentary procedure have been set up since that time, and a good many rules have been adopted, most of which are designed to check the freedom of discussion on the one hand, and to secure the certainty of business on the other. In the earlier times, as we have seen, every member had the right to initiate legislation. Prior to the nineteenth century, as is pointed out by Sir William Anson,[4] the rules of the House were devised for two purposes only: to protect the House from hasty and ill-considered action pressed forward by the King's ministers, and to secure fair play between the parties in the chamber and a hearing for all. All this is

---

[1] Porritt, *op. cit.*, pp. 535, 537-542.

[2] *Ibid.*, pp. 535-536, 542.

[3] Redlich, *Procedure of the House of Commons,* Introduction by Ilbert, p. xvii.

[4] Anson, W., *Law and Custom of the Constitution* (5th edition, 1922) vol. i, p. 265.

now changed. Since 1811 Government business has been given precedence on certain days. The changes brought about during the last century have sharply reduced the chance for private member's legislation. Under the present rules, the Government has precedence at every sitting throughout the session except the evening sittings (after a quarter past eight) on Tuesday and Wednesday and the sittings on Friday. Priority is given to Private Members' motions on Tuesdays and Wednesdays (after quarter past eight), and to Private Members' bills on Fridays. After Easter, the Government takes nearly all the sittings.[1] Appendix B shows the division of time between private members and the Government. On the whole, discounting a few years, the number of Government sittings has increased while that of Private Members' sittings has decreased in recent years. Even on the days when private members have precedence, their freedom of discussion is further restricted by the " Twelve O'clock Rule " and by the automatic suspension of the sittings of the House at half past five on Fridays. (Now the interruption occurs at eleven on Mondays, Tuesdays, Wednesdays, and Thursdays, and at five on Fridays.) [2] Thus private members have very little chance of independent legislation.

The influence and usefulness of private members with regard to legislation and control of the Government has steadily declined. One of the reasons for the appointment of the Select Committee on Procedure in 1914, which, unlike other Committees of the same nature, consisted entirely of private members, was the feeling among private members that their power and influence in connection with legisla-

---

[1] Low, S., *Governance of England,* (1920), pp. 70-71. Also *Manual of Procedure in the Public Business of the House of Commons* (1919), sec. xli, p. 37.

[2] *Manual of Procedure* (1919), sec. xxxiv, p. 30.

tion, and their control over finance and administration had
been very much curtailed.[1]   In his evidence before the
Committee, Mr. Lough, a member of Parliament, describes
the nature of the general changes as follows:

When I came in, the theory was that we had a free and independent Parliament, and that the House of Commons had retained its liberties practically in its own hands.  The tendency of
the changes has been to place all liberty with reference to what
shall be done, and almost everything that shall be said, in the
hands of the Administration.  The old Standing Orders were
generally adopted unanimously and were of great interest, and
we could follow them.  But since 1902 a code of regulations
was suddenly prepared for the House and issued as new Standing Orders, suddenly and very hurriedly drawn up, as will be
seen particularly if you look at Standing Order 18, which was
never finished; the consideration of paragraph 2 was broken
off in the middle of it, and never resumed. . . . The New Rules
were not unanimously adopted, but by a Party majority in 1902.
I think that is a great distinction between them and the old
rules.[2]

Another result of the changes in the rules of procedure
has been the increasing limitation of the opportunity for
raising general questions at the various stages of Government business.  The purpose of " questions " is two-fold:
to obtain information from the Government, and to preci-
pitate discussions on the policy of the administration.  Questions are of two kinds, namely, questions for oral answers,
notice of which must be given in advance, and questions not
for oral answers.[3]  According to Standing Order number

[1] Report of Select Committee on Procedure, *Parliamentary Papers,*
Reports Committees, 1914, vol. i, p. vii.

[2] *Ibid.,* p. i, questions 3 and 4.

[3] Lees-Smith, H. B., " The Time Table of the House of Commons,"
*Economica,* June, 1924, pp. 143-144.

9(2), questions are taken on Mondays, Tuesdays, Wednesdays, and Thursdays after private business and begin from three o'clock.[1] A minister may, on the ground of public interest or on some other ground, decline to answer any question, and not more than three questions for oral answers may be placed upon the paper by any member for the same day. Answers to questions for written answers, or the so-called " unstarred " questions, are printed in the official reports in the Parliamentary Debates. Theoretically, the asking of questions is a very important function of the House, a method which enables the members to control the executive. But practically, it is much restricted. No less than seventeen rules have been adopted for the regulation of questions,[2] and, besides, the allowance or rejection of a

[1] The Order of Business is as follows: After prayer, (1) Private business, (2) new writs, (3) Presentation of Public Petitions orally, (4) Unopposed motions for returns, motions for new writs, and other formal business, (5) questions, (6) request for leave to make any motion for adjournment under Standing Order 10, (7) introduction of new members, (8) matters taken " at the commencement of public business," (9) Orders of the Day and Notices of Motion as set down on the notice paper. (Lees-Smith, *loc. cit.*, p. 142.)

[2] Lees-Smith, *ibid.*, pp. 145-146. The rules are as follows: (1) A question addressed to a minister of the Crown must relate to public affairs with which he is officially connected, or to a matter of administration for which he is responsible. (2) A question addressed to an unofficial member must relate to some bill, motion, or other matter connected with the business of the House for which he is responsible. (3) A question must not contain names of persons or statements of fact, unless they are necessary to make it intelligible. (4) If a question contains a statement, the member asking it must make himself responsible for its accuracy. (5) A question must not contain any argument. (6) A question must not contain any epithet or ironical expression. (7) Quotations are not permitted in questions. (8) A question must not be asked about proceedings in a Committee which have not been placed before the House by a report from the Committee, (9) A question must not ask for an expression of opinion. (10) A question must not ask for the solution of an abstract legal question. (11) A question must not ask for an answer to a hypothetical proposition.

question is mostly at the discretion of the Speaker. Another trouble is that all questions must stop at a certain time. In the evidence before the Procedural Committee of 1914, Mr. Lough declared :

As regards questions, the vice of the present system is that they close at 3 :45; that is to say, when there are more questions than can be asked in an hour, they are suddenly cut off because the five or ten minutes cannot be spared to finish them. Very bad answers may be given by Ministers, time is too short for supplemental questions, and too many are put down for each day. There is no arrangement or organization of questions, indeed the House has no machinery for organizing anything except through the Ministry, which may organize everything to suit its own convenience and to strengthen their control over the House at all.[1]

Questions may possibly have two results: publicity of important governmental matters, and emergency motions for the adjournment of the House " for the purpose of discussing a definite matter of urgent public importance." The first is not of much importance now, since a public man outside the House can do the same thing, and since the press can perform the same function. The second is not very practicable, for the present rules with regard to adjournment require: (1) forty members must concur; (2) not more than one such motion can be made at the same sitting;

(12) A question must not be asked as to the character or conduct of any person except in his official or public capacity. (13) A question must not be asked which reflects on the character or conduct of any person, whose conduct can only be challenged on a substantive motion. (14) A question making or implying a charge of a personal character may be disallowed. (15) A question fully answered must not be asked again. (16) A question must not relate to the internal affairs of a friendly state. (17) A question which might prejudice a pending trial should not be asked.

[1] *Report of Select Committee on Procedure*, p. 3, question 32.

(3) not more than one matter can be discussed on the same motion; (4) such a motion must not revive discussion on a matter which has been discussed in the same session and (5) it must not anticipate a matter which has already been appointed for consideration by the House or with reference to which a notice of motion has been previously given.   Thus the Government can always block discussion on any subject by giving a previous notice of motion.[1] (6) The motion must not raise a question of privilege, or any other question which according to the rules of the House, can only be debated on a distinct motion after notice; (7) and lastly the Speaker may not allow the motion to be made if in his opinion it is not definite, or the matter is not important or not urgent.[2]   Speaking of the right to move the adjournment before the Procedural Committee of 1914, Mr. Lough made this remark:

That was a very great right which Parliament retained in its own hands, and when I came in, if the adjournment was granted, the debate upon it took place immediately and Government business stood aside.   Now, of however great importance the matter may be, it stands till 8:15, till the dinner hour, which has obviously been selected because it is the very worst time.[3]

In short, it was claimed that the method of adjournment as a means of criticism had broken down.   And a change in the rules seems necessary if it is to be effective.   Thus in the evidence before the Committee, Lord R. Cecil was of the opinion that he should certainly like to see the rule against anticipations  modified, so as to give greater freedom for moving the adjournment of the House.[4]

[1] Low, *op. cit.*, pp. 36-87.

[2] *Manual of Procedure* (1919), sec. lix, p. 62; Lees-Smith, *loc. cit.*, pp. 147-148.

[3] *Report of Select Committee on Procedure*, p. 3, question 31.

[4] *Ibid.*, p. 55, Question 907.

A third result of the changes in the procedure has been the cutting down of the time allowed for debate on measures proposed by the Government. This is accomplished by the " simple closure," the " guillotine," and the " kangaroo." The simple closure was introduced in 1881, became one of the Standing Orders in 1882, and assumed its present form in 1887.[1]    As used in the present form, the rule reads according to Standing Order 26 thus: " After a question has been proposed, a member rising in his place may claim to move ' that the question be now put ', and unless it shall appear to the Chair that such a motion is an abuse of the Rules of the House, or an infringement of the rights of the minority, the question ' that the question be now put ' shall be put forthwith and decided without amendment or debate." [2]    A majority vote of at least one hundred in the House, and of at least twenty in a standing committee, is necessary for its adoption.    The guillotine is also known as " closure by compartments." [3]    By this method, the House agrees beforehand upon an allotment of time to the various parts or stages of a measure, and at the expiration of each period, debate is instantly closed, and a vote taken.    This is a more drastic device than the ordinary closure.    The kangaroo is a method whereby the Speaker is authorized to pick out for discussion from the amendments proposed for any clause of a given bill those which he deems most important.    Only such amendments as are thus picked out may be debated.    This power was at first given to the Chair by special authorization, but in 1919 it was incorporated into the Standing Order 27A, whereby the power was made permanent.    The use of the various forms of closures is shown in Appendix C.

[1] Lowell, *op. cit.*, vol. i, pp. 293, 294, 295.

[2] *Ibid.*, pp. 298-299.

As a result of these innovations, the deliberative function of the House of Commons has been seriously curtailed. This was the view of Mr. Robert Harcourt before the same Procedural Committee. He said:

I think that fundamental rights and privileges exercised by Members of Parliament from the earliest times have been recently withdrawn, the effect being that we may get laws passed through which have not been considered by the House or by even any Party in the House; I would go to the length almost of saying, which Ministers themselves sometimes do not completely understand—the facilities being so great for rushing these measures through by the Ministry.[1]

It is not necessary to describe the further details of the procedure of the House, such as those relating to the various stages of Money Bills, Public Bills, and Private Bills, with which we are not chiefly interested. The foregoing account of some of the important changes will suffice to show that the House of Commons is overburdened. The only purpose of these procedural devices is to enable the House to get through with its business. If business were not congested, the rules of the closure, the guillotine, and the kangaroo would not have been tolerated for a moment. There is no member, I believer, who does not regret the drastic infringement upon the freedom of debate, and yet every minister, every member, has acquiesced in these rules, simply because the business of the Government must be carried on, and this cannot be done unless such rules be enforced. It has been contended that the congestion of business originated in the wilful obstruction which was cultivated to its perfect form by the Irish Nationalist members in the eighties, and that closure was introduced as a means to check it. This was true; but, even if there had been no Nationalist ob-

[1] *Report of Select Committee on Procedure*, p. 4, Question 52.

struction, such measures would have been adopted just the same. Furthermore, if the changes we have described were caused by obstruction alone, the simple closure would be sufficient for the purpose, and there would be no occasion for the introduction of the guillotine and the kangaroo. Besides, obstruction in the nature of things can never be eliminated and should not be eliminated, because under the English system of Government, the opposition in the House is supposed to obstruct the business of the Government. This point was brought out by Viscount Bryce in the House of Lords on March 5, 1919 in the following passage:

At the bottom of the whole Party system is this, that we set up a Government to carry Bills, and we set up an Opposition to prevent the carrying of those Bills, and the Opposition which is set up is animated not merely with the desire to get rid of a particular measure, to which it may upon legitimate grounds be opposed, but with a desire to discredit and disparage the Government by showing it, before the country, to be unable to carry its measures, and then of being able to turn round, when a General Election approaches, and to contrast the promises of the Government, with its performances. That is, I think the root defect of our system, and I do not think that any one has ever proposed a means of escape from it under our Parliamentary system, which makes it the interest of nearly half the House of Commons to prevent the other half from doing something, quite irrespective of the merits of the particular question. Therefore I cannot share the hopes of the noble and learned Lord (Lord Birkenhead) that we shall have much relief in the future, while human nature continues to be what it is, from the evils which belong to what is called Parliamentary Obstruction.[1]

## 2. *The Failure of Legislation*

The most cogent evidence of the congestion of business in the House of Commons is the failure or delay of certain

[1] *Parliamentary Debates*, Lords, vol. 33, pp. 532-533.

legislation. For the purpose of proving this failure, we may take the period from 1900 to 1910 as the best example, because these ten years came shortly after the introduction of various changes in the procedure we have described, and just a few years before the War. If it can be shown that Parliament failed to legislate during this period in spite of the changes in the procedure, then the congestion of business must be taken as fairly well established.

First, let us take the Government legislation. It was estimated [as shown in Appendix D(1)], that, during the ten years from 1900 to 1910, 115 bills were mentioned in the King's speeches, of which only 57, or exactly 50 per cent passed through the House of Commons in the same session. Thirty-one of them or more than 25 per cent were never introduced at all, although they had been put in the forefront of the Government's political programme. Thus the Government achieved on the average only 50 per cent of its legislative programme, and this certainly cannot be considered as a success.[1]

The minor Government Bills show a slightly better result. During the same period, a total number of 526 such bills were introduced or brought from the House of Lords, and of these 331 or about 63 per cent were passed in the House of Commons. If we exclude the 60 Financial Bills, the proportion between the bills introduced and those passed stands 466 to 271, the success being only 58 per cent. Besides, not all of these bills were passed in the same session. Some of them were reintroduced in more than one session. During the two Parliaments of 1900 and 1906, for instance, the number of separate bills which failed to pass on one or more occasions numbered 154, of which 65 had succeeded in reaching the Statute Book by the end of 1910;

[1] *The Round Table*, vol. ii (December, 1911 to September, 1912), pp. 65-66.

the other 90 Government Bills were lost in the pressure of business.[1]

Speaking before the Procedural Committee of the failure of small Government Bills Mr. Gulland observed:

The difficulty at present is to find time for them. They are very often measures which have begun at the instigation of some private member; there has been a Departmental Committee or a Royal Commission about them, or something of that sort, and they are usually very useful measures. With big measures on in the House up till eleven it is very difficult to find time before eleven for these Bills, because if you put more than one of them down on a day there is a great deal of interest, and people who are interested in the second Bill are interested to discuss the first, and so on, and it is extremely difficult to get these through. One or two men can hold up a measure. I suggest very humbly that it is not the Government that is the tyrant, it is the men who quite rightly, quite fairly make use of the existing rules of the House, and the result is that these Bills which are called for by a large section of the Community either are not passed or are reached at the end of the Session, when no discussion ever takes place.[2]

The failure of Public Bill legislation is shown in Appendix D(2) and D(3) where the figures for later years have been added. Appendix D(2) shows that, taking all the Public Bills introduced each year, only an average of 61 per cent was passed, and Appendix D(3) shows that, taking the Government Bills alone, only an average of 76.88 per cent was passed. Even taking those that were passed, the success was more apparent than real. Many of those bills, which were all necessary and uncontentious, should have been passed much earlier, had Parliament had the time. Take for instance the Lunacy Bill and the Scottish Education Bill.

[1] *The Round Table*, vol. ii (Dec., 1911 to Sept., 1912), p. 66.
[2] *Report of Select Committee on Procedure*, p. 98, Question 1393.

The former was mentioned no less than three times, and the latter, twice in the King's speech; yet it was not until 8 years afterwards that they were finally passed.[1]  Furthermore, the bills that were passed were not all given adequate consideration.  From 1900 to 1910, altogether 388 Government Bills passed through the House of Commons.  Sixty of these were purely financial measures and hence must be excluded.  The remaining 328 bills occupied 483 days of parliamentary time.  Of these 328, ten were very contentious bills which occupied a total of 207 days.[2]  The remaining 318 bills were passed in 276 days, less than one day for each bill.  The time occupied by these bills, however uncontentious they might be, was utterly inadequate.  A great many of them were rushed through in the small hours of the morning or at the week-ends.  Hence much of the legislation of the House is piece-meal and defective.[3]

As to Private Members' bills the failure is more marked. In recent years, the Government has practically occupied all the legislative time of the House.  Only on Fridays can Private Members' bills be discussed, and even these days may be appropriated by the Government towards the latter part of the session.  The practice of balloting is very hazardous and it has been suggested that the order of these Bills should be determined by the amount of support they each possess rather than by the chance of balloting.  Besides, a single member can defeat a Bill at the close of the sitting by saying, " I object ".  Very often the closure may be

---

[1] *The Round Table* (Dec., 1911 to Sept., 1912), vol. ii, p. 67.

[2] *Ibid.*, p. 62. The principal bills were (1) Education Bill in 1902, which occupied 52 days; (2) Irish Land Bill in 1903, 15 days; (3) Licensing Bill in 1904, 18 days; (4) Aliens Bill in 1905, 10 days; (5) Plural Voting Bill in 1906, 12 days; (6) Educational Bill in 1906, 31 days; (7) Territorial and Reserve Forces Bill in 1907, 14 days; (8) Licensing Bill in 1908, 30 days; (9) Old Age Pension Bill in 1908, 10 days; and (10) Irish Land Bill in 1909, 15 days.

[3] *Ibid.*, p. 63.

withheld by the Speaker whereby such Bills are automatic-
ally slaughtered.   The total number of Private Members'
bills introduced each year is far greater than the number
of bills introduced by the Government.   But only a very
small number of Private Members' bills succeed in becoming laws.   This fact may be clearly brought out by taking
an earlier period even before 1900.   For illustration we take
the figures between 1895 and 1900 as shown in the following Table: [1]

| Session | Total No. of bills introduced | Government Bills | Members' Bills | Royal Assent G. B. | M. B. |
|---------|------|------|------|------|------|
| 1895.... | 263 | 66 | 197 | 38 | 12 |
| 1896.... | 256 | 65 | 191 | 44 | 16 |
| 1897.... | 263 | 67 | 196 | 54 | 16 |
| 1898.... | 259 | 65 | 194 | 40 | 17 |
| 1899.... | 224 | 53 | 171 | 37 | 16 |
| 1900.... | 238 | 66 | 172 | 49 | 15 |

Again, the figures since 1900 [See Appendix D(3)]
show that the failure of Private Members' Bills each year
is greater than the failure of Government Bills: on the
average only 6.71 per cent of Private Members' bills was
passed each year from 1900 to 1923.

What has been said thus far relates mostly to subjects of
a definite political importance with which the Government
wished to deal.   There were, however, quite a number of
other subjects of an urgent and important character that the
House had never considered.   Take for example the case
of the adjustment of local and Imperial taxation.[2]   For
many years there was a dire need for reform.   The local
authorities depended upon one single tax for their revenue,

---

[1] Ilbert, *op. cit.*, p. 215.

[2] *The Round Table* (Dec., 1911 to Sept., 1912), vol. ii, pp. 68-71.

and out of this tax, they had to meet, not only local expenditures, but also part of the expenses of police and criminal prosecution, main roads, poor relief and education, all of which are admittedly national expenditures.  The tax was levied on the amount of rateable property owned by a men, which was a fallacious test, resulting in gross inequalities throughout the country.  In 1896 Lord Salisbury's Government appointed a commission to investigate the whole problem.  A final report was made in 1901, recommending certain immediate reforms.  For ten years nothing was done for the simple reason that the House could not afford the prolonged debate that such a measure would call for.[1]

Even in the field of private bill legislation the failure is quite noticeable.  Appendix E shows all the private bills introduced and passed in the House of Commons, from 1901 to 1914.  The total number of bills introduced in the House of Commons or sent down from the House of Lords was 3,115, of which only 2,741 received the royal assent.  Even if we eliminate those bills that were passed by the House of Commons but not by the House of Lords, those abandoned by the parties, and those rejected in the House or in the Committee, numbering a total of 253, there was still a failure of 121 bills.  The failure to pass these 121 bills cannot be attributed to any other reason except the congestion of business.

Again let us take a few other matters wherein Parliament has failed.  For instance, the Public Health Acts were very defective in many respects,[2] and yet for more than sixty years no change was made.  The sale of patent medicines with all their attendant evils and frauds has been regulated by the Pharmacy Act of 1869.[3]  The purity of water supply

[1] *The Round Table*, vol. ii (Dec., 1911 to Sept., 1912), p. 71.

[2] *Ibid.*, pp. 72-73.

[3] *Ibid.*, p. 74.

has been regulated by an act of 1878.[1]   Dental quacks
flourish under an act of the same year.   Obscene publica-
tions were regulated by acts of 1824, and 1857.   In short,
Parliament has failed to deal with many things that vitally
affect the well-being of the people.   This is another evidence
of the congestion of business in the House of Commons.

### 3. *The Neglect of Other Functions of Parliament*

(a) *The financial function.*   Parliament, or the House
of Commons, has several important functions other than the
making of laws.   The first of these is the financial function which is partly legislative and partly administrative.   It
involves two things, namely, to grant money for the public
service, specifying the purposes for which that money is to
be appropriated, and to impose taxes and to authorize loans.
The exercise of this function is governed by four principles:[2]  First, the Crown acting through its Ministers cannot raise money by taxation, borrowing, or otherwise, or
spend money, without the authority of Parliament.   Secondly, the financial power both of raising money by taxation
or loans and of authorizing expenditure, belongs exclusively
to the House of Commons.   Thirdly, the House of Commons cannot vote money for any purpose whatsoever except
at the demand and upon the responsibility of Ministers of the
Crown.   And, lastly, the House of Commons cannot impose
a tax except upon the recommendation of the Crown.

The national revenue is derived chiefly from taxation.
Most of these taxes are regulated by permanent statutes and
hence called permanent taxes; and some of them are of an
annual duration and hence called temporary taxes, such as
the Tea Duty and the Income tax.[3]   All the national revenue

---

[1] *The Round Table*, vol. ii (Dec., 1911 to Sept., 1912), p. 74.

[2] Ilbert, *Parliament*, pp. 91-92.

[3] Higgs, Henry, *The Financial System of the United Kingdom*, p. 40.

with a few slight exceptions is paid into the so-called Consolidated Fund of Great Britain and Ireland at the Bank of England, and out of this all the national payments are made. All the payments are watched over by an independent officer, called Comptroller and Auditor General, who is appointed by the Crown, holds office during good behaviour, and cannot be a member of either House.

The national expenditure like the national revenue is of two kinds, one regulated by standing laws, and the other by annual votes or appropriations. The latter includes the annual charges authorized by Parliament each year, while the former includes the annual charges for the national debt, for the Civil List, for judicial salaries, and for other charges of a permanent character.[1]

Thus the financial function of the House of Commons relates to two things only, namely, the annual authorization of such money as has to be provided by the annual votes, and the imposition of such taxes as are required to meet the expenditure. The latter results in the Financial Act of the year, and the former in the Appropriations Act. The procedure of passing these Acts may be briefly noted.

The financial year of the United Kingdom begins on the 1st of April. On the 1st of October of the preceding year, a circular is issued by the Treasury to the several departments, requesting them to furnish on or before the 1st of December the Estimates of their financial requirements for the ensuing financial year. For some reasons the Estimates may be delayed until the 13th of January, after which date no Estimate or alterations of an Estimate can be received.[2] These Estimates are first submitted to, and scrutinized by, the Treasury, and then approved by the Cabinet. The various Estimates, consisting of four volumes for the Navy,

[1] Ilbert, *Parliament*, pp. 93-94.
[2] Higgs, *op. cit.*, pp. 1-2.

the Army, the Civil Service, and the Revenue Departments
are submitted to the Committee of Supply.  Supply is the
first order of the day in the House of Commons on Thursdays, but it is also set down on Mondays and Wednesdays.
The Business of supply extends over about ten weeks, usually
until the end of July or the beginning of August.  Thus a
large part of the Parliamentary session is occupied by the
consideration of the Estimates.[1]  At least twenty days must
be set aside for the Committee of Supply, whose function is
is to consider the Estimates and vote such grants of money
as are required.  The debate in the Committee is mainly
critical.  As a means of controling finance its value is
practically nil.  Often great sums of money are granted
without the slightest scrutiny or discussion.  Standing
Order 15 provides:[2]

Section 2: Not more than twenty days, being days before the
5th of August, shall be allotted for the consideration of the
annual Estimates for the Army, Navy and Civil Service, including Votes on Account.  The days allotted shall not include
any day on which the question has to be put that the Speaker
do leave the Chair, or any day on which the business of supply
does not stand as first order.

Section 7: At 10 of the clock on the last day but one of the
days so allotted the Chairman shall forthwith put every question
necessary to dispose of the Votes then under consideration, and
shall then forthwith put the question with respect to each class
of the Civil Service Estimates, that the total amount of the
Votes outstanding in that Class be granted for the services
defined in the Class, and shall in like manner put severally the
questions that the total amounts of the Votes outstanding in the
Estimates for the Navy, the Army, and the Revenue Departments, be granted for the services defined in those Estimates.

[1] Higgs, *op. cit.*, p. 34.
[2] *Ibid.*, pp. 31-32.

After the various Votes have been passed by the Committees they are reported to the House, following the regular procedure of other public bills.   Section 8 of the same Order provides:

At 10 of the clock of the last, not being earlier than the twentieth, of the allotted days, the Speaker shall forthwith put every question necessary to dispose of the report of the resolutions then under consideration, and shall then forthwith put, with respect to each class of the Civil Service Estimates, the question that the House doth agree with the Committee in all the outstanding resolutions reported in respect of that class, and shall then put a like question with respect to all the resolutions outstanding in the Estimates for the Navy, the Army, the Revenue Departments, and other outstanding resolutions severally.

In pursuance of such a process of guillotine, millions of pounds are voted each year without a single word of debate. The following is a list of the sums thus voted:[1]

| | | | |
|---|---|---|---|
| 1900 ........ | 3,591,877 | 1906 ........ | 15,727,746 |
| 1901 ........ | 67,706,671 | 1907 ........ | 50,844,895 |
| 1902 ........ | 12,088,571 | 1908 ........ | 33,157,478 |
| 1903 ........ | 5,231,117 | 1909 ........ | 57,836,901 |
| 1904 ........ | 31,124,231 | 1910 ........ | 52,615,286 |
| 1905 ........ | 50,619,241 | 1911 ........ | 67,046,752 |

At the end of each year, the Controller prepares the appropriation Accounts.   They are submitted to a Committee of Public Accounts, which examines them and then makes a report to the House.

So much for the business of Supply.   Let us now consider the question of taxation.   Once in every year, usually soon after Easter, the Chancellor of the Exchequer makes a budgetary statement in the Committee of Ways and Means, fol-

---

[1] *The Round Table*, vol. ii (Dec., 1911 to Sept., 1912), p. 79.

lowed by his budget resolutions. Legally these resolutions take administrative effect immediately under directions given to the revenue authorities. These resolutions are discussed in the Committee of Ways and Means, which can reject or amend them, but cannot increase the amounts. When passed by the Committee and agreed to by the House, they become the Financial Act of the year.

From the foregoing considerations, it must be clear that the control over the public purse by the House of Commons cannot be regarded as satisfactory. Sir Courtenay Ilbert says that the control of the House over the amount of expenditure is not very effective, although the control over irregularity of expenditure and over taxation is said to be substantial.[1] The failure to control the amount of expenditure is undoubtedly due to a number of causes. First of all, the House of Commons is hampered by its ancient procedure. Secondly, the financial discussions and debates are primarily for political, rather than for financial, purposes. Lastly, the members have no adequate and accurate information regarding financial matters. Added to all these is the fundamental fact of the lack of time. These shortcomings of the present system are admitted by recent writers on the subject.[2] The Select Committee on National Expenditure in 1917-1918 came to the same conclusion. The Committee was of the opinion " that the existing procedure of the House of Commons is inadequate to secure proper Parliamentary control over the national expenditure." [3]  " A so-called Committee of 670 members," the Committee observed, " cannot effectively consider the details of finance. The time at its disposal is closely restricted. It cannot examine wit-

[1] Ilbert, *Parliament*, p. 110.

[2] Davenport, E. H., *Parliament and the Tax-payer*, p. 116; Higgs, H., *Financial Reform*, pp. 62-64.

[3] Quoted in Davenport, p. 185.

nesses.  It has no information before it but the bulky volumes of the Estimates themselves, the answers of a Minister to questions addressed to him in debate, and such facts as some private member may happen to be in a position to impart.  A body so large, so limited in its time, so ill-equipped for inquiry, would be a very imperfect instrument for the control of expenditure even if the discussions in Committee of Supply were devoted entirely to that end.  But those discussions afforded the chief, sometimes the only, opportunity in the course of the year for the debate of grievances and of many questions of policy.  In the competition of time, those matters of greater interest, and often of greater importance, usually take precedence, and questions of finance are crowded out." [1]  The same Committee recommended various measures of reform.  Among others it suggested the establishment of two Standing Committees on Estimates.  But unless the House of Commons can find more time than it has, such reforms cannot be effective.

(b) *The critical function.*  The practical usefulness of Parliament nowadays lies first in the selection of a Cabinet that is responsible to the House and must have the confidence of the majority of the House, and secondly, in the constant control of the Ministry by criticism.  Without either of these functions, efficient parliamentary government would be impossible.  The control of the executive is considered by some as even more important than legislation.  But in recent years the critical function of the House of Commons has considerably declined.  Criticism is abandoned because of the technical character of the subject matter, the lack of sufficient knowledge on the part of members, and the congestion of business.  Besides, the development of the party system has rendered independent criticisms inadvisable, if not impossible.  Nowadays the Prime Minister may threaten

[1] Quoted, *ibid.*, pp. 185-186.

a dissolution of Parliament whenever he pleases for the purpose of reducing disobedience of his party members and of strengthening his power; and of late years ministries have been turned out of office as a result of a general election rather than of the adverse criticisms of the House. " In the eighteenth century," says Sir Sidney Low, " Ministries went out of office because they lost the confidence of the King; in the great Parliamentary period of the nineteenth century, because they had lost that of the House of Commons; and under the democratic franchise they have usually taken their dismissal from the elector." [1]

Parliamentary criticism may be exercised through many ways. First, a debate may be had in answer to the King's speech. This is, however, not of great importance. Secondly, questions are asked of the ministers from day to day. The usefulness of this method of control has already been described. Thirdly, there are motions to adjourn for the purpose of discussing a matter of urgent public importance. This has also been considered on previous pages. Fourthly, private members may make motions. Aside from voicing some opinion on the part of private members, the device has very little practical consequence on the conduct of the Ministry. Fifthly, there are the debates on going into the Committee of Supply, and the Committee of Ways and Means. Sixthly, there are the various debates in the Committee of Supply, the debates on the Consolidated Fund resolutions, on the Appropriation Bill, on the Budget, and on the Motions to adjourn for the holidays. These are perhaps the only occasions when the policies of the administrative departments may be criticised. All these have been restricted by the use of the various forms of closure and other rules of debate. Theoretically, the House can compel the resigna-

[1] *The Governance of England*, p. 101.

tion of the Ministry by refusing to grant supplies, but in practice it has never been applied.[1]

(c) *Foreign affairs.* In respect to foreign affairs, the failure of Parliament is most complete. Parliament has the general duty to control the Executive, and foreign affairs, being an executive function, should undoubtedly be controlled by Parliament. But Parliament has failed to perform this duty, because it has no time and no adequate information. There are two methods through which Parliament can obtain information in this respect, namely, Blue Books, and questions.[2] The former consist of carefully edited dispatches concerning negotiations, which have taken place long ago, and are, therefore, not of much value as a method of controlling foreign affairs. The latter afford little information, inasmuch as the foreign secretary can always avoid the answer to a question on the ground of public policy. Secrecy has always been the policy of the diplomat. The foreign secretary has almost the sole control of foreign affairs. Before the war more than one day in the session was seldom devoted to a debate on this important matter.[3] Consequently, treaties can be contracted and obligations undertaken without consulting Parliament. " Parliament is," says Mr. Ponsonby, " ignorant and powerless. More than that, it has been content to remain ignorant and powerless. A marked diminution in the time devoted to foreign affairs in the House of Commons has been noticeable within the last twenty years or so." [4] Various reasons are given for this. Some of the evidence before the Procedural Commiteee of 1914 on Foreign Affairs is worth noting.

[1] *Ibid.*, p. 90.
[2] Ponsonby, A., *Democracy and Diplomacy*, p. 52.
[3] *Ibid.*, p. 117.
[4] *Ibid.*, p. 48.

With regard to Foreign affairs, Mr. Speaker [Mr. Ponsonby asked Mr. Lowther] is it your experience since you have been in the House that they are less discussed now than they used to be?—I should say during the last few years, certainly less, but I attribute that to the fact that there is no violent Party discord on Foreign affairs.[1]

You think it is more the absence of disagreement between the Parties than the pressure of other work?—Yes, for instance during the time of the Armenian Massacres, the Bulgarian Atrocities, and the series of crises in Egypt in 1881-82, there were constant discussions on Foreign Affairs. That was because Parties were very sharply divided on the Government policy at those respective times.[2]

Mr. Ponsonby asked Ramsay MacDonald:

Do you think that Foreign Affairs are sufficiently discussed in the House of Commons at present?[3]—Not nearly—What would you suggest for making more frequent opportunities? —This proposal I make for having general Departmental discussion several times. I suggest in the course of the Session would make that possible. You would have two or three discussions perhaps on Foreign Affairs as the need arises. Then you have got the usual methods, supply and resolutions.[4]

On the other hand, Mr. Balfour declared that frequent discussion of Foreign Affairs in the House of Commons is undesirable. Thus he answered Mr. Ponsonby:

I think neither Indian Affairs nor Foreign Affairs are very fitting subjects for constant discussion and debate. Indiscreet speeches, the value of which we can perfectly weigh within the House, get reported and circulated abroad, or in India, or even

[1] *Report of Select Committee on Procedure*, p. 212, Question 3002.

[2] *Ibid.*, p. 212, Question 3003.

[3] *Ibid.*, p. 146, Question 2088.

[4] *Ibid.*, p. 146, Question 2089.

at home in the provinces, and very often make bad blood quite
unnecessarily, and raise difficulties which might easily have been
avoided.[1]

In general, then, it is very hard for the House of Commons to control foreign affairs.   The obstacles are several:
first, nearly all the diplomats of the old school believe that
secrecy in foreign affairs should be maintained; second,
there is a lack of public opinion on this topic and the members usually are ignorant about it too; third, there is no
adequate machinery.   Before the war, foreign affairs, if
debated at all, were only debated during the Foreign Office
Vote, and this was admittedly inadequate.   It is suggested
that a Foreign Affairs Committee may be created.   This
might be possible, but there is a fourth obstacle, namely, the
lack of time in the House itself.   Unless the House can have
more time, no important change seems possible.

Closely connected with foreign affairs is the question of
the dominions, over the international relations of which
Parliament is supposed to have complete control.   Appendix
F shows that for the ten years from 1900 to 1909 inclusive
an average of only .2 of a day was devoted to a debate on
Canada and Newfoundland, 0.1 of a day to Australia, nothing to New Zealand, 4.8 days to South Africa, and 1.5 days
to Egype and the Crown Colonies.   Thus dominion affairs
have been practically neglected.   Such a state of affairs has
been deplored.   " We shall not long continue," says Mr.
Murray Macdonald, " to hold the Empire together, unless
we give more time and sympathy to its affairs than is possible at the present time." [2]   Earl Brassey sounded the same
warning in the House of Lords on March 5, 1919.   In the
course of a debate on a motion for devolution, he quoted the
opinion of the dominion representatives as follows:

[1] *Report of Select Committee on Procedure*, pp. 116-117, Question 1707.

[2] *Parliamentary Debates* (Commons), 5th ser., vol. 116, June 3, 1919,
p. 1883.

We find Parliament engaged upon what we regard as parochial legislation to the entire exclusion of the greater question which affects us so closely, and it makes us despair of the future of the Empire. We are compelled to consider our own position. There is no fear that we shall ever desert the Crown or the Flag, but we want to go further than this; we want to act hand in hand with the Mother country in certain questions on certain lines, and if we are forced to the conviction that there is no prospect of the Imperial Parliament finding time to deal with these matters we shall then be compelled, very much against our will, to strike a line of our own, and to embark upon a programme which otherwise we should not adopt.[1]

So far we have been considering the evidences of the congestion of business in the House of Commons. We have adduced a number of important facts from procedure, legislation, and other functions of Parliament such as finance, criticism, and foreign affairs, for the purpose of showing that the alleged failures of the House of Commons are due primarily to the congestion of business. Of course, many other causes may be mentioned, which are, however, beyond the control of Parliament, such as the growing complexity of the issues with which Parliament has to deal, the tightening of the party machine with the result of transferring the powers to the Cabinet, and the increasing enlightenment of the electors—all these tend to weaken the authority of Parliament. But one thing at least is within its control and that is to relieve its congestion by one way or another, and much has been done already. Four ways are open, namely, further changes of parliamentary procedure, economizing of parliamentary time, prolongation of parliamentary sessions, and devolution of parliamentary functions. Let us next consider which method will afford the most effective relief.

[1] *Parliamentary Debates* (Lords), March 15, 1919, vol. 33, p. 510.

# CHAPTER III

## The Case for Devolution

### (Continued)

#### IV. ALTERNATIVE AND CONCURRENT REMEDIES

WITH regard to the first method, the change of procedure, there is very little hope. Under the present Standing Orders, private members' legislation has almost disappeared. Parliamentary debates have already been too much restricted. Appendix F shows that the time allotted for debate on the various subjects is far from being adequate. The use of the closure, the guillotine, and the kangaroo has already curtailed the freedom of discussion in Parliament. Any further restriction of debate would have only one effect, namely, to reduce Parliament to a mere registering machine of the will of the Cabinet, and it would thereby cease being a deliberative assembly. Even then, the method may not be practicable. Of the 95 Standing Orders, no less than 34 deal in one form or another with the restrictions on debate.[1] Any further change of procedure is limited to only two forms, namely, closure and devolution to Committees. Appendix C shows that there has been a marked increase in the use of guillotine, but there has not been a proportionate diminution in the use of the ordinary closure. The Select Committee on Procedure in 1914 recommended among other things that the Chairman of Ways and Means and the Deputy Chairman should have the power, without a motion being made, to select the amendments and new clauses that may be considered, and, at any time, to put to the House, without amendment or debate, the question that the words

---

[1] *The Round Table*, vol. ii (Dec., 1911 to Sept., 1912), p. 82.

down to a point selected by him stand part of the Bill or resolution. It also recommended that the Chairman of Ways and Means and the Deputy Chairman should have the same power with regard to the closure as the Speaker has, without notification of unavoidable absence being required.[1] In 1919 these provisions were pretty nearly all carried out and thus the kangaroo closure was further strengthened and extended. This perhaps saves some time for the House, but it adds more to the burdens of the Speaker and the Chairman who already have too many duties to perform.

Various suggestions have also been made with regard to devolution to Standing Committees, to National Committees, and to Parliamentary Committees. With regard to Standing Committees the possibility is rather limited, because of the pressure of time in the House of Commons. Two standing committees were created in 1882 on bills relating to law and to trade; their deliberations were to take the place of debate in the Committee of the Whole. They were made permanent in 1888, each committee being composed of not less than sixty and not more than eighty members.[2] The number of these committees was increased to four in 1907.[3] All bills except money bills and bills for confirming provisional orders were to be referred to one of the Standing Committees, unless the House ordered otherwise. In 1914 the Select Committee also recommended that the Standing Committes should be increased, and that they should be allowed to sit, while the House was sitting. All these proposals have been introduced into the procedure. In 1919, the number of Standing Committees was increased to six and they were allowed to sit while the House was

---

[1] *Report of Select Committee on Procedure*, p. ix.
[2] Lowell, *op. cit.*, vol. i, p. 269.
[3] *Ibid.*, p. 273.

sitting.  On the whole, they have been very useful, but subject to certain disadvantages: first, they are useful only regarding non-political bills; bills involving party policies must be discussed in the whole House.  Secondly, they are manned by the same members who have to get through the work of the House itself.  A great strain has been thus imposed upon the members.  Appendix G shows the number of members appointed to the various committees and the number of sittings of the same.  The number appointed to Standing Committees is increasing in recent years.  Mr. Marriott has calculated in 1919, as has already been alluded to in a previous section, that there were only 480 working members out of a total of little more than 700.  And out of these 480, 427 were on committees of one kind or another.[1]  Often a member may belong to several committees at the same time.  Here is the testimony of Captain Ormsby-Gore, a member of the House of Commons:

I have been on two Standing Committees at once and had to choose which I would attend, while at the same time I have been on an important Government Committee at the Indian Office, examining the Indian Bill and doing what I could to prepare for the Indian constitutional reforms.  It is utterly impossible to expect Members of Parliament to work fourteen hours a day and do decent work.  We cannot do it.  That is what the Government is asking us to do today.  The present procedure of this House is absolutely ruining this House.  It is ruining debates on the floor of the House.  It means that a large amount of legislation is going upstairs, and instead of being within the knowledge of Members of Parliament and of the people of this country, it is done by twenty or thirty Members in a Committee Room.[2]

As to National Committees to be composed entirely of the members from England, Scotland, and Wales, respectively,

[1] *Parliamentary Debates* (Commons), 5th ser., vol. 116, p. 2102.
[2] *Ibid.*, pp. 1958-1959.

as was suggested by the Procedural Committee, the same objections to Standing Committees may be applied. It may save the time of Parliament to some extent, but the trouble is that the same set of men are required to perform two jobs at the same time, and that Parliamentary responsibility will be further divided. On this point Mr. Balfour testified before the Procedural Committee as follows;

I think if we are to have National Committees really governing the opinion of the House I would rather have some form of Home Rule all round. Take the Scotch Committee; if you have some form of federation then the people sent to the Central Parliament by the constituencies are probably different from those who would be sent to the Local Parliament, and I would much rather, if I were a Scotchman, a Welshman, an Irishman, or an Englishman, have my affairs dealt with by a local parliament than I would by Members sent there from a particular area, not because they are particularly qualified to deal with the affairs of that area but because they are, or are supposed to be qualified to deal with Imperial matters as a whole. It seems to me if we are to be really nominally one Parliament but really a collection of separate little parliaments each of which is to govern the whole Parliament, it would be much better frankly to have federation in some form or another, as being the least of what I should regard as two evils, because as the Committee knows, I do not love these things in any shape, but I am very confident that you do not get a good tribunal for dealing with the affairs of a particular locality merely by choosing the representatives sent from that locality to the Central Assembly. I do not think that is the way to do it.[1]

Parliamentary committees have been suggested primarily as a means of controlling administration; incidentally they are useful in improving on legislation. But this raises grave questions of Cabinet responsibility. Such Committees

[1] *Report of Select Committee on Procedure*, p. 88, Question 1281.

are found in France and the United States Congress.
" There is little question," as Professor Lindsay Rogers
has pointed out, " of the utility of Committees in the work
of legislation.   Business is now so congested and problems
are so technical that some division of labor is absolutely
essential." [1]   But it is doubtful whether they would be
practicable in Great Britain.   The question has aroused
considerable interest in recent years in the House of Commons as a possible means of controlling the Executive Departments.   The Government has been on the whole opposed
to it on various grounds.   Thus Lord Robert Cecil declared
in the House of Commons:

The real difficulty of the present administrative system of
this country is, not that we have a reckless set of administrators
who are always trying to rush through experiments, but the
difficulty is to get anything done at all.   The complications of
business are so great and so increasing, and the time of the
individuals who are in control of the various Departments is
so much occupied that it is almost impossible to get any administrative reforms carried through, except those that are absolutely and vitally necessary.[2]

It is therefore plain that no great help can be expected
from changes in procedure.   Nor is it feasible to cut down
the non-legislative activities of Parliament in order to extend the time allowed for legislation.   The average session
before the war consisted of about 140 working days.   A
certain number of these days were taken up with the necessities of administration or by the express provisions of the
Standing Orders, and were therefore not available for ordinary legislation.   Appendix H shows the distribution of time
occupied by the routine work of the session.   First as to
the matter of finance.   The finance bill usually would take

[1] " Parliamentary Commissions in France," *Political Science Quarterly*,
Dec., 1923, pp. 622-632.
[2] Quoted, *ibid.*, p. 631.

nine or ten days. The Appropriation Bill was limited by
the Standing Order to 20 days, or by special order of the
House, to 23 days; but in practice no less than 26 days were
required for this item.[1] Furthermore, two days must be
spent on the Consolidated Fund Bills, and another day on
the Indian Budget. Thus altogether 38 days must be allowed to finance. There were only 16.2 days allowed for
debate on this item as shown by Appendix F. Therefore
under the head of finance there would be little room for
reduction.

Then take the Notices of Motions. At least seven days
must be allowed to the debates on the address. Two days
must be allowed under the urgency Motion to Adjourn.
Nine days must be allowed to private members' motions.
Two days must be allowed for various adjournments, three
more days for declaratory resolutions, and two days for
miscellaneous things. Thus a total number of 25 days must
be spent under the heading of Notices of Motions. It was
not feasible to economise under this heading.

Again take Appendix F. The time allowed for debates
on the various subjects could not be further reduced. Under
the heading of Empire were included the discussion of Army
and Navy Estimates, of the fiscal question, questions of
inter-Imperial communication, and of Imperial and foreign
policy. Under miscellaneous were included the Votes of
Supply for the Home Office, Local Government Board,
Board of Trade, Board of Education, and Board of Agriculture and the minor departments and home industrial
problems, such as unemployment, strikes and lockouts, shipping, mining, and factories; it also includes parliamentary
procedure and the relations between the two Houses. Nine-
teen and five tenths days for the Empire were already inadequate for the discussion of the manifold Imperial problems.

---

[1] *The Round Table*, vol. ii (Dec., 1911 to Sept., 1912), pp. 58-59.

And 21.6 days for the miscellaneous were by no means a disproportionate allowance. Take the other figures. India received less than two days a year. The three dominions of Canada, Australia, and New Zealand received only 3 days in a period of ten years. Egypt and the Crown Colonies received practically no attention. The time allowed to Ireland seemed to have been rather disproportionate, while Scotland received only 1.7 days, and Wales less than a day.

What was true before the war is, with a few exceptions, still true today. If any reduction is to be made, it must be at the expense of private members. Great encroachments have already been made upon the time allowed for private members' legislation. At the present time private members' legislation is almost negligible. Appendix I shows the days devoted to private members' bills each year, and the number of bills passed. During 1900 to 1909, an average of 13.6 days were devoted to private member's bills each year, and average of 11.7 bills are passed. Even if private members' legislation could be entirely abolished, the time thus saved would hardly amount to anything.

As to the third method of the prolongation of the sessions of Parliament, the same conclusion holds true. Appendix J shows that there has been an increase of the number of days in recent years, and an even greater increase in the number of hours. Any further increase of the number of days or of the number of hours would be at once impracticable and disadvantageous. Moreover, in recent years Autumn sessions have become more frequent. In the evidence before the Select Committee in 1914, it was suggested that Parliament should meet in November to get through a certain amount of formal business, so as to be able to go on directly with legislation at the end of January or beginning of February. There were, however, serious objections to this. For instance, Mr. Asquith said:

The difficulty is that you have not got a dead end at the other end of the Session. What I am afraid of is that if it was made habitual to meet, say, in November, you would go on sitting just as long as you do now in the summer. There is no dead-end which you have to come up against. I believe you might find that it would mean the prolongation of the Session. I think the Session is too long now; I think it is having a very serious effect not only on the health of Members and the efficiency of Ministers and Departments, but also on the attractiveness of Parliament to the kind of man we want to have here. I think our Sessions are too long, and I should deprecate anything which had the effect of even indirectly, although unintentionally, adding to the average duration of the Session.[1]

From what we have said, it may be concluded that although some further changes in the procedure may be still possible in one way or another, which may be desirable on their own account, yet they will not be able to rid the House of its congestion of business. Since 1837 many drastic changes, as we have seen, have been introduced into the House and yet the congestion, instead of decreasing, has steadily grown from bad to worse. The chief trouble is not the way of handling the business but the business itself. Mr. Murray Macdonald said in the House of Commons on June 3, 1919:

We have made I do not know how many changes in procedure during the last forty years, and all have failed to accomplish their purpose. The mass of business has steadily outgrown our capacity to deal with it. Without claiming any deep insight into the future, and without taking any very comprehensive views of the state of things in the Empire, we can confidently say the business of Parliament is not likely to go on accumulating more slowly in the years that lie in front of us than it has done in the years that are behind us.[2]

Again Earl Brassey said in the House of Lords in the same year:

[1] *Report of Select Committee on Procedure*, p. 152, Question 2178.
[2] *Parliamentary Debates*, 5th ser. (Commons), vol. 116, p. 1885.

A reform in procedure has been suggested to relieve the congestion and enable Parliament to do its business more effectively.  I venture to think that the reform in procedure now proposed will prove as ineffective and as futile as other reforms of a similar nature have proved to be in the past.[1]

The only way, then, of relieving the congestion of business in the House of Commons is through devolution.  The necessity of devolution has long been recognized.  In the procedural reforms of 1906, the Committee on Procedure thought it necessary but did not discuss it because that was not within its scope of inquiry.  Again the Select Committee in 1914 suggested two remedies, " first, those which aim at relieving Parliament of part of the business which now clogs its machinery and renders necessary the curtailment of the freedom of debate by devolving upon other bodies some of the duties which it now retains under its own immediate control, and, second, those which are designed to so amend the procedure and practice of the House of Commons as to enable it to get through more legislative work in the time at its disposal and also increase its efficiency as a critical and controlling assembly, and, as a result, to restore to some extent the independence, authority and interest of the Private Members." [2]  Thus although the Committee recognized devolution as a concurrent remedy or perhaps as a primary remedy, it, however, declined to discuss it because it fell outside the scope of the Committee's reference.  But the Committee did suggest that Bills applicable to only part of the United Kingdom should all be referred to Standing Committees composed entirely of English, Scotland, Irish, or Welsh Members.  The Committee recommended: " Your Committee, however, see no reason why the principle of Standing Order 47(2) with regard to Scottish Bills, and

---

[1] *Parliamentary Debates*, 5th ser. (Lords), vol. 33, p. 504.

[2] *Report of Select Committee on Procedure*, p. vii.

Standing Order 48 with regard to Welsh Bills, should not be extended to Bills which refer exclusively to England, or to England and Wales, or to Ireland." [1]

Again, in the debate on procedural rules on February 18, 1919, Major Wood said that in these circumstances, the Government had two alternatives before them, either to retain the present business and change the rules of procedure or to limit the business of the House through Federal Devolution. The difference between these two methods of saving Parliament's time is, as he points out, " that the Government says, ' Reduce the amount of attention you pay to your work,' whereas I would say, ' Reduce the amount of work to which you pay attention and do it properly.' " [2]

Mr. Murray Macdonald also touched upon the same point:

I contend, and I do not think that any old member of the House will dispute the contention, that no amendment of procedure can ever enable this House to accomplish the work that falls to it, and if that is accepted then it is very difficult to dispute the view that while we are ready to accept the Government proposals for this session we ought in the meantime to consider the alternative proposal with a view to bringing it into operation at the earliest possible moment, I will not go further than that. I have risen for the purpose of supporting the proposal that we should limit these changes in procedure to the present Session and to urge the Government and the House to consider what in my view is the only permanently satisfactory remedy for the congestion of business from which the House has so long suffered, namely, the remedy of a devolution of powers and functions to subordinate legislatures of the United Kingdom.[3]

To conclude the case for devolution, let us briefly recapitulate the points made in these two chapters. We have

---

[1] *Report of Select Committee on Procedure*, p. viii.

[2] *Parliamentary Debates*, 5th ser. (Commons), vol. 112, pp. 839-840.

[3] *Ibid.*, pp. 991-992.

seen that Parliament is really and actually congested and
that the congestion is daily growing. The causes of this
phenomenon are not far to seek. In the first place, there
was the development of the Empire which brought upon
Parliament an enormous burden of an unparalleled character.
Secondly, there was the development of modern legislation
which has tremendously augmented the legislative functions
of Parliament and which has been mainly responsible for
the growing congestion. In the way of positive evidence,
we have mentioned the facts of the changes in procedure
whose purpose has been to curtail discussions and to get
through business; of the failure of legislation which is a
chief function of Parliament, and of the neglect of other
functions which are no less important than legislation itself.
There is no doubt that, as a result of this state of things,
the prestige and influence of the House of Commons have
suffered. There are of course many other causes of the
general impotency of Parliament such as the development
of the party system, the development of the press and the
enlightenment of the people. Some defects again are inherent in the parliamentary system over which members
have no control. The proposed remedy of devolution aims
at one thing, namely, to remove the congestion of parliamentary business and thereby to enable the House of Commons to discharge its functions more adequately and effectively with regard to matters concerning the nation as a
whole and the Empire at large. Hitherto the remedy has
been confined to the reform of procedure. The latter has
been to some extent necessary but has proved ineffective.
Besides, the changes in procedure have brought in many
undesirable features which further threaten the independence and prestige of the House of Commons. Therefore,
the only effective remedy must be found in the devolution
of parliamentary functions to subordinate legislatures for
England, Scotland, and Wales.

## APPENDIX A

### Showing the Number of Acts Passed Since 1800

| Year | Session | Public Acts | Local and Personal Acts | Private Acts | | Total |
|------|---------|-------------|-------------------------|--------------|------|-------|
| | | | | Printed | Not Printed | |
| 1801.... | 41 Geo. 3......... | 109 | 146 | .. | 131 | 386 |
| 1801-02. | 42 Geo. 3......... | 120 | 119 | .. | 120 | 359 |
| 1802-03. | 43 Geo. 3......... | 162 | 147 | .. | 120 | 429 |
| 1803-04. | 44 Geo. 3......... | 110 | 89 | .. | 72 | 271 |
| 1805.... | 45 Geo. 3......... | 129 | 119 | .. | 105 | 353 |
| 1806.... | 46 Geo. 3......... | 158 | 147 | .. | 79 | 384 |
| 1807.... | 47 Geo. 3 S. 1.... | 56 | 43 | .. | 30 | 129 |
| 1807.... | 47 Geo. 3 S. 2.... | 78 | 134 | .. | 61 | 273 |
| 1808.... | 48 Geo. 3......... | 152 | 157 | .. | 77 | 386 |
| 1809.... | 49 Geo. 3......... | 129 | 192 | .. | 112 | 433 |
| 1810.... | 50 Geo. 3......... | 119 | 218 | .. | 96 | 433 |
| 1811.... | 51 Geo. 3......... | 128 | 221 | .. | 74 | 423 |
| 1812.... | 52 Geo. 3......... | 165 | 212 | .. | 77 | 454 |
| 1812-13. | 53 Geo. 3......... | 162 | 216 | .. | 79 | 457 |
| 1813-14. | 54 Geo. 3......... | 190 | 233 | .. | 65 | 488 |
| | | | Local Acts | | | |
| 1814-15. | 55 Geo. 3......... | 196 | 100 | 71 | 41 | 408 |
| 1816.... | 56 Geo. 3......... | 142 | 87 | 47 | 29 | 305 |
| 1817.... | 57 Geo. 3......... | 132 | 76 | 38 | 26 | 272 |
| 1818.... | 58 Geo. 3......... | 101 | 87 | 39 | 27 | 254 |
| 1819.... | 59 Geo. 3......... | 138 | 128 | 49 | 44 | 359 |
| 1819-20. | 60 Geo. 3 & 1 Geo. 4 | 14 | 6 | .. | 3 | 23 |
| 1820.... | 1 Geo. 4 ........ | 119 | 90 | 50 | 18 | 277 |
| 1821.... | 1 & 2 Geo. 4 .... | 123 | 128 | 45 | 14 | 310 |
| 1822.... | 3 Geo. 4 ....... | 127 | 114 | 36 | 11 | 288 |
| 1823.... | 4 Geo. 4 ........ | 100 | 126 | 29 | 12 | 267 |
| 1824.... | 5 Geo. 4 ........ | 115 | 160 | 40 | 13 | 328 |
| 1825.... | 6 Geo. 4 ........ | 134 | 202 | 59 | 21 | 416 |
| 1826.... | 7 Geo. 4 ........ | 79 | 142 | 46 | 13 | 280 |
| 1826-27. | 7 & 8 Geo. 4 .... | 75 | 112 | 61 | 11 | 259 |
| 1828.... | 9 Geo. 4 ........ | 95 | 122 | 45 | 8 | 270 |
| 1829.... | 10 Geo. 4......... | 63 | 136 | 50 | 19 | 268 |
| 1830.... | 11 Geo. 4 & 1 Will. 4 | 75 | 138 | 50 | 16 | 279 |
| 1830-31. | 1 Will. 4......... | 27 | 70 | 7 | 3 | 107 |
| 1831.... | 1 & 2 Will. 4 .... | 60 | 76 | 22 | 16 | 174 |
| 1832.... | 2 & 3 Will. 4 .... | 127 | 113 | 34 | 10 | 284 |
| 1833.... | 3 & 4 Will. 4 .... | 106 | 122 | 30 | 13 | 271 |
| 1834.... | 4 & 5 Will. 4 .... | 96 | 96 | 36 | 10 | 238 |
| 1835.... | 5 & 6 Will. 4 .... | 84 | 112 | 27 | 21 | 244 |
| 1836.... | 6 & 7 Will. 4 .... | 117 | 138 | 35 | 18 | 308 |
| 1837.... | 7 Will. 4 & 1 Vict. | 91 | 133 | 43 | 16 | 283 |
| 1837-38. | 1 & 2 Vict. ...... | 120 | 102 | 35 | 15 | 272 |
| 1839.... | 2 & 3 Vict. ...... | 97 | 107 | 46 | 16 | 266 |
| 1840.... | 3 & 4 Vict. ...... | 113 | 131 | 36 | 17 | 297 |
| 1841.... | 4 & 5 Vict. ...... | 72 | 114 | 49 | 14 | 249 |

APPENDIX A—*Continued*

| Year | Session | Public Acts | Local and Personal Acts | Private Acts | | Total |
|---|---|---|---|---|---|---|
| | | | | Printed | Not Printed | |
| 1842.... | 5 & 6 Vict. .... | 123 | 113 | 40 | 19 | 295 |
| 1843.... | 6 & 7 Vict. .... | 99 | 110 | 29 | 10 | 248 |
| 1844.... | 7 & 8 Vict. .... | 113 | 108 | 34 | 15 | 270 |
| 1845.... | 8 & 9 Vict. .... | 130 | 204 | 33 | 4 | 371 |
| 1846.... | 9 & 10 Vict. .... | 117 | 402 | 43 | 8 | 570 |
| 1847.... | 10 & 11 Vict. .... | 115 | 297 | 35 | 3 | 450 |
| 1847-8.. | 11 & 12 Vict. .... | 133 | 163 | 22 | 5 | 323 |
| 1849.... | 12 & 13 Vict. .... | 111 | 95 | 26 | 8 | 240 |
| 1850.... | 13 & 14 Vict. .... | 116 | 112 | 18 | 7 | 253 |
| 1851.... | 14 & 15 Vict. .... | 106 | 146 | 23 | 3 | 278 |
| 1852.... | 15 & 16 Vict. .... | 88 | 168 | 21 | 1 | 278 |
| 1853.... | 16 & 17 Vict. .... | 137 | 227 | 29 | 6 | 399 |
| 1854.... | 17 & 18 Vict. .... | 125 | 222 | 38 | 3 | 388 |
| 1854-5.. | 18 & 19 Vict. .... | 134 | 198 | 16 | 7 | 355 |
| 1856[1]... | 19 & 20 Vict. .... | 120 | 139 | 14 | 3 | 276 |
| 1857-8.. | 20 & 21 Vict. .... | 105 | 165 | 7 | 8 | 285 |
| 1858.... | 21 & 22 Vict. .... | 110 | 150 | 10 | 1 | 271 |
| 1859-60. | 22 & 23 Vict. .... | 101 | 174 | 6 | 2 | 283 |
| 1860.... | 23 & 24 Vict. .... | 154 | 203 | 9 | 1 | 367 |
| 1861.... | 24 & 25 Vict. .... | 134 | 249 | 10 | .. | 393 |
| 1862.... | 25 & 26 Vict. .... | 114 | 227 | 6 | 2 | 349 |
| 1863.... | 26 & 27 Vict. .... | 125 | 238 | 8 | .. | 371 |
| 1864.... | 27 & 28 Vict. .... | 121 | 329 | 14 | 1 | 465 |
| 1865.... | 28 & 29 Vict. .... | 127 | 372 | 9 | 1 | 509 |
| 1866.... | 29 & 30 Vict. .... | 122 | 363 | 11 | 3 | 499 |
| 1867[2]... | 30 & 31 Vict. .... | 146 | 209 | 9 | 4 | 368 |
| 1868.... | 31 & 32 Vict. .... | 130 | 182 | 8 | 3 | 323 |
| 1869.... | 32 & 33 Vict. .... | 117 | 159 | 10 | 2 | 288 |
| 1870.... | 33 & 34 Vict. .... | 112 | 177 | 4 | .. | 293 |
| 1871.... | 34 & 35 Vict. .... | 117 | 206 | 9 | 2 | 334 |
| 1872.... | 35 & 36 Vict. .... | 98 | 200 | 7 | 1 | 306 |
| 1873.... | 36 & 37 Vict. .... | 91 | 253 | 2 | 1 | 347 |
| 1874.... | 37 & 38 Vict. .... | 96 | 200 | 9 | .. | 305 |
| 1875.... | 38 & 39 Vict. .... | 96 | 215 | 7 | .. | 318 |
| 1876.... | 39 & 40 Vict. .. . | 81 | 243 | 2 | 1 | 327 |
| 1877.... | 40 & 41 Vict. .... | 69 | 242 | 11 | 4 | 326 |
| 1878.... | 41 & 42 Vict. .... | 79 | 238 | 7 | .. | 324 |
| 1879.... | 42 & 43 Vict. .... | 78 | 225 | 8 | .. | 311 |
| 1880.... | 43 & 44 Vict. .... | 67 | 211 | 5 | 5 | 288 |
| 1881.... | 44 & 45 Vict. .... | 72 | 219 | 6 | .. | 297 |
| 1882.... | 45 & 46 Vict. .... | 82 | 266 | 5 | .. | 353 |
| 1883.... | 46 & 47 Vict. .... | 62 | 232 | 5 | .. | 299 |
| 1884.... | 47 & 48 Vict. .... | 78 | 262 | 6 | .. | 346 |
| | | 9,556 | 14,774 | 1,786 | 1,937 | 28,053 |

The above table was taken from Clifford's "History of Private Bill Legisla⁻tion," Vol. I, pp. 491–492. The figures before 1856 were based upon a Return of the Acts of Parliament in the House of Commons Paper number 34, session 1857.

[1] From 1856 to 1884 the figures were compiled by Mr. Clifford from the Statute Book for each year.

[2] Since 1867 the Acts for confirming Provisional Orders have been transferred from the list of Public to that of Local Acts.

| Year | Session | Public Acts | Local and Personal Acts | | Private Acts | | Total |
|---|---|---|---|---|---|---|---|
| | | | Prov. Order Confirm. | Local Acts | Printed | Not Printed | |
| 1884–85. | 48 & 49 Vict. ...... | 80 | 47 | 153 | 7 | .. | 287 |
| 1886.... | 49 & 50 Vict. ...... | 59 | 25 | 94 | 1 | 1 | 180 |
| 1887.... | 50 & 51 Vict. ...... | 73 | 41 | 160 | 1 | 3 | 278 |
| 1888.... | 51 & 52 Vict. ...... | 66 | 49 | 153 | 1 | 1 | 270 |
| 1889.... | 52 & 53 Vict. ...... | 76 | 49 | 165 | 5 | 1 | 296 |
| 1890.... | 53 & 54 Vict. ...... | 72 | 68 | 179 | .. | 1 | 320 |
| 1891.... | 54 & 55 Vict. ...... | 76 | 78 | 145 | 2 | .. | 301 |
| 1892.... | 55 & 56 Vict. ...... | 65 | 79 | 163 | 1 | .. | 308 |
| 1893–94. | 56 & 57 Vict. ...... | 73 | 67 | 162 | 1 | 1 | 304 |
| 1894.... | 57 & 58 Vict. ...... | 60 | 70 | 140 | 2 | 3 | 275 |
| 1895.... | 58 & 59 Vict. ...... | 50 | 70 | 103 | .. | .. | 223 |
| 1896.... | 59 & 60 Vict. ...... | 59 | 79 | 154 | 2 | 4 | 298 |
| 1897.... | 60 & 61 Vict· ...... | 67 | 63 | 197 | 2 | 4 | 333 |
| 1898.... | 61 & 62 Vict. ...... | 62 | 59 | 203 | 1 | 2 | 327 |
| 1899.... | 62 & 63 Vict. ...... | 51 | 65 | 212 | 1 | 2 | 331 |
| 1900.... | 63 & 64 Vict. ...... | 63 | 61 | 230 | 1 | .. | 355 |
| 1901.... | 64 Vict. & 1 Edward VII ............ | 40 | 80 | 201 | .. | .. | 321 |
| 1902.... | 2 Edward VII...... | 42 | 78 | 183 | .. | .. | 303 |
| 1903.... | 3 Edward VII...... | 47 | 84 | 179 | 2 | .. | 312 |
| 1904.... | 4 Edward VII...... | 36 | 84 | 161 | 3 | .. | 284 |
| 1905.... | 5 Edward VII...... | 23 | 63 | 150 | 3 | 5 | 244 |
| 1906.... | 6 Edward VII...... | 58 | 63 | 149 | 2 | 1 | 273 |
| 1907.... | 7 Edward VII...... | 56 | 60 | 116 | .. | 7 | 239 |
| 1908.... | 8 Edward VII...... | 69 | 60 | 108 | 1 | 1 | 239 |
| 1909.... | 9 Edward VII...... | 49 | 61 | 103 | .. | 1 | 214 |
| 1910.... | 10 Edward VII & 1 Geo. V.......... | 38 | 63 | 82 | .. | 1 | 184 |
| 1911.... | 1 & 2 Geo. V ...... | 58 | 76 | 114 | 1 | 4 | 253 |
| 1912–13. | 2 & 3 Geo. V ...... | 31 | 70 | 103 | 1 | 1 | 206 |
| 1913.... | 3 & 4 Geo. V ...... | 38 | 69 | 105 | 4 | 4 | 220 |
| 1914.... | 4 & 5 Geo. V ...... | 91 | 77 | 116 | 3 | .. | 287 |
| 1915.... | 5 & 6 Geo. V ...... | 105 | 47 | 62 | .. | 4 | 218 |
| 1916.... | 6 & 7 Geo. V ...... | 71 | 34 | 32 | 1 | 4 | 142 |
| 1917 18. | 7 & 8 Geo, V ...... | 67 | 24 | 36 | .. | 3 | 132 |
| 1918.... | 8 & 9 Geo. V ...... | 61 | 26 | 36 | 4 | 1 | 138 |
| 1919.... | 9 & 10 George V .... | 102 | 48 | 74 | 1 | 4 | 229 |
| 1920.... | 10 & 11 Geo. V .... | 82 | | | | | |
| 1921.... | 11 & 12 Geo. V .... | 67 | | | | | |
| 1922.... | 12 & 13 Geo. V .... | 60 | | | | | |
| 1922.... | 13 Geo. V.......... | 5 | | | | | |
| 1923.... | 13 & 14 Geo. V .... | 43 | | | | | |
| | Total from 1884 to 1914.. | 1,728 | 6,441 | | 96 | | 8,265 |

The above Table was compiled from the Statute Book of each year. The Local and Private Acts since 1920 did not appear in the Statute Books and hence were left out.

## APPENDIX B

### SHOWING THE DIVISION OF PARLIAMENT'S TIME

| sion | Government Sittings | | | | | | Private Members' Sittings |
|---|---|---|---|---|---|---|---|
| | Under the Standing Orders | Monday & Thursday | Tuesday, Wednesday, & Friday | Saturdays | Total No. of Sittings | Total No. of Days | |
| ..... | | 63 | 69 | 6 | 138 | | 35 |
| ..... | | 48 | 56 | 2 | 106 | | 33 |
| ..... | | 49 | 53 | 4 | 106 | | 25 |
| –91.. | | 57 | 54 | 1 | 112 | | 39 |
| (i) .. | | 36 | 32 | .. | 68 | | 39 |
| –94.. | | 90 | 118 | 7 | 215 | | 31 |
| ..... | | 44 | 53 | 3 | 100 | | 17 |
| (i) .. | | 38 | 38 | 1 | 77 | | 29 |
| (ii) .. | | 7 | 9 | 1 | 17 | | .. |
| ..... | | 49 | 57 | 2 | 108 | | 17 |
| ..... | | 51 | 54 | 1 | 106 | | 21 |
| ..... | | 47 | 55 | 1 | 103 | | 17 |
| (i) .. | | 46 | 52 | .. | 98 | | 18 |
| (ii) .. | | 3 | 5 | .. | 8 | | .. |
| (i) .. | | 46 | 45 | .. | 91 | | 21 |
| (ii) .. | | 3 | 4 | 1 | 8 | | .. |
| ..... | | 45 | 55 | 2 | 102 | | 18 |
| 1 a .. | | 27 | 29 | .. | 56 | | 13 |
| b ... | | 45 | 62 | .. | 107 | | 6 |
| ..... | | 45 | 56 | .. | 101 | | 30 |
| ..... | | 49 | 61 | 1 | 111 | | 29 |
| ..... | | 44 | 58 | 0 | 102 | | 34 |

| sion | Under the Standing Orders | Tuesdays & Wednesdays up till 8:15 | Under Special Order | Saturdays | Total No. of Sittings | Total No. of Days | Private Members' Sittings | | |
|---|---|---|---|---|---|---|---|---|---|
| | | | | | | | Tues. & Wed. at 8:15 | F. & spec. | Total |
| 5..... | 89 | 22 | 29 | 2 | 140 | 156 | 19 | 14 | 33 |
| 7..... | 93 | 16 | 9 | 1 | 119 | 131 | 16 | 12 | 28 |
| 8..... | 84 | 23 | 46 | 3 | 156 | 171 | 21 | 17 | 38 |
| 9..... | 81 | 16 | 68 | .. | 165 | 179 | 15 | 13 | 28 |
| 0..... | 44 | 5 | 45 | 1 | 95 | 103 | 5 | 6 | 11 |
| 1..... | 58 | 6 | 97 | 1 | 162 | 172 | 2 | 8 | 10 |
| 2..... | 68 | 15 | 109 | 1 | 193 | 206 | 14 | 12 | 26 |
| 3..... | 51 | 6 | 35 | .. | 92 | 102 | 6 | 9 | 15 |
| 4..... | 53 | 18 | 43 | .. | 114 | 130 | 18 | 15 | 33 |

The above Table was taken from Redlich's "History of the Procedure of the House of Commons", Vol. III, p. 18.

*a* before and *b* after the change of Standing Orders.

Since 1902 the Standing Orders have been amended. The figures from 1906 were compiled from the Returns of the Business in the House of Commons in the Accounts and Papers of Parliament. The figures since 1914 were not given and hence were left out.

## APPENDIX C

### Showing the Use of Closure in the House and in the Committee of the Whole House

| Session | Number of Times Ordinary Closure Carried | Number of Bills Guillotined | Number of Times Kangaroo Closure Carried |
|---|---|---|---|
| 1900 | 19 | .. | .. |
| 1901 | 74 | .. | .. |
| 1902 | 81 | 1 | .. |
| 1903 | 13 | .. | .. |
| 1904 | 44 | 1 | .. |
| 1905 | 45 | .. | .. |
| 1906 | 61 | 2 | .. |
| 1907 | 45 | 4 | .. |
| 1908 | 40 | 5 | .. |
| 1909 | 124 | 2 | 9 |
| 1910 | 13 | 3 | 1 |
| 1911 | 66 | .. | 1 |
| 1912 | 68 | .. | 1 |
| 1913 | 58 | .. | 1 |
| 1914 | 28 | .. | .. |
| 1914–16 | 1 | .. | .. |
| 1916 | 2 | .. | .. |
| 1917–18 | 18 | .. | .. |
| 1918 | 11 | .. | .. |
| 1919 | 7 | .. | .. |
| 1920 | 41 | .. | .. |
| 1921 | 35 | .. | .. |
| 1922 | 12 | .. | .. |
| 1923 | 53 | .. | .. |
| Total | 959 | 18 | 13 |

The figures from 1900 to 1909 were taken from the Round Table, Vol. 2, p. 93. Those for the later years were compiled from the Returns of the business of the House of Commons in the Accounts and Papers of Parliament for each year.

## APPENDIX D—I

SHOWING BILLS MENTIONED IN KING'S SPEECH, INTRODUCED AND PASSED, TOGETHER WITH TIME SPENT ON ABORTIVE LEGISLATION (EXCEPT HYBRID BILLS)

| Session | 1900 2 Sessions | 1901 | 1902 | 1903 | 1904 | 1905 | 1906 | 1907 | 1908 | 1909 | Total |
|---|---|---|---|---|---|---|---|---|---|---|---|
| Bills mentioned in speech from the throne | 11 | 10 | 7 | 10 | 12 | 13 | 16 | 13 | 11 | 12 | 115 |
| Introduced or brought from Lords | 10 | 3 | 5 | 8 | 7 | 11 | 10 | 9 | 11 | 10 | 84 |
| Rejected in House of Commons | .. | 3 | .. | .. | .. | .. | .. | .. | .. | .. | .. |
| Passed House of Commons | 7 | 3 | 4 | 6 | 3 | 4 | 9 | 7 | 7 | 7 | 57 |
| Percentage passed | 63.63 | 33.33 | 57.14 | 60.00 | 25.00 | 30.76 | 56.25 | 53.84 | 63.63 | 58.33 | 49.56 |
| Other Government Bills: | | | | | | | | | | | |
| Introduced or brought from Lords | 56 | 49 | 40 | 47 | 46 | 57 | 67 | 55 | 60 | 49 | 526 |
| Rejected by House of Commons | .. | .. | .. | .. | .. | .. | .. | .. | .. | .. | .. |
| Passed House of Commons | 42 | 32 | 22 | 29 | 23 | 13 | 45 | 41 | 47 | 37 | 331 |
| All Government Bills—Percentage passed | 74.27 | 67.30 | 57.77 | 63.63 | 49.05 | 25.00 | 70.13 | 75.00 | 76.05 | 74.57 | 63.60 |
| Private Members' Bills: | | | | | | | | | | | |
| Introduced in to House of Commons | 162 | 152 | 174 | 174 | 144 | 165 | 198 | 165 | 225 | 198 | 1757 |
| Rejected by House of Commons | 5 | 4 | 3 | 3 | 2 | 4 | 2 | 1 | 2 | 3 | 29 |
| Passed by House of Commons | 15 | 4 | 14 | 14 | 10 | 8 | 5 | 10 | 18 | 9 | 107 |
| Percentage passed | 9.24 | 2.63 | 8.05 | 8.05 | 6.94 | 4.84 | 2.52 | 6.06 | 8.00 | 4.54 | 6.09 |
| Time spent on abortive legislation: | | | | | | | | | | | |
| Government Bills | 1 | 2 | .. | 1 | 8 | 3 | 1 | 1 | 13 | 1 | 31 |
| Private Members' Bills | 7 | 6 | 8 | 9 | 6 | 9 | 6 | 8 | 12 | 11 | 82 |

The above Table was taken from the Round Table, Vol. 2, p. 88.

## APPENDIX D—2

### SHOWING NUMBER OF PUBLIC BILLS PASSED AND FAILED EACH YEAR

| | 1910 | 1911 | 1912 | 1913 | 1914 | 1914–16 | 1916 | 1917–18 | 1918 | 1919 | 1920 | 1921 | 1922 | 1923 | Average |
|---|---|---|---|---|---|---|---|---|---|---|---|---|---|---|---|
| **I. Bills which received Royal Assent:** | | | | | | | | | | | | | | | |
| 1. Introduced into the House of Commons | 38 | 54 | 33 | 46 | 91 | 100 | 76 | 69 | 56 | 90 | 71 | 61 | 52 | 36 | |
| 2. Brought from the Lords | 2 | 11 | 4 | 5 | 5 | 5 | 7 | 4 | 5 | 22 | 16 | 7 | 16 | 9 | |
| 3. Provisional Orders and Confirmation Bills | 61 | 69 | 64 | 57 | 72 | 47 | 22 | 18 | 25 | 40 | 51 | 57 | 47 | 33 | |
| Total passed | 101 | 134 | 101 | 108 | 168 | 152 | 105 | 91 | 86 | 152 | 138 | 125 | 115 | 78 | |
| **II. Bills which failed:** | | | | | | | | | | | | | | | |
| 1. Introduced into but not passed by the House of Commons | 178 | 224 | 224 | 193 | 206 | 7 | 4 | 9 | 7 | 43 | 68 | 67 | 82 | 91 | |
| 2. Provisional Orders and Confirmation Bills | 5 | … | … | 3 | 4 | … | 1 | 1 | 1 | 6 | … | 5 | 8 | … | |
| 3. Passed by Lords but not by Commons | 4 | 13 | 15 | 8 | 11 | 3 | 2 | 1 | 5 | 1 | 6 | 4 | 1 | 10 | |
| 4. Passed by Commons but not Lords | 1 | 2 | 2 | 3 | 2 | … | … | … | … | 1 | 3 | 1 | … | 2 | |
| Total failed | 188 | 239 | 241 | 207 | 223 | 10 | 7 | 11 | 13 | 51 | 77 | 77 | 91 | 103 | |
| III. Total Number of Bills | 289 | 373 | 342 | 315 | 391 | 162 | 112 | 102 | 99 | 203 | 215 | 202 | 206 | 181 | |
| IV. Percentage Passed | 34% | 36% | 29% | 34% | 43% | 94% | 94% | 89% | 87% | 74% | 64% | 61% | 56% | 43% | 61% |

The above figures were compiled from the Returns of the business of the House of Commons for each year in the Accounts and Papers of Parliament.

## APPENDIX D—3

SHOWING NUMBER OF GOVERNMENT AND PRIVATE MEMBERS' BILLS
INTRODUCED AND THE PERCENTAGE PASSED IN THE
HOUSE OF COMMONS

| Year | Government Bills | | | Private Members' Bills | | |
|------|------------|--------|------------|------------|--------|------------|
| | Introduced | Passed | Percentage | Introduced | Passed | Percentage |
| 1900 ......... | 58 | 49 | 84.48 | 162 | 15 | 9.25 |
| 1901 ......... | 46 | 38 | 82.60 | 152 | 4 | 2.63 |
| 1902 ......... | 48 | 30 | 62.50 | 168 | 15 | 8.93 |
| 1903 ......... | 49 | 38 | 77.55 | 163 | 12 | 7.30 |
| 1904 ......... | 55 | 29 | 52.72 | 145 | 10 | 6.89 |
| 1905 ......... | 53 | 17 | 32.07 | 165 | 6 | 3.63 |
| 1906 ......... | 78 | 55 | 70.51 | 188 | 5 | 2.66 |
| 1907 ......... | 61 | 47 | 77.05 | 169 | 14 | 8.29 |
| 1908 ......... | 68 | 53 | 77.94 | 228 | 21 | 9.21 |
| 1909 ......... | 55 | 41 | 74.54 | 204 | 15 | 7.35 |
| 1910 ......... | 42 | 32 | 76.43 | 176 | 8 | 4.54 |
| 1911 ......... | 64 | 49 | 76.72 | 225 | 16 | 7.11 |
| 1912–13 ...... | 44 | 29 | 65.90 | 217 | 8 | 3.68 |
| 1913 ......... | 59 | 35 | 59.32 | 185 | 16 | 8.65 |
| 1914 ......... | 97 | 80 | 86.95 | 205 | 16 | 7.84 |
| 1914–16 ...... | 113 | 105 | 92.92 | 7 | .. | .... |
| 1916 ......... | 86 | 82 | 95.35 | .... | .. | .... |
| 1917–18 ...... | 82 | 73 | 89.02 | .... | .. | .... |
| 1918 ......... | 68 | 61 | 88.82 | .... | .. | .... |
| 1919 ......... | 122 | 107 | 87.70 | 33 | 5 | 15.15 |
| 1920 ......... | 96 | 82 | 85.42 | 59 | 5 | 8.47 |
| 1921 ......... | 62 | 54 | 87.09 | 73 | 14 | 19.18 |
| 1922 S. 1 & 2 . | 74 | 61 | 81.35 | 73 | 7 | 9.58 |
| 1923 ......... | 43 | 35 | 81.39 | 92 | 10 | 10.87 |
| Average .... | .. | .. | 76.88 | .... | .. | 6.71 |

The above figures were compiled from the Returns of the Business of the
House of Commons for each year in the Accounts and Papers of Parliament.

## APPENDIX E—1

### SHOWING PRIVATE BILLS INTRODUCED AND PASSED FROM 1901 TO 1922

| Session | 1901 | 1902 | 1903 | 1904 | 1905 | 1906 | 1907 | 1908 | 1909 | 1910 | 1911 | 1912 | 1913 | 1914 | 1920 | 1921 | 1922 |
|---|---|---|---|---|---|---|---|---|---|---|---|---|---|---|---|---|---|
| Private Bills introduced on petition in the House of Commons | 129 | 115 | 116 | 95 | 95 | 96 | 67 | 72 | 61 | 52 | 68 | 53 | 63 | 65 | 59 | 40 | 36 |
| Private Bills sent down from the House of Lords including Estate Bills | 94 | 82 | 98 | 91 | 77 | 88 | 62 | 52 | 68 | 59 | 52 | 55 | 63 | 70 | 64 | 42 | 37 |
| Divorce Bills | .. | .. | .. | .. | 3 | .. | 5 | 1 | 1 | 1 | 3 | .. | 4 | 1 | 7 | .. | .. |
| Other Bills | .. | .. | .. | .. | .. | 2 | 3 | .. | .. | 1 | 1 | .. | .. | .. | .. | .. | .. |
| Provisional Order Confirmation Bills | 85 | 76 | 79 | 79 | 50 | 61 | 32 | 56 | 54 | 65 | 69 | 63 | 58 | 77 | 51 | 59 | 51 |
| Hybrid Bills | .. | .. | 4 | 6 | .. | 3 | 2 | 2 | 1 | . | 2 | 3 | 1 | 2 | 1 | .. | 3 |
| **Total** | **308** | **273** | **297** | **271** | **225** | **251** | **171** | **183** | **185** | **178** | **195** | **174** | **189** | **215** | **182** | **141** | **127** |
| Royal Assent | | | | | | | | | | | | | | | | | |
|   Private Bills | 196 | 182 | 184 | 163 | 157 | 152 | 123 | 110 | 104 | 83 | 119 | 105 | 122 | 119 | 124 | 78 | 70 |
|   Provisional Order Confirmation Bills | 85 | 76 | 78 | 53 | 50 | 61 | 55 | 55 | 54 | 61 | 69 | 63 | 57 | 72 | 51 | 57 | 47 |
|   Hybrid Bills | .. | .. | 1 | 4 | .. | 3 | 1 | 1 | 1 | 1 | 2 | 3 | .. | 1 | 1 | 1 | 3 |
|   Passed by Commons, not by Lords | 1 | .. | 3 | .. | 1 | 1 | .. | 1 | 2 | 2 | 2 | 2 | 4 | 2 | 6 | 2 | 1 |
|   Withdrawn or abandoned by Parties | 9 | 6 | 14 | 12 | 7 | 16 | 10 | 11 | 23 | 20 | 2 | 2 | 3 | 18 | 5 | 1 | 2 |
|   Rejected in House or by St. Ord. Comm. | 6 | 3 | 3 | 2 | 6 | 2 | 2 | .. | 1 | 1 | .. | 2 | 5 | 5 | 1 | 1 | 1 |
|   Rejected in Comm. | 8 | 5 | 8 | 6 | 6 | 6 | 3 | 4 | 3 | 3 | 1 | .. | 2 | 4 | .. | 1 | 1 |

These two Tables were compiled from the Accounts and Papers of Parliament.

## APPENDIX E—2

### CLASSIFICATION OF PRIVATE BILLS WHICH RECEIVED ROYAL ASSENT

| Session | Railways | Tramways | Tramroads | Subways | Canals & Navigation | Roads & Bridges | Water | Water works | Gas | Gas & Water | Lighting & improvement | Police & sanitation | Corporations | Ports, piers, etc. |
|---|---|---|---|---|---|---|---|---|---|---|---|---|---|---|
| 1904.... | 30 | 16 | 3 | : | 4 | 1 | 13 | : | 26 | 4 | 4 | 22 | 7 | 7 |
| 1905.... | 38 | 10 | : | : | 5 | 2 | 7 | : | 17 | 3 | 2 | 26 | 8 | 2 |
| 1906.... | 36 | 10 | 1 | : | 1 | 1 | 9 | : | 22 | 2 | 3 | 11 | 6 | 9 |
| 1907.... | 20 | 7 | : | : | 2 | 1 | 16 | 3 | 13 | 1 | : | 11 | 6 | 5 |
| 1908.... | 22 | 6 | : | : | 1 | 9 | 3 | 1 | 9 | 1 | : | 18 | 6 | 6 |
| 1909.... | 26 | 9 | 1 | : | : | 9 | 8 | 6 | 13 | 3 | : | 12 | 6 | 2 |
| 1910.... | 17 | 4 | : | : | : | : | 10 | 1 | 16 | 1 | 1 | 10 | 3 | 3 |
| 1911.... | 21 | 8 | : | : | 2 | 2 | 11 | 1 | 13 | 1 | : | 18 | 7 | 6 |
| 1912–13. | 20 | 4 | : | : | 1 | 1 | 11 | 1 | 22 | 4 | : | 8 | 5 | 5 |
| 1913.... | 21 | 4 | : | : | 1 | : | 10 | 1 | 17 | 1 | 1 | 18 | 12 | 8 |
| 1914.... | 23 | 6 | : | : | 4 | 1 | 6 | : | 23 | 1 | 1 | 22 | 15 | 3 |
| ........ | 8 | 5 | : | : | 3 | 2 | 8 | 6 | 10 | : | 3 | 23 | 18 | 11 |
| 1921.... | 5 | 1 | : | : | 1 | 1 | 13 | 8 | 7 | 2 | 1 | 15 | 5 | 2 |
| 1922.... | 5 | 4 | : | : | 4 | : | 5 | 4 | 6 | : | 6 | 15 | 6 | 3 |

APPENDIX E—2—*Continued*

| Session | Churches, Chapels, etc. | Markets & Fairs | Gaols other Blds. | Enclosures, drainage | Estate | Divorce | Naturalization | Nationality | Hospitals | Patent | Name | Legitimation | Miscellaneous | Total |
|---|---|---|---|---|---|---|---|---|---|---|---|---|---|---|
| 1904.... | 3 | | | 1 | 3 | | | | 2 | | | | 17 | 163 |
| 1905.... | 2 | | | | 3 | 5 | | | 1 | | | | 27 | 157 |
| 1906.... | 1 | | | 1 | 2 | 1 | | | | 2 | | | 34 | 152 |
| 1907.... | 1 | | | | | 5 | | | 2 | 1 | 3 | 1 | 25 | 123 |
| 1908.... | | | | | 1 | 1 | | | | | | | 26 | 110 |
| 1909.... | | | | 2 | | 1 | | | | | | | 15 | 104 |
| 1910.... | | | | | | 1 | | | | | | | 16 | 83 |
| 1911.... | | | | 2 | 1 | 3 | | 1 | | | | | 22 | 119 |
| 1912–13. | | | | 1 | 1 | 1 | | | | | | | 20 | 105 |
| 1913.... | | | | 2 | 4 | 4 | | | | | | | 18 | 122 |
| 1914.... | 1 | | | 1 | 3 | | | | | | | | 8 | 119 |
| ........ | | | | | | | | | | | | | | |
| 1920.... | | | | 1 | | 7 | | | | 1 | | | 19 | 125 |
| 1921.... | 1 | | | 1 | 2 | 5 | | | | | | | 8 | 78 |
| 1922.... | | | 1 | | 1 | 4 | | | | | | | 6 | 66 |

APPENDIX F

SHOWING DISTRIBUTION OF TIME OVER VARIOUS SUBJECTS OF DEBATE

| Session | 1900 | 1901 | 1902 | 1903 | 1904 | 1905 | 1906 | 1907 | 1908 | 1909 | Average |
|---|---|---|---|---|---|---|---|---|---|---|---|
| Finance (exclusive of Supply and Consolidated Fund Bills) | 9 | 19 | 13 | 6 | 14 | 9 | 4 | 11 | 8 | 69 | 16.2 |
| General Debate relating to: | | | | | | | | | | | |
| Empire (including Imp. Forces) | 20 | 18 | 21 | 23 | 27 | 24 | 17 | 12 | 15 | 18 | 19.5 |
| Scotland | 3 | 2 | 3 | 1 | 1 | 1 | 2 | 2 | 1 | 1 | 1.7 |
| Ireland | 8 | 12 | 13 | 3 | 8 | 14 | 7 | 8 | 10 | 5 | 8.8 |
| Wales | 1 | : | 2 | 3 | : | : | : | 1 | : | : | .7 |
| India | 2 | 2 | 2 | 1 | 1 | : | 2 | 2 | 3 | 2 | 1.8 |
| Canada and New Foundland | : | : | : | 1 | 1 | : | : | : | : | : | .2 |
| Austria | : | : | : | 1 | : | : | : | : | : | : | .1 |
| New Zealand | : | : | : | : | : | : | : | : | : | : | .. |
| South Africa | 13 | 8 | 6 | : | 7 | 4 | 5 | 1 | 3 | 1 | 4.8 |
| Egypt, Crown Colonies, etc. | 3 | 3 | 1 | 2 | 1 | 1 | 1 | 1 | 1 | 1 | 1.5 |
| Miscellaneous (including Supply for English Services and Procedure) | 15 | 20 | 34 | 20 | 20 | 18 | 18 | 28 | 20 | 23 | 21.6 |
| Legislation: | | | | | | | | | | | |
| Government Bills relating to Empire (including Imp. Forces) | 4 | 7 | 1 | 7 | 1 | 3 | 1 | 14 | 1 | 2 | 4.1 |
| United Kingdom | 7 | 5 | 2 | 5 | 4 | 13 | 28 | 9 | 25 | 12 | 11 |
| Parts of United Kingdom | 17 | 5 | 67 | 28 | 27 | 9 | 53 | 27 | 63 | 25 | 32.1 |
| India, Dominions, etc. | 3 | 1 | : | : | : | : | 1 | 1 | 1 | 5 | 1.1 |
| Private Members' Bills | 14 | 13 | 15 | 13 | 12 | 15 | 14 | 12 | 16 | 13 | 13.7 |
| Blank days | 3 | 3 | 1 | 1 | 1 | 2 | 4 | 1 | 4 | 2 | 2.2 |
| Total number of sitting days | 122 | 118 | 181 | 115 | 124 | 114 | 156 | 131 | 171 | 179 | 141.1 |

The above Table was taken from the Round Table, Vol. 2, p. 92.

## APPENDIX G

SHOWING NO. OF MEMBERS APPOINTED TO AND NO. OF SITTINGS OF COMMITTEES

| Session | 1900 | 1901 | 1902 | 1903 | 1904 | 1905 | 1906 | 1907 | 1908 | 1909 | 1 |
|---|---|---|---|---|---|---|---|---|---|---|---|
| No. of members appointed to: | | | | | | | | | | | |
| Standing Committees ....... } | 381 | 342 | 342 | 338 | 349 | 318 | 412 | { 502 | 496 | 441 | |
| Select Committees.......... } | | | | | | | | 146 | 226 | 155 | |
| Private Bill Committees ....... | 127 | 133 | 116 | 122 | 127 | 99 | 102 | 118 | 105 | 88 | |
| No. of days Committee sat: | | | | | | | | | | | |
| Standing Committees ......... | 31 | 26 | 20 | 43 | 26 | 24 | 52 | 88 | 115 | 59 | |
| Select Committees............ | 197 | 189 | 262 | 158 | 140 | 165 | 321 | 171 | 301 | 176 | |
| Private Bill Committees ....... | 378 | 289 | 241 | 255 | 264 | 250 | 182 | 205 | 208 | 240 | |

Appendix G was taken from The Round Table, Vol. 2, p. 94.

## APPENDIX H

SHOWING AMOUNT OF TIME SPENT ON THE ROUTINE WORK

| Session | 1904 | 1905 | 1906 | 1907 | 1908 | Average |
|---|---|---|---|---|---|---|
| Finance: | | | | | | |
| Budget and Financial Legislation... | 14 | 9 | 4 | 11 | 8 | 9.2 |
| Indian Budget ......... ........ | 1 | 1 | 1 | 2 | 1 | 1.2 |
| Supply and Consolidated Fund Bills. | 34.5 | 33.5 | 27 | 25.5 | 26.5 | 29.4 |
| Notices of Motions: | | | | | | |
| Address ....................... | 14 | 11.5 | 6 | 7 | 7 | 9.1 |
| Adjournment under Standing Order 10 | 3.5 | 4.5 | 2.5 | 1.5 | 1 | 2.6 |
| Private Members' Motions . ........ | 8.5 | 9.5 | 9.5 | 8 | 10.5 | 9.2 |
| Adjournments (Easter, Whitsuntide, | | | | | | |
| etc.) ...................... | 1.5 | 1.5 | 3 | 1.5 | 3 | 2.1 |
| Declaratory Resolutions, Votes of | | | | | | |
| Censure, etc. .................. | 2 | 2 | 2 | 5.5 | 4 | 3.1 |
| Days unavailable for business....... | 1 | 2 | 4 | 1 | 4 | 2.4 |
| Total ..................... | 80 | 74.5 | 59 | 63 | 65 | 68.3 |
| Government Legislation ............ | 32 | 24.5 | 83 | 56 | 90 | 57.1 |
| Private Members' Eegislation ........ | 12 | 15 | 14 | 12 | 16 | 13.8 |
| Total No. of sitting days ...... | 124 | 114 | 156 | 131 | 171 | 139.2 |

Appendix H was taken from The Round Table, Vol. 2, p. 87.

## APPENDIX I
### SHOWING PRIVATE MEMBERS' LEGISLATION

|  | 1900 | 1901 | 1902 | 1903 | 1904 | 1905 | 1906 | 1907 | 1908 | 1909 |
|---|---|---|---|---|---|---|---|---|---|---|
| Fridays devoted to Private Members' Bills........ | 14 | 13 | 15 | 13 | 12 | 14 | 14 | 12 | 16 | 13 |
| Bills discussed which passed | 3 | 2 | 5 | 3 | 3 | 2 | .. | 4 | 9 | 1 |
| Total No. passed......... | 15 | 4 | 14 | 14 | 10 | 8 | 5 | 10 | 18 | 9 |

The above Table was taken from The Round Table, Vol. 2, p. 81.

## APPENDIX J
### SHOWING THE INCREASE OF DAYS AND HOURS IN THE SESSIONS OF THE HOUSE

| Year | Average No. of Days | Average No. of Hours |
|---|---|---|
| 1831–32–1841 ........... | 131.3 | 1000.65 |
| 1842–1851 .............. | 128.1 | 1015.17 |
| 1852–1861 .............. | 120.3 | 933.08 |
| 1862–1871 .............. | 115.3 | 894.69 |
| 1872–1881 .............. | 123.9 | 1042.22 |
| 1882–1891 .............. | 137.4 | 1186.13 |
| 1892–1901 .............. | 128.6 | 1078.74 |
| 1902–1910 .............. | 141.5 | 1203.76 |
| 1911–1921 ............ ... | 149.1 | ...... |

The above Table was taken from The Round Table, Vol. 2, p. 75. The figure from 1911 to 1921 was based upon the Returns of the business of the House of Commons for each year in the Accounts and Papers of Parliament.

# CHAPTER IV

## Parliamentary Resolutions and Proposals for Devolution—From 1874 to 1914

### I. BEFORE 1900

THE purpose of this and the following chapters is to make a general survey of the attitude of the House of Commons towards devolution and of the resolutions and proposals it has considered. We shall not concern ourselves with the Irish Home Rule movement, which, so far as its historical connections are concerned, has been briefly touched upon in the introductory chapter. We shall, therefore, confine ourselves in these chapters to a survey of the movement for Home Rule in Scotland and Wales and for Home Rule all round, or devolution.

As we have seen, the first exponent of the doctrine of devolution was Sir Isaac Butt. His ideas of a federal arrangement for the United Kingdom were substantially in line with the recent proposals for devolution. It was also he who first brought this problem to the attention of the House of Commons. On June 30, 1874, he moved the following resolution in the House:

That this House resolve itself into a Committee of the Whole House, to consider the present Parliamentary relations between Great Britain and Ireland.[1]

Although this motion was made primarily for Ireland, yet Butt's proposal did not stop with Ireland. His proposal

[1] *Parliamentary Debates*, Commons, 3rd ser., vol. 220, p. 700.

was, as we have seen, for an Irish Parliament " under a Federal arrangement, which would secure to that Parliament the power of regulating all the internal affairs of the country, while leaving all Imperial questions to be decided by the Imperial Legislature, such as all matters relating to the defence of the Empire and the providing of supplies for Imperial purposes." [1]  Besides the right of self-government, Sir Isaac mentioned another reason for his proposal. This was the congestion of business in the House of Commons.  He said:

Was any Irishman satisfied with the way in which Irish business was conducted in that House?  Why, if it was only for the physical impossibility of the House transacting such business in a satisfactory manner he would have made out his case.  Were Scotchmen satisfied with the way Scotch business was done, or indeed were Englishmen satisfied with the way English business was done?  English business was hurried through at 2 or 3 o'clock in the morning, without discussion, because the House was overburdened with work.[2]

Because of this congestion of business, which was then already noticeable, he would favour a devolution not only of Irish business but of English and Scotch business as well. The latter was, however, up to the English and Scotch Members.  " If the Scotch Members wished to be separated from the English he would be ready to support them," continued Sir Isaac, " but if they were satisfied with the English Legislature he should not wish to disturb the existing arrangements so far as they were concerned, and he would in that event propose that the House should meet without Irish Members for the discussion of English and Scottish affairs." [3]  But in the discussion of Imperial affairs, Irish Members would take part.

[1] *Ibid.*, p. 702.
[2] *Ibid.*, p. 714.
[3] *Ibid.*, p. 715.

This mild proposal was the beginning of Home Rule for Ireland and Home Rule all round for England and Scotland. The motion was, however, defeated by a vote of 61 to 458.[1]

Shortly after the Irish Home Rule Bill of 1886, the question of Home Rule for Scotland began to be advocated in the House of Commons. It was casually referred to on August 20, 1886 for the first time in the debate on the address.[2] On April 9, 1889, Dr. G. B. Clark made a motion for Scottish Home Rule. The motion reads:

That, in the opinion of this House, it is desirable that arrangements be made for giving to the people of Scotland, by their representatives in a National Parliament, the management and control of Scottish affairs.[3]

After alluding to the fact that Home Rule did not mean separation and that there were strong national feelings in Scotland, Dr. Clark presented two reasons for the motion: first, " that Scottish business is neglected;" [4] and second, that the House of Commons was overburdened. On the last point he made this observation:

It must be admitted that the House does its work very badly and inadequately, and that something is required to be done to enable Parliament to discharge its duty to the whole country. Every year more work is thrown upon Parliament, and the probability is that the aggregate amount of the work that ought to be done will go on increasing. Everybody, even old Tories on the other side, must admit that some change is necessary. Then what is the remedy to be? It must, I think, take

[1] *Ibid.*, p. 965.

[2] Referred to in *Parliamentary Debates*, Commons, 3rd ser., vol. 335, p. 74.

[3] *Ibid.*, p. 74.

[4] *Ibid.*, pp. 69-70.

the form of devolution. The Government themselves propose
some devolution in their Local Government Bill, referring
Private Bill legislation inquiries to a local Commission. For
my own part, I think that is a bad system, and I do not think
it will save the time of the House. It is possible even that
more time will be occupied, for probably the Committee discussions would be resumed in this House on the Report stage
of Private Bills. I think the only solution of the present state
of affairs in this House is to have devolution upon lines of
nationality, to devolve on each of the National elements, of
which this Great Empire is composed, its own local or National
business.[1]

Referring to the question of Irish Home Rule, Dr. Clark
expressed the opinion that it could be settled in one of two
ways, on the principle of dualism, or by the method of
federalism. By federalism he meant Home Rule all round.
Dualism was impossible, because the country would never
consent to Irish Members being driven out of Parliament;
nor would it consent to Irish Members, while settling their
own National affairs, having a finger in the Scottish and
English pie. " So under the circumstances," concluded Dr.
Clark, " it seems to me that we are logically bound, and I
have long held this view, to have Home Rule All Round,
and a Federal Parliament representing every section of the
Empire." [2]

Mr. Gladstone supported the motion. He was of the
opinion that devolution would not weaken the authority of
Parliament, as its opponents would suppose. His argument is as follows:

I do not think that judicial devolution weakens Parliament;
I say it strengthens it . . . I hold that all judicious devolution
which hands over to subordinate bodies duties for which they

[1] *Ibid.*, pp. 71-72.
[2] *Ibid.*, p. 73.

are better qualified by local knowledge, and which at the same time sets free the hands of Parliament for the pursuit of its proper business, does not weaken it but strengthens it, gives vitality to it, and makes the people more then ever disposed to support the supremacy of Parliament.[1]

Mr. Balfour and the Government were against the motion. Consequently it was defeated by a vote of 79 to 200.[2]  Subsequently the same motion was brought in again in 1890 and was again defeated by a majority of 40. It was then brought in in 1892 for a third time and was again defeated by a majority of 20.  It was brought in for a fourth time in 1893 and was also defeated by a majority of 18.[3]

On April 3, 1894, Mr. Henry Dalziel made another motion for Scottish Home Rule.  It is as follows:

That it is desirable, while retaining intact the power and supremacy of the Imperial Parliament, to establish a legislature in Scotland for dealing with purely Scottish affairs.[4]

In support of the motion he gave the following arguments: first, that Parliament was overburdened and that relief was necessary.  On this point he said:

We are agreed that the disease from which the patient is suffering is congestion.  We only differ as to the remedy that is to be applied.  If there was any doubt about the nature of the disease, I would mention one fact and call one witness.  Having taken pains to ascertain the number of Bills introduced last Session, I find that there are no fewer than 386, and that, putting aside purely Departmental Bills, only 58 come under the consideration of the House.  I do not claim that that is an absolutely reliable test, but it is fair to assume that every one

[1] *Ibid.*, p. 106.
[2] *Ibid.*, p. 124.
[3] Referred to in *Parliamentary Debates*, Commons, 4th ser., vol. 22, p. 1289.
[4] *Ibid.*, p. 1287.

of the 386 Bills embodied a proposal desired by a certain section
of the Community, and the fact that only 58 of them were even
discussed is an indication that further time is necessary for the
Debates in this House.[1]

Then Mr. Dalziel quoted a Unionist opinion from the
*Scotsman* newspaper as a witness for his proposition:

The Imperial Parliament cannot adequately cope with the
legislative requirements of the different parts of the United
Kingdom.   The Imperial Parliament has admitted its own in-
capacity to deal with all the subjects it once used to take in hand.
It has parted with some of its work from time to time, delegating
it to other hands.   Still the pressure increases, and it is simple
fatuity to suppose the question of further and wider delegation
can be long delayed.[2]

Secondly, Scottish interests had been neglected in the past,
and there was no prospect that they would be better attended
in the future.   On this point he quoted the following authorities:

The form in which our affairs have been administered for
well-nigh 100 years [wrote Professor Aytoun in 1853] is quite
inadequate for the purpose for which it was originally intended,
and the rapid development of the wealth and population of the
country ought long ago to have suggested the propriety of a
more rational arrangement.   The case is a very clear one,
founded upon justice and public policy; and if properly argued
no Government can venture to treat it lightly.[3]

I admit without the least hesitation [said the late Prime
Minister, when receiving the freedom of Aberdeen twenty-three
years ago] that the present condition of the action of Parliament with regard to Scottish business is unsatisfactory.   You
have much more reason to complain that we have not been able

[1] *Ibid.*, p. 1287.
[2] *Ibid.*, p. 1288.
[3] *Ibid.*, p. 1289.

to deal with several subjects interesting to the people of Scotland, and material to its welfare, with the promptitude that we should all have desired.[1]

Thirdly, the principles of representative Government demanded that Scottish opinion should be supreme in Scottish affairs, and this was only possible by the establishment of a Scottish legislature. In the Local Government Bill of 1886, it was pointed out, the opinion of the Scottish Members was practically set aside, and the fatal accident Bill of 1893, though desired by the Scottish Members, was lost through lack of time. There were many other Bills which were not dealt with according to their views.[2]

Lastly, it was urged that Scotland was an ideal field for a great experiment in local self-government Then Mr. Dalziel concluded his argument in these words:

I am in favour of Home Rule all round. I believe that is the only possible way in which we can properly carry forward the legislation of the country. My idea is that this House will have to undergo a very great and material change so far as the business laid before it is concerned. We are too much occupied in discussing purely local questions which can be better settled in the localities concerned. Let this House devote itself —first, to the consideration of all the great questions which have the same application to all portions of the Kingdom; and, in the second place, to the consideration of the great Colonial, Indian and Imperial questions which ought to engage more than they do at present the close attention of the House. It is because I believe my Resolution is a step in that direction that I submit it to the House.[3]

Mr. Birrell seconded the motion. Mr. Herbert Lewis spoke in favour of the motion from the standpoint of Wales.

[1] *Ibid.*, pp. 1289-1290.

[2] *Ibid.*, pp. 1290-1291.

[3] *Ibid.*, pp. 1293-1294.

He believed that Home Rule for Scotland would be a certainty at no distant date and he would impress on the House that Home Rule for Wales must not be left out of the question.[1]  The Secretary for Scotland, Sir G. Trevelyan also spoke in favour of the motion.[2]

The motion was, however, severely criticised by Mr. Balfour.  He argued that if Scotland were to have her own legislature, Wales might have one, London might have one, and Lancashire and Yorkshire might each have one.  That would be very ridiculous.[3]  In spite of this attack by Mr. Balfour and a few others, the motion was carried by a vote of 180 to 170.[4]

On March 29, 1895, on the Motion to go into Committee of Supply, Mr. Dalziel moved the following amendment:

That, in the opinion of this House, in order to give speedier and fuller effect to the special desires and wants of the respective Nationalities constituting the United Kingdom, and with a view to increase the efficiency of the Imperial Parliament to deal with Imperial affairs, it is desirable to devolve upon Legislatures in Ireland, Scotland, Wales and England respectively the management and control of their domestic affairs.[5]

This was the first time that a proposal for a general devolution or Home Rule all round was made in the House of Commons.  Ireland was included in the motion, because Mr. Dalziel thought that, if Home Rule was to be extended to England, Scotland, and Wales, the objection to Home Rule for Ireland would disappear.[6]  With regard to Scot-

[1] *Ibid.*, p. 1294.
[2] *Ibid.*, pp. 1307-1308.
[3] *Ibid.*, pp. 1313-1314.
[4] *Ibid.*, p. 1315.
[5] *Parliamentary Debates*, Commons, 4th ser., vol. 32, p. 523.
[6] *Ibid.*, p. 525.

land he admitted that, although " there was not in Scotland
that passionate feeling with regard to Home Rule which
existed in Ireland ", yet there was an unmistakeable demand
for Home Rule in Scotland. He summed up the case for
the latter in two sentences. First, " it was utterly impossible, under the present condition of things, to obtain the
legislation for Scotland desired by the Scotch people; and
secondly, " the legislation which they were able to secure
was not in accordance with the desire of the majority of
the Scotch Representatives ".[1]  With regard to Wales, he
said that, " if there was to be a general devolution of business, Wales should come up for separate treatment." [2]  As
to Home Rule for England, his opinion was that it " could
not come into force immediately," but " would have to be
left for final treatment." [3]  But most important of all was the
Imperial view of the matter.  " There could be no doubt,"
added Mr. Dalziel, " that the House was unable properly
to discharge all the work required of it.  No matter how
many hours they might sit, nor how much time was taken by
the Government, there was always a large number of Bills
of great importance which never got discussed at all." [4]

Mr. Lloyd George seconded the motion.  He said that
heretofore, the parties had adopted a policy of non-inter-
ference in matters of trade and commerce; but now all was
changed.  It was impossible for the House of Commons to
meet all the legislative demands of the people, and such measures as were got through the House were very often incomplete and imperfect.[5]  He said also that the present system
was not businesslike and was absurd.  He pointed out that

[1] *Ibid.*, p. 526.
[2] *Ibid.*, p. 527.
[3] *Ibid.*, p. 528.
[4] *Ibid.*, p. 528.
[5] *Ibid.*, p. 532.

" two thirds of the time of that House was taken up by questions which affected separate and distinct parts of the Kingdom.    In 1880, for example, about half the time of Parliament was devoted to Irish questions.    In 1886 the best part of the first Session was spent in discussion of the Irish Coercion Bill; then there were two or three Sessions devoted to an Irish Land Bill, and subsequently the last part of one or two Sessions was spent in an attempt to force poor little Wales to pay tithes.    The result was the great Unionist Parliament found no time at all for English business.    Even in the present Parliament the same state of things had prevailed, and it would prevail so long as the present system was allowed to continue." [1]

Mr. John Redmond disliked the Amendment, because he believed that the Home Rule question was rather an academic question to England and Wales, but a vital reality to Ireland. The Irish question should not, therefore, be discussed in such an academic Resolution.[2]   The rest of his opinion was as follows:

For his part, although he had no hesitation in saying he believed in the principle of federalism and that in the principle of federalism all these international difficulties would eventually find solution, at the same time he was convinced it would be a grievous injury to the cause of Home Rule for Ireland if it were now complicated by coupling with it the demand for the creation of local assemblies for England, Scotland and Wales. Further, he believed that in granting Home Rule to Ireland, in the first instance, care ought to be taken that Home Rule should be conceded to Ireland in such a shape and form that it would be possible to fit in afterwards with a complete system of federalism for all these Islands.[3]

[1] *Ibid.*, p. 533.
[2] *Ibid.*, p. 536.
[3] *Ibid.*, p. 538.

The Secretary for Scotland Sir G. Trevelyan supported the motion. Mr. Balfour opposed it. The tendency of all the great countries of the world, in Mr. Balfour's judgment, was " to bind together and not to loosen." " It appears to be absolute lunacy for this country," said he, " to pursue alone among the nations of the world an opposite course to that which has built up every other great Empire with which we have to compete." [1]  The motion was defeated by a vote of 128 to 102.[2]

Again, on March 15, 1898, Mr. J. Herbert Roberts made another motion for local self-government. The motion reads :

That, in the opinion of this House, in order to relieve the congestion of business in the Imperial Parliament and in the various Public Departments, and in order to give speedier and fuller effect to local requirements, it is urgently necessary that there should be devolved upon bodies representative of the different parts of the United Kingdom a large measure of self-government.[3]

Although this motion was counted out, because forty Members [4] were not present, it was nevertheless discussed at some length. " The only issue," as stated by the mover, is the issue as to whether it is desirable or undesirable to apply the principle of delegation to the solution of the congestion of public business in Parliament." [5]  In concluding the case, Mr. Roberts declared :

We stand today face to face with a great problem, for which, in justice to the country we represent, and for the honor and dignity of Parliament, some remedy must be found (this remedy was devolution) . . .

[1] *Ibid.*, p. 558.
[2] *Ibid.*, p. 560.
[3] *Parliamentary Debates*, Commons, 4th ser., vol. 54, p. 1680.
[4] *Ibid.*, p. 1744.
[5] *Ibid.*, p. 1682.

The main objection of the first Lord of the Treasury is . . . that the adoption of it (devolution) would have the effect of dividing the country and creating rival interests, instead of unifying and keeping together the Kingdom as a whole. I venture, Mr. Speaker, to predict that the right Honorable Gentleman opposite will live to see the day when he will have been taught by national experience that that view is entirely wrong. I speak, as I have the right to speak, on behalf of Wales, and I say that there is no portion of the United Kingdom which is prouder of the British Empire than Wales. Wales has played an important part in the building up of the Empire, and it values and claims the privilege of having had an active participation both in the responsibility and glory of the Empire, and I wish to make it perfectly clear, and there should not be even a momentary impression or suspicion that there lurks within this Motion I am now making, so far as Wales is concerned, the shadow of a desire to impair the supreme authority of this Parliament, or to advance one single step along the road to separation.[1]

Mr. Robert T. Reid (later Lord Loreburn) seconded the motion. He said that there could not be any controversy as to the congestion of business in the House of Commons. To support this contention he cited many legislative proposals which had failed to secure the attention of the House. He pointed out, for instance, that there had been a Royal Commisison for over ten years with regard to the housing of the working classes.[2] The Commission had revealed a horrible state of things—disease, death, drunkenness, etc.— due to the overcrowding in London and other districts. Yet little had been done since 1886, when the reports were made. Then there was the Sweating Committee of the House of Lords which revealed another state of things— excessive hours, inadequacy of subsistence among a large

[1] *Ibid.*, p. 1690.

[2] *Ibid.*, p. 1692.

class of helpless people, especially women. Nothing was done for that.[1] There were also commissions in regard to joint holdings, and in regard to agriculture, a Royal Commission on Labour and an Inquiry into the conditions of the poor.[2] Finally, there was the Liquor problem in Scotland, which had been a most crying grievance for many years. But nothing was done for that either. Thus declared Mr. Reid:

We have for the last ten, twelve, or fourteen years been making attempts to get that evil remedied. I recollect that in 1884, Mr. Maclagan . . . succeeded in getting the second Reading of the Local Veto Bill, which had the support not only of the Liberals in Scotland but of many of the Conservatives there also, and on the back of that Bill was the name of the Member for Kirkcaldy, a conservative. Unfortunately, the Bill was not passed the second time. From that time to this the Scotch Members have been trying to pass that Bill, or a Bill like it. We are now in the year 1898, we were then in the year 1884; and this Bill, affecting the most vital interests of the people of Scotland, has never been able to reach a Second Reading.[3]

Mr. D. A. Thomas, the Chairman of the Welsh Party moved an Amendment to the effect, first of giving Ireland the priority of Home Rule, and secondly of changing the word "urgently necessary" into "desirable".[4] Mr. Thomas Lough seconded this Amendment.[5]

Sir H. Campbell-Bannerman spoke for the motion in the capacity of a Scotch Member. He said that in any scheme of devolution, Ireland would naturally be accorded priority.[6]

[1] *Ibid.*, pp. 1692-1693.
[2] *Ibid.*, p. 1693.
[3] *Ibid.*, pp. 1693-1694.
[4] *Ibid.*, p. 1706.
[5] *Ibid.*, p. 1711.
[6] *Ibid.*, p. 1724.

On Scottish business he made a very strong argument, because he said that he knew it best.   The argument runs as follows:

The complaint we make as regards Scotch business is twofold.   In the first place, we complain that there is insufficient time given for the full discussion of Scotch affairs owing to the pressure of public business. . . . But then, again, this is not the principal ground upon which I, for my part, base my adherence to this Motion.   Our principal grievance is that on purely Scotch matters Scotch opinion is by the present system allowed to be overborne.   In the House a discussion takes place, and we have an opportunity of stating our views, but when it comes to the decisive vote Members come in who have no knowledge of Scotch affairs, and who have not heard the Debate, and it is they who determine the conclusion of the House.[1]

Mr. A. J. Balfour, the first Lord of the Treasury, spoke for the opposition against both the Resolution and the Amendment.   " We object to Home Rule," he said, " whether it begins with Ireland and ends with Wales, or begins with Wales and ends with Ireland.   We object to the whole thing; . . ."[2]   Then with regard to the congestion of business in the House, he replied:

There are times when undoubtedly this House has so many measures of first-class importance it desires to pass that we cannot make the progress we desire with many Bills which not only individual Members, but the Government of the day itself, are anxious to make progress with.   But, so long as the House is fortunate enough to avoid those periods of stress and storm in which controversy is long and business is slow, I do not think that our annual crop of legislative work is really so small as some of our critics who have spoken in this Debate seem to

[1] *Ibid.*, pp. 1727, 1728-1729.
[2] *Ibid.*, p. 1732.

think. . . . The House of Commons is like a great steam engine, which will have a great output so long as the working parts are cool, but as soon as, from some error in construction or defects in oiling, or some similar cause, the working parts become warm, undoubtedly the labour is great, but the result is small.  But, Sir, granted—and I am quite prepared to grant it— that there are times and seasons in which our legislative work is in serious arrears, surely a more inaccurate method of remedying that defect was never proposed than the suggestion that we should at once begin to pass Home Rule Bills for Ireland, Wales and Scotland, as well as one for England alone, which would inevitably follow, as I shall presently point out.[1]

In this Mr. Balfour virtually conceded that there was such a thing as the congestion of business in the House of Commons.  That was in his opinion due to the fact that the working parts of the machine sometimes got warm.  It is, however, difficult to see how such an engine as the House of Commons, in which controversy is constant and competition is keen, can ever keep itself cool.  The real fear in the mind of Mr. Balfour and of many other conservatives was that devolution or Home Rule would stimulate the separatist movement in all directions.[2]

## II. SINCE 1900

In the first decade of the present century, there was very little discussion of Home Rule or devolution in the House of Commons.  The only time, perhaps, when these questions were discussed was on May 26, 1908, when Mr. D. V. Pirie introduced a Bill for the Government of Scotland.[3] The Bill was to give effect to a Resolution passed in 1894. It provided for devolution upon a legislative body in Scotland of matters exclusively relating to Scotland.  The pow-

---

[1] *Ibid.*, pp. 1733-1734.

[2] *Ibid.*, p. 1737.

[3] *Parliamentary Debates*, Commons, 4th ser., vol. 189, p. 968.

ers of the Scottish Legislature were specifically enumerated.
The Executive power continued with the Crown. It was proposed that the old Scottish Privy Council might be revived,
so that an executive committee might advise His Majesty as
to what was most required for the Government of Scotland.
Power was given to the Scottish Legislature to impose taxes,
except duties of customs and excise. Arrangements were
made for the adjustment of Scottish and Imperial finances.
Finally it was provided that the supreme authority of Parliament was to remain unaffected by the Bill.[1]

In introducing the above Bill, Mr. Pirie mentioned that in
1892, Dr. Hunter introduced a similar measure, and that
in 1899 he himself introduced one. He asked leave only to
have the Bill printed. Leave was signified by a vote of
257 to 102.[2]

After 1910 the discussions on Home Rule and devolution become more and more frequent as well as important.
Thus on August 16, 1911, another Government for Scotland Bill was ordered to be brought in by Sir Henry Dalziel,
Mr. Munro-Ferguson, Mr. Pirie, Mr. Watt, Mr. Cowan,
Mr. Munro, Mr. Pringle, Mr. Hope, Mr. Rainy, Mr. Mor-
ton, Mr. Cathcart Wason, and Mr. Barnes, to be read a
second time on the 25th of October and to be printed.[3]

In introducing the Bill, Mr. Dalziel declared: " The question is not a new one in this House. Twenty years ago I
had the honor of making a proposition that the time had
then arrived when Scotland should have control of her
purely domestic affairs in a Parliament sitting in Scotland.
. . . During the twenty years that have since elapsed the
case which was then accepted by the House of Commons

[1] *Ibid.*, pp. 969-970.
[2] *Ibid.*, p. 972.
[3] *Parliamentary Debates*, Commons, 5th ser., vol. 29, p. 1935.

has in no way weakened.   Every year has supplied fresh
facts and fresh arguments in favor of the proposition." [1]
The case for Scotch Home Rule rests upon the following
grounds: [2] First, " it is impossible under the prevailing
system for Scotland to carry into legislative effect the will
of the people as expressed at the poll."   Second, " in all
matters of purely domestic concern Scottish opinion should
be predominant."   And lastly, while the supremacy of the
Imperial Parliament must be maintained, its congestion of
business should be relieved.   On the last point he said:

In the interest of the Imperial Parliament itself our measure
ought to be accepted by the House.   Any one who has observed
the working of this House will admit that the Parliamentary
machine has broken down completely and absolutely.   The work
at the present time is not in any sense consistent with any
reasonable idea of Parliamentary institutions.   Members start
sitting on Committees at eleven o'clock in the morning, and
continue in attendance until two or three o'clock the next morning.   It is impossible for them to give proper consideration to
the work expected of them. [3]

The Bill provided for a legislature in Scotland, consisting
of His Majesty the King and a House of Representatives.
The latter should consist of 140 Members, two from each
constituency, and should be elected for five years.   The
powers of the Scottish Parliament should concern such matters as local government, public health, criminal law, administration of justice, bankruptcy, gaols and prisons, marriage and divorce, education, railways and canals, land, and
other matters of purely local concern.   The powers reserved to the imperial Parliament should be matters relating

[1] *Ibid.*, p. 1929.
[2] *Ibid.*, pp. 1929-1930.
[3] *Ibid.*, p. 1930.

to the making of treaties, Imperial forces and all other matters which properly belong to a purely Imperial Parliament. The Bill also provided for the establishment of a consolidated Fund for Scotland, and a Commission to adjust the financial relations. The supreme power of Parliament should be left undisturbed.[1]

Again, on February 28, 1912, Dr. Chapple made another motion for Scottish Home Rule. It reads:

That, in the opinion of this House, any measure providing for the delegation of Parliamentary powers to Ireland should be followed in this Parliament by the granting of similar powers of self-government to Scotland as part of a general scheme of devolution.[2]

The motion was expressly conditioned upon the granting of Home Rule to Ireland first, as the latter was then being considered by the Government. In introducing the motion, Dr. Chapple said that there had been an unbroken policy in Scotland for self-government ever since the Union. That policy had no doubt ebbed and flowed, but it had always been kept to the front.[3] He described his proposal as one for federalism, and he thought there had been a movement towards federalism all over the world.[4]

Mr. Munro-Ferguson, who seconded the motion, pointed out the fact that devolution was favored not only by the Liberals, but by the Unionists and Laborites as well. " The evils of congestion are patent to us all ". The reasons for opposing devolution are not far to seek. First of all, there was the prejudice excited by the idea of Home Rule and its past associations. Secondly, there was the conception

---

[1] *Ibid.*, pp. 1930-1931.
[2] *Parliamentary Debates*, Commons, 5th ser., vol. 34, p. 1446.
[3] *Ibid.*, p. 1447.
[4] *Ibid.*, pp. 1447-1449.

on the part of England of the Empire as a greater England controlled by the English Parliament. Thirdly, there was the opposition of property. And lastly, there was the difficulty of Ulster.[1] With regard to the Irish question, he remarked that, unless devolution to local Parliaments be adopted, the Irish problem could not be satisfactorily solved.

Mr. Wilkie made a very interesting speech on Federal Home Rule. He thought that the Private Bill legislation under the present system was very costly. " I think the expenditure in connection with private bill procedure," said he, " is a useless waste of public money. All that could be done by devolution if we had, as we ought to have, an authority in the district where it is required, and which would know far better the necessities of the district than a Private Committee upstairs." [2] The most important part of his speech was of the neglect of Parliament in the control over finance and foreign affairs.[3] Then he concluded:

Federal Home Home solves many of the difficulties that came up when the previous Home Rule Bills were before this House. It relieves the question of the ins and the outs and the comings and the goings. We are, in fact, already a Home Rule Empire. Our different Colonies have adopted the method of devolution. We appear to be like a wheel. At the outer end of the spokes we have our self-governing colonies. Then let us have at the inner end of the spokes self-government for the four countries comprising the United Kingdom, leaving the hub, the center of all, to the Imperial Government for the whole Empire. Scotland is by nature's laws designed to be the northern part of this Kingdom, but that is no reason why we should be subject to neglect, or why the wishes of the majority of the people should be ignored. Therefore, I hope the Government will take

[1] *Ibid.*, p. 1456.

[2] *Ibid.*, p. 1464.

[3] *Ibid.*, p. 1465.

its courage in both hands and will make Irish Home Rule the beginning for all the other four round the hub, so that we can have Home Rule at the extreme end of the spokes and at the inner end, with one central Parliament of the whole Empire at the hub in the center.[1]

The Secretary for Scotland, Mr. McKinnon Wood, spoke in favor of the motion for three reasons: first, that it would increase Imperial efficiency; second, that it would increase local efficiency; and third, that it would satisfy local sentiments.[2]

Several Members were against the motion. The chief speaker for the opposition was Mr. Bonar Law, whose main contention was that there was no public demand for Home Rule in Scotland. He said:

What can Scotland possibly gain by a change of this kind? We can gain nothing from the point of view of national characteristics, or love of national traditions. . . . I am bound to say, from the point of view of the integrity of the country as a whole, the very worst way in which you can set up devolution is by putting it on a national basis.[3]

From whatever point of view you look at it, if you look at it from the point of view of the interests of Scotland you will find that Scotland stands to lose by any weakening of the arrangement by which the countries are now linked together. It stands to lose far more, whether it be a trade interest or a personal interest, and I say, without the slightest hesitation, that so far as I am able to judge there is not the smallest desire for this change in Scotland.[4]

The motion was carried by a vote of 226 to 128.[5]

[1] *Ibid.*, pp. 1465-1466.
[2] *Ibid.*, p. 1486.
[3] *Ibid.*, pp. 1487-1488.
[4] *Ibid.*, pp. 1489-1490.
[5] *Ibid.*, p. 1490.

On July 3, 1912, Mr. MacCallum Scott moved to introduce a Government of the United Kingdom Bill, providing for devolution upon four Local Parliaments in England, Scotland, Ireland, and Wales of local administration and local legislation.[1] The motion was carried by a vote of 264 to 212. It was ordered to be read a second time and to be printed. This was the third proposal in Parliament for a comprehensive scheme of devolution. The Bill provided for four local Parliaments in England, Scotland, Ireland, and Wales. It was based upon the Government of Ireland Bill, being an adaptation of the latter to a scheme of Home Rule all round. The principle features of the Bill were: (1) In addition to the powers specifically referred to the Imperial Parliament, the Post Office, and the imposition of duties on Customs and Excise were reserved to that Parliament. Three other matters, namely, old Age Pensions, National Insurance, and Labour Exchanges were also reserved. (2) With regard to the composition of the Local Parliament, the proposal was as follows: that the Senate shall be retained in Ireland in accordance with the wishes of the Irish Representatives. But in the case of England, Scotland, and Wales, the Local Parliament shall consist of one chamber only, elected by existing constituencies with the exception of the Universities. In England, each constituency shall return the same number of representatives as at present. In Scotland, Ireland and Wales, each constituency shall return one representative for the first 6000 electors, and an additional one for every additional 5000, or portion of 5000, electors. This would give a House of Commons to each country, consisting of the following numbers: England, 456; Scotland, 175; Ireland, 169; and Wales, 84. (3) With regard to finance, it was proposed that a commission be appointed, after the passing of

[1] *Parliamentary Debates*, Commons. 5th ser., vol. 40, p. 1155.

the Act, to inquire into the financial relations which should exist between the United Kingdom and the several countries. Meanwhile, the Imperial Parliament should undertake the full cost of the existing services transferred together with a margin based on population. Each country should have further powers to raise revenue by means of direct taxation. And (4) A Court of Appeal was to be created in Wales.[1]

In 1913, another Home Rule Bill for Scotland was introduced by Mr. Cowan, supported by Mr. Eugene Wason, Mr. Pirie, Dr. Chapple, Mr. Cathcart Wason, Mr. Wilkie, Mr. Lyell, Mr. J. Hogge, Mr. R. Munro, Mr. J. Duncan Millar, and Mr. Murray Macdonald. It was read a first time on March 17, and a second time on May 30, 1913.[2] The Bill, as stated by its Memorandum, was to represent a further installment of the policy of devolution, as initiated by the Government of Ireland Bill. It was practically a reproduction of the latter. It provided for the establishment in Scotland of a single-chamber Parliament subordinate to the Imperial Parliament, and consisting of 140 members representing the existing constituencies except the Universities, and returned by the Parliamentary electors with the addition of Peers. The representation of Scotland was to continue in the House of Commons for the time being, until separate provision was made for devolution in England and Wales, when the representation of the United Kingdom should be reconsidered and readjusted. The powers of the Scots Parliament were to include all those conferred upon the Irish Parliament in the Government of Ireland Bill, except the control over the Post Office and the power to vary customs and excise. The said Parliament would also have the administration of Old Age Pensions,

[1] *Ibid.*, pp. 1155-1156.
[2] *Parliamentary Debates*, Commons, 5th ser., vol. 53, p. 471.

National Insurance, and Labour Exchanges. The executive power was to continue vested in His Majesty the King, who would be represented in Scotland by a Lord High Commissioner. The administration was to be carried on by the High Lord Commissioner advised by an Executive Committee of a Scottish Privy Council. The power of varying Imperial taxes, except customs and excise, was conferred upon the Scots Parliament, which was, in addition, to have the exclusive power of levying the existing Imperial taxes on inheritable property in Scotland. Provision was made for the payment by the Imperial Exchequer to the Scottish Exchequer, out of the proceeds of Scottish taxes, of an annual sum towards defraying the expenses of Scottish services. A Joint Exchequer Board should be established to determine all questions arising under the financial provisions. Finally, the Judicial Committee of the Privy Council was to be substituted for the House of Lords as a final court of appeal, which would also determine all constitutional questions.

In introducing the Bill on its second reading, Mr. Cowan declared that he was not introducing it as an individual private member nor on behalf of any small group or section of Members, but on behalf of the whole body of Liberal Scottish Members in the House.[2] They represented 85 per cent of the total Scottish representation in the House. He said also that there had been a great awakening in Scotland on the subject of Home Rule.[3] Thirty years ago a body called the Scottish Home Rule Association was formed. There was also the Young Scots Society, which had put Home Rule in the forefront of its programme. The latter had carried on a wide campaign for Home Rule in Scotland

[1] *Ibid.*, pp. 479-482.
[2] *Ibid.*, p. 471.
[3] *Ibid.*, p. 474.

for many years.   There had also been much discussion of
the subject in the Scottish press.   Then, lastly, there was
the Scottish Liberal Association, which had always stood
for the same object.   Therefore, Mr. Cowan concluded that
there was no doubt about the demand for Home Rule in
Scotland.

The arguments for Scottish Home Rule were those which
had been made over and over again, such as the neglect of
Scottish business and the congestion in Parliament.   In
connection with the last point he pointed out that 75 per
cent of the money voted by the House of Commons was
voted under closure and without a word of debate, and that
half of the Bills the government introduced each year were
jettisoned because they had not the time to carry them
through.[1]

Mr. Murray Macdonald supported the measure.   He based
his case solely on the ground of the congestion of business
in the House of Commons.   That the congestion existed was
admitted on all hands.   The only dispute was regarding its
cause and remedy.   On the latter point he said:

On this point two opinions prevail amongst us.   One is that
it is due to obstruction either on the part of individual Members or groups of Members, which can be remedied by an
Amendment of our procedure; the other opinion is that it is
due to a steady and continuous growth in the actual volume of
business, for which the only remedy is to devolve on subordinate
Legislatures some of the work which this House at present
attempts hopelessly to get through.   I hold the second of those
two opinions.   I support this Bill not exclusively in the interests of the people of Scotland, but as a part of a general scheme
of devolution promoted in the interests of the Parliament of
the United Kingdom as a whole.[2]

[1] *Ibid.*, p. 479.
[2] *Ibid.*, p. 482.

This is perhaps the best and the most clearcut statement
of the policy of devolution ever made in the House of Commons. Mr. Macdonald has been one of the chief advocates
of devolution. His opinion is, on the whole, authoritative
as well as illuminating. In these few words he touched on
the core of the whole problem.

Mr. Balfour opposed the measure as usual. He disagreed
with Mr. Macdonald on the proposition that devolution is
the only remedy for the congestion of business in the House
of Commons. Granted that the evil existed, the right way
to remedy it was not devolution upon national bodies, but
devolution upon regional areas. In that event, you must
consider the United Kingdom as a whole, and cut the country
into convenient units or districts, each of which would have,
" not a Parliament—of course, that is absurd,—but something in the nature of a glorified country council." This
suggestion, however, might not be feasible; but, at any rate,
that would be a better way of relieving the congestion of
Parliament than devolution to nationalities.[1] Furthermore,
in the opinion of Mr. Balfour, the latter scheme would be
utterly impracticable. The greatest difficulty was England.
He thus declared:

A Parliament which really adequately represented England,
would be a Parliament which would hardly sit side by side in a
position of admitted inferiority to another assembly sitting
within these walls. A collision with an Irish Parliament would
be bad enough. A collision with a Scottish Parliament is not a
desirable thing to think of. But conceive a collision with an
English Parliament! I believe that directly you face the question of England's position in your ideal federal system, you
will see the utter absurdity of it. To cut up England would
be greatly unfair to England, on your own principles. . . .
Therefore England will remain as a unit, I presume. A system

[1] *Ibid.*, p. 532.

of four provinces, of which England is one, is so lopsided, so top-heavy, and so unequal a system, that it is impossible that it should retain its equilibrium for any great length of time, and your whole federal system would fall into the grossest absurdity.[1]

The Secretary for Scotland, Mr. McKinnon Wood, spoke in favor of the measure. The motion was carried by a vote of 204-159.[2]

During recent years the policy of devolution found many ardent supporters also in the House of Lords. In 1914 on the second reading of the Government of Ireland Bill, Lord Dunraven declared in the House of Lords (January 27):

I believe devolution to be necessary, not by any means only for the welfare of Ireland, but for the welfare of the United Kingdom, for the restoration of efficiency to Parliament, and for the permanency of representative institutions, and I do not believe that without the adoption of the principle of devolution any scheme or any device ever will bring together the component parts of the Empire. It is for these reasons, my Lords, that I go so far as to support the second reading of the Bill.[3]

In the same debate, Earl Grey expressed the opinion that he favored the federal plan. His idea of a federal plan was a system which would combine local autonomy on domestic matters with unity of government in all matters of common interest.[4] Such a plan would have the following advantages:

" First, the federal plan follows established precedent. It is a plan which has been proved to work smoothly in our self-governing Dominions. Secondly, it gives Home Rule

---

[1] *Ibid.*, p. 538.

[2] *Ibid.*, p. 550.

[3] *Parliamentary Debates*, Lords, 5th ser., vol. xiii, pp. 469-470.

[4] *Ibid.*, p. 500.

in a manner that ensures, not only the possession of liberty
to the people, but the growth of loyalty to the state. Thirdly,
it would give the people of England the power, which is now
denied them, of managing their own local and domestic affairs. Fourthly, it would also necessitate the immediate
establishment of a Second Chamber which as a coordinate
branch of the Legislature would restore to our Constitution
the balance which has been removed." [1]

On the other hand, Viscount Haldane (the Lord Chancellor) was of the opinion that the underlying idea of the
Home Rule Bill was devolution and not federalism. The
distinction between the two is clearly brought out in the
following passage:

The theory of the Bill is this—devolution, retaining Imperial
supremacy over the Legislature, over the Executive, and over
the Judiciary. Under the Bill you have true devolution as
distinguished from true federalism. . . . The best example of
federalism is the United States Constitution. You will see
how radically this Bill differs from that. The United States
Federal Parliament cannot interfere with the jurisdiction of
the State Legislature. If it does, its legislation is at once
declared invalid by the supreme Tribunal; nor can the Federal
Judiciary interfere with the decision of a State Judge. There
is not interference of any sort or kind. The relation is that
of co-ordination, which is the basis of federalism, and we felt
that that was something quite impossible and not to be looked
for in a Constitution such as we were seeking to set up in
Ireland, and which might form a model for setting up similar
Constitutions in other parts of the United Kingdom. What
makes Imperial legislative supremacy certain under this Bill
is that every British Statute is intra vires and cannot be changed
on the ground that it is ultra vires, and the power of the
Imperial Parliament remains by express declaration unimpaired.
The proposition that you cannot interfere when once you de-

[1] *Ibid.*, p. 507.

volve is one which must be taken with qualifications. If you have successfully devolved to a local Legislature and things are working well, you attain the object at which you are aiming, and you do not require or desire to interfere. In that sense de facto supremacy is diminished. But if, on the other hand, things do not go well, and there are Acts which have to be vetoed and executive dealings to be controlled, those powers of control remain intact and can be put into operation.[1]

This is certainly a remarkable opinion. Nowhere else in the debates on the subject had such a clear-cut distinction been conceived or made. As we have seen, all the proposals for Home Rule and devolution ever since the time of Butt were built upon the idea of devolution and not federalism. But many of them were called federal and this resulted in a considerable amount of confusion and conflict. If people had grasped this distinction made by Viscount Haldane, a good deal of the unnecessary fight over the proposals would have been avoided.

### SUMMARY

Devolution is, from what we have seen, certainly not a new movement. Its beginnings reached back as far as 1874, when Mr. Butt, for the first time, voiced the demand for Home Rule for Ireland in the House of Commons. But the House was not prepared to listen to him, and consequently his motion was defeated by a majority of 397 votes. Subsequently, from 1874 to 1894, all the resolutions on Home Rule were turned down, but all the time more Members were getting interested in the subject. This was shown by the relative votes on Scottish Home Rule during this period. The Resolution on Scottish Home Rule was defeated in 1889 by a majority of 121; in 1890, by a majority of 40; in 1892, by a majority of 20; and in

[1] *Ibid.*, pp. 540-541.

1893, by a majority of 18. In 1894, however, it scored a victory by a majority of 10. Thus the interest of the Members in Home Rule for Scotland was gaining. In 1895 the first motion for devolution was made in the House of Commons. It was, however, defeated by a majority of 26. At that time, both the Unionists and the Irish Nationalists disliked such a proposal. The former opposed it anyway, while the latter thought it disadvantageous to Home Rule for Ireland. A second motion for devolution was made in 1898. It was unfortunately counted out.

During the opening decade of the present century, the questions of Home Rule and of devolution were virtually dead. This was to be expected, because during this period of Unionist ascendency such proposals could hardly be entertained. But no sooner had the Liberals come into power again, than these questions were revived with even greater enthusiasm than before. From now on, not only abstract resolutions, but definite Bills, were introduced. The first definite Bill for Scottish Home Rule was introduced in 1908 and was ordered to be printed. The second Bill was introduced in 1911, was read a second time and printed. In 1912, another motion on Scottish Home Rule was made, which was carried by a majority of 98. Then in 1912, the first Bill on devolution was introduced. The motion to introduce the Bill was carried by a majority of 52. In 1913, a third Bill for Government of Scotland was introduced and was read a second time. Thus before 1914, the problem of devolution had passed beyond the first stage of development.

Nor was the interest confined to the House of Commons. During the Irish Home Rule crisis, devolution was favored by several noted Members in the House of Lords. Some of them supported the Irish Home Rule Bill, simply because it was an installment of devolution. This was indeed the view of Mr. Asquith who introduced it. Although the Irish

Bill was defeated by the House of Lords, it would have become law in accordance with the Parliament Act, had the War not intervened. Then devolution to other countries of the United Kingdom might soon have followed according to the expressed views of the Liberal Government. We shall continue the survey of the movement during and since the War in the next chapter.

# CHAPTER V

FROM 1914 TO 1924

During the War the movement for devolution in Parliament was temporarily suspended. Immediately after the War the question was brought up again with renewed interest and added conviction. All parties came to realise the necessity for devolution, not only as a measure to satisfy the demand for Home Rule of the several nationalities, but primarily as a remedy for the congestion of the business in the House of Commons, which congestion as a result of war conditions had become well nigh intolerable. On June 26, 1918, a large deputation composed of representatives of all parties from both Houses of Parliament was introduced to the Prime Minister by Earl Brassey. They urged the government to take steps for the immediate establishment of subordinate legislatures in England, Scotland, and Wales as well as Ireland. In reply, Mr. Lloyd George said that he had always been a strong federalist. But he thought that for a change of this kind, there must be practical unanimity. He was sure that unanimity could be obtained in Scotland and Wales, but he was not so clear about public opinion in England. He suggested that a campaign on this subject in England might not be inadvisable, but could not promise any immediate action during the War.[1]

[1] *London Times*, July 1, 1918, p. 9d.

152

On March 5, 1919, Earl Brassey moved the following resolution in the House of Lords:

That for the purpose of (a) securing prompt and efficient handling of pressing domestic problems and better control over public expenditure, and (b) enabling the Imperial Parliament to devote more attention to the general interests of the United Kingdom and matters of common Imperial concern than is possible under the present system of a single Parliament and Cabinet, the establishment of local legislatures throughout the United Kingdom is an urgent necessity.[1]

Concerning the history of the movement Earl Brassey declared:

The policy of Federal Devolution, as it is generally described, was referred to by Mr. Joseph Chamberlain on the Home Rule Bill of 1886 as affording the best solution of the Irish question. It was brought before your Lordships' House in the discussion on the Home Rule Bill in February, 1913, by the late Earl Grey and by Lord Dunraven, and it was alluded to by many speakers in the course of that debate. In the discussion that went on in the country during the following winter the noble Marquess, Lord Lansdowne, Mr. Austen Chamberlain and others also made reference to the question, while Sir Edward Carson over and over again stated that Ulstermen would not consent to be placed in a position of inferiority as compared with Englishmen and Scotsmen in their relation to the Imperial Parliament—in other words, that the only form of Home Rule which Ulstermen might possibly be induced to accept would be a form which was part of a general scheme of devolution applicable to the whole of the United Kingdom.[2]

Speaking of the congestion of business, after referring to congestion in former times, Earl Brassey added:

[1] *Parliamentary Debates*, 5th ser. (Lords), vol. 33, pp. 501-502.
[2] *Ibid.*, p. 502.

The situation is ten times more serious today that it ever was before. During the last two and a quarter years a large number of new Ministries, a large number of new Departments, and a vast bureaucracy have been created, a bureaucracy which, we know from the Estimates published a few days ago, will cost the country the appalling sum of £500,000,000 a year, or more than two and a half times the total national expenditure of the country before the war.

The extension of Government Departments has not ceased with the War. Within the last few days Bills have been introduced for the establishment of a Ministry of Health and a Ministry for Transport. The Government apparently propose to control mines. There are pressing for consideration vast problems of housing, and so forth, affecting the life of the people in their homes, and then there are big questions of more than home interest affecting the trade and the defence of the country, and the vast problem of the government of India, all pressing for consideration. If Parliament is to be a mere machine for registering the decrees of the Cabinet; if Ministers are to spend public money at will; if the Ministry of Munitions is to be permitted to add at least £40,000,000 to the labour bill of his Ministry without even consulting the Labour Advisors of the Government, if £2,000,000 is to be spent on a motor depot at Slough, to which Lord Desborough called attention last summer; if fourteen Departments each with its own Minister are to be allowed to interfere in the question of demobilization—if this sort of thing is to be allowed to go on you may say there is no congestion of business in Parliament. Many excuses may be advanced for extravagance and maladministration during the War, but those excuses can no longer be made. I submit that under present conditions it is impossible for Parliament to discharge its functions as a Parliament, that democratic principles cannot be maintained, and that the people through their representatives cannot control administration, legislation, or public expenditure owing to the congestion of business in Parliament.[1]

[1] *Ibid.*, pp. 503-504.

With regard to the principle of devolution, Earl Brassey made the following observations:

(1) "No change is suggested in the Imperial Parliament as constituted at present. It is possible, assuming these subordinate Legislatures are established, that there will be some reduction in the number of members of the House of Commons." (2) "The supremacy of the Imperial Parliament is indefeasible, and it can always, if necessary, override the acts of the subordinate legislatures." (3) "That the devolution of powers to subordinate Legislatures should be as extensive as possible, consistently with the maintenance of the security and integrity of the United Kingdom." Generally speaking, the powers to be retained would be questions affecting the Crown, the Army and Navy, Foreign policy, questions of coinage, weights and measures, the control of harbours of Naval or Military importance, lighthouses, and so on. The powers to be handed over will include questions connected with local government, agriculture, education, licensing, and so on. Certain questions are on the border line, such as factory legislation. The powers transferred need not be identical in every case. There is no necessity that the constitution of the subordinate Legislatures should be similar in all cases.[2]

After speaking from the Imperial, and the Irish point of view, Earl Brassey pointed out that devolution would produce salutary effects upon the House of Lords:

The effect of carrying through a policy of Federal Devolution would be to remove from the control of your Lordships' House practically every question on which there has hitherto been a difference of opinion between the two Houses, questions affecting the church, the land, licensing, and education. I think it would strengthen very much the position of your Lordships' House in that it would diminish hostility to the continued existence of your Lordships' House. Further, it would alter

[1] *Ibid.*, pp. 505-506.

the whole problem of reforming the composition of your Lordships' House. If I may say so, with all deference to the noble Viscount who is sitting below me (Lord Bryce) it has always seemed to me that it is a grave mistake to attempt to reform the composition of your Lordships' House until we have settled what form of government we are going to have in the United Kingdom.[1]

The Earl of Selborne seconded the Motion. On the reasons for his support of the Motion he said in part:

. . . and my argument in favour of Devolution arises not from a sense that this has always been the way to settle the Irish problem, but from my sense that the interests and the welfare, and indeed the safety, of Great Britain demand some such change in our constitutional procedure.[2]

After alluding to the breakdown of Cabinet responsibility and the Parliamentary system as a result of congestion, Lord Selborne continued:

I submit that the case is made out that Parliament is not competent by its present organization to deal with the work with which the nation expects it to deal, and I entirely agree with my noble friend (Brassey) that no mere change of procedure in the House of Commons will effect the necessary reform. We have seen the problem tinkered with (I can use no other expression) by the process of reform of procedure again and again, and I confidently join with him in the opinion that this attempt will be no more successful than previous ones.[3]

The Lord Chancellor (Lord Birkenhead) spoke on behalf of the Government against the Motion. His objections were: (1) The congestion of business is not merely due to the number of subjects which were placed before the House

[1] *Ibid.*, pp. 509-526.
[2] *Ibid.*, p. 513.
[3] *Ibid.*, p. 517.

for consideration, but is largely due to obstruction.[1]   (2)
There is no public opinion in favor of the proposal.[2]   (3)
Devolution would either not relieve the congestion or make
the Law Courts the masters of Parliament.   He said:

It is obvious that under such a scheme as that which has been
discussed, . . . the highest Legislature of all (that is to say,
the Imperial Legislature) obviously from the nature of the thing
could not be given powers to overrule the others. . . . If it were
given powers to override the others on the ground that any of
the subordinate Legislatures had exceeded their constitutional
powers, this consequence would immediately follow—that so
far from having got rid of any congestion, the congestion
would be increased at least twenty-fold; because the whole
time they were discussing it there would be an Irish or a Welsh
or a Scottish orator, or a deputation of orators, from each
of these Chambers on important occasions; therefore, we should
listen to deputations from these various subordinate Assemblies
in order to establish that certain powers were intra legem, and
therefore constitutional.   Therefore, that course could not be
adopted.[3]

What is the alternative?   There is only one alternative—
namely, that there must be a statutory definition of the powers
of each inferior Legislature.   That is an immense revolution
in all our habits of thought.   It never has been our custom
in this country that the Law Courts should assume the right of
defining what were the constitutional functions of our Assemblies.   That makes the whole difference between what is
sometimes called a rigid constitution and a flexible constitution;
and it has always been the peculiar type and character of our
legislature that it should be flexible, and reject and refuse to
submit to the decisions of the Law Courts.   As your Lordships know, the American Constitution, and all Federal systems,

[1] *Ibid.*, pp. 522-523.
[2] *Ibid.*, pp. 525-526.
[3] *Ibid.*, p. 529.

from their very nature are driven to adopt the other solution. Does anybody really suppose that at this period of time, after muddling on tolerably well for ten centuries, having regulated our policy upon centripetal lines for that period of time, we are suddenly to resort to centrifugal lines, involving as this involves, the adoption of a policy which for the first time makes the Law Courts the masters of Parliament? [1]

He concluded by saying that neither of these countries wanted devolution, and that the introduction of the motion was altogether inopportune. It was rather for the advocates to go to the country and convince the people first. [2]

Viscount Bryce's speech was the most interesting as well as the most scholarly. He spoke in very friendly terms of Lord Brassey's proposals but raised several practical objections to it. He disagreed with the Lord Chancellor on several points. In the first place, he did not think that there was no public opinion on the subject. [3] Secondly, as to the evils of the present system he said there could be no doubt whatever, and he did not believe that they were the result of obstruction. Obstruction in the nature of things could not be eliminated; it was inherent in the system of party Government. [4]

Lord Bryce's main point was, " Whether this remedy which they propose is the only remedy, or whether it will prove an effective remedy." In this connection, he pointed out esveral difficulties of the scheme. In the first place, he said that devolution or the proposal of devolution means federalism, in which the most difficult problem is the division of powers. [5] Secondly, it means the multiplicity of new execu-

---

[1] *Ibid.*, pp. 529-530.

[2] *Ibid.*, p. 531.

[3] *Ibid.*, p. 532.

[4] *Ibid.*, pp. 532-533.

[5] *Ibid.*, pp. 335-337.

tives.[1]  Thirdly, there is the preponderance of England which would render the proposal unworkable if not impossible.[2]

Lord Charnwood answered Lord Bryce.  He said first, that he was surprised that Lord Bryce should have treated this proposal as if there were any question of creating in this country what can properly be called a Federation, something analogous to the Constitution of the United States or of Canada or Australia.  ". . . . and as I understand," said he, " the proposal which my noble friend's motion adumbrates is emphatically not anything in the nature of a strict Federation like that of the United States, but is what might be more correctly expressed by the phrase with which one is familiar of Home Rule All Round."  Consequently there would not be any difficulty in distributing the powers because the Imperial Legislature would legally still be supreme. Secondly, with regard to the setting up of new Executives, he said that there was already much guidance in the legislation of Parliament and that to a large extent these executives already existed.[3]  Thirdly, as to preponderance of England, he remarked:

There is one other point which has seemed to present to the noble Viscount a great difficulty, and which I must say I cannot understand at all.  He pointed out the great inequality of size between England and Scotland, or England and Wales.  What does that matter?  The difficulty would equally have arisen in the case of the existing Federations.  Take the actual Federation of the United States at the present day.  You have a State like New York, or like Illinois, which in the matter of population are as big as Scotland, or as big as the whole of Canada perhaps, and a little State like Rhode Island, which in

[1] *Ibid.*, pp. 537-538.
[2] *Ibid.*, pp. 538-539.
[3] *Ibid.*, pp. 544, 545-546.

area and population is about the same as a good-sized English county. What does it matter to them? Each manages its own affairs. What element of friction does it introduce that one of them happens to legislate for a larger and the other for a smaller area? Or what does it matter either, supposing instead of being independent Legislatures they should be subordinate Legislatures exercising delegated powers? I confess that I am amazed that such a point should be put forward as one which occasions serious practical difficulty.[1]

The Motion was, by leave, withdrawn.

Again on June 3, of the same year, a motion on Federal Devolution was introduced in the House of Commons by Major Edward Wood, supported by Mr. Murray Macdonald. The motion reads:[2]

That with a view to enabling the Imperial Parliament to devote more attention to the general interests of the United Kingdom, and, in collaboration with the other governments of the Empire, to matters of common Imperial concern, this House is of the opinion that the time has come for the creation of subordinate legislatures within the United Kingdom, and that, to this end, the Government, without prejudice to the proposals it may have to make with regard to Ireland, should forthwith appoint a parliamentary body to consider and report:

1. Upon a measure of Federal Devolution applicable to England, Scotland and Ireland, defined in its general outlines by existing differences in law and administration between the three countries;
2. upon the extent to which these differences are applicable to Welsh conditions and requirements; and
3. upon the financial aspects and requirements of the measure.

This motion was the most important of those that had been made on the subject. In the first place, it differed from

[1] *Ibid.*, p. 547.
[2] *Parliamentary Debates* (Commons), 5th ser., vol. 116, p. 1873.

the other motions in two important respects.   First, the sole purpose of the motion was " to enable the Imperial Parliament to devote more attention to the general interests of the United Kingdom, etc." and second, it was not an abstract motion but one that called for a definite action on the part of the Government, namely, to appoint a Parliamentary body for the investigation of the problem.   In the second place, there was an almost unanimous agreement on the motion that had never existed before.   Only Sir Henry Craik and one or two others were absolutely opposed to it.   The representative of the Government, Mr. Long, supported the motion too, but he took exception to its wording.   The debates on the motion may be summarized as follows :

In support of the motion Mr. Wood declared :

I do not think it is too much to say that, in the times immediately in front of us, what may tilt the scale between civilization and disruption may be the confidence that our people have in their institutions.   That confidence, let us be very sure of it, depends upon the ability and efficiency with which those institutions do their work.   Therefore, if it be at all true, as I think it is, that this House has receded in public estimation, the case that I wish to submit to honorable members is that that is due to the fact that we have been asking too much of our machinery.[1]

After mentioning the breakdown of Cabinet responsibility and the congestion of the House, he went on to say :

Therefore, my conclusion is that it is as groundless to suppose that we can remedy our defects by tinkering in this way or that with our present system as it is to suppose that you can make a horse pull more than a certain load by merely refitting the harness in which he pulls it.   It is not the way he is pulling that is wrong, it is the load you are asking him to pull.   If that

[1] *Ibid.*, p. 1874.

be so, what we suggest is that we should inquire and inform ourselves as to the extent to which it may be possible to delegate a good deal of the business that we do here to subordinate assemblies, perhaps, in different parts of the country.[1]

Mr. Macdonald seconded the motion. He made a number of important points. First, as respects the congestion of business he said that it was not a thing of today nor of yesterday. It was an evil which had been slowly and almost insensibly accumulating upon us for at least eighty years, and it was an evil which we must in some way get rid of.[2]

He pointed out that there was only two remedies, namely, a change in the rules of procedure and devolution of functions. The first method had already proved ineffective.[3] Therefore the only remedy must be sought in devolution.

He also alluded to the fact that the word Federal devolution had given rise to some doubts. But he pointed out that the effect of devolution would not be federalism in the strict sense.[4] However, in a loose sense of the word federal, it is to some extent already true of the constitution of the United Kingdom.[5]

Finally, he made a few remarks on the motion. First, the motion calls for a federal devolution applicable to England, Scotland, and Ireland. The question of Wales is left open for the decision of Wales.[6] With regard to Ireland, he said there were then three sections of public opinion on the question of Home Rule, namely, first, a minority extreme view in favor of independence; second, a majority view in favor of dominion rule; and lastly, the Ulster

[1] Ibid., pp. 1877-1878.
[2] Ibid., p. 1885.
[3] Ibid., p. 1885.
[4] Ibid., p. 1886.
[5] Ibid., pp. 1887-1888.
[6] Ibid., p. 1888.

point of view for Union.  None of these views was desirable.  The best solution for the Irish question would be devolution.  " For my part," he concluded, " I believe that the acceptance of this proposal lies deep in the truest interest of Ireland, of Great Britain, and the Empire, and in that belief I second the motion." [1]

Sir Edward Carson also spoke in favor of devolution, but did not believe that it should be based upon nationality. He declared:

While I agree that you must have these local bodies with certain powers conferred upon them by way of devolution, I entirely dissent from the proposition that the unit must be in accordance with nationality.  I see no reason for it.  I see no reason why England should be only one part.  I see great difficulties in having England only one part.  I see no reason why Ireland should be only one part.  I see great difficulties in that also.[2]

He dissented also from that part of the Motion which excepted Ireland from the scope of inquiry.

Sir Henry Craik was the only person who was absolutely against the motion.  After alluding to the difficulties of allocation of powers and praising the strength of Parliament, he concluded by saying:

Let us do what we can to expedite our measures, let us do what we can to entrust a very wide share of administration to local authorities, but let us pause before we strip this House of a great part of the functions that have made it great in the past, and let us pause before we divide the unity of legislative authority and make two competing legislative authorities in the Kingdom.[3]

[1] *Ibid.*, p. 1894.
[2] *Ibid.*, p. 1897.
[3] *Ibid.*, p. 1904.

Mr. Long spoke for the Government. He was personally in favor of the Motion, but took exception to its wording. He said:

So far as the Government are concerned, they do not propose as a Government either to try to affect the vote of, or to offer advice to, the House of Commons. But individually we shall, of course, express our views, whether we are for or against the subject of the Resolution. As a supporter of the Federal system, I confess that the precise wording of this Motion places me in somewhat the same difficulty in which my right honorable and learned Friend, the leader of the Irish Unionist Party, who spoke a few moments ago, found himself. . . . The Motion, as I understand it, the Motion that I am anxious to support, is a Motion advising that there shall be a Parliament body set up to inquire into and make recommendations upon a system of subordinate Parliaments for the United Kingdom. It seems to me, if that be the decision of the House of Commons, as I hope it may be, to be a contradiction of terms to say that that action is not to prejudice in any way action regarding Ireland. One of the reasons why I am a strong Federalist is because I have always maintained that if you find it necessary to alter your Parliamentary system by some devolution of business, whatever may be your governing reasons, you should treat the United Kingdom as a whole, on the same terms and in the same way, and that you should give to all members of the United Kingdom the same privileges and the same Parliamentary rights and the same Parliamentary powers, and if it is suggested that in setting up a Federal system there is to be, because there is an Irish Act on the Statute Book, some separate treatment for Ireland, I could not vote for the Resolution.[1]

In other respects, he was in favor of the Motion. There is no doubt in his opinion that the House of Commons is no longer capable of meeting the demands of the United Kingdom for legislation. This is not due to the system,

[1] *Ibid.*, p. 1905.

but because the business of Parliament has increased. He declared: " In the debates we have had, so far, and in previous debates on this subject in and out of the House of Commons, has there been found anybody to deny that our system today is not sufficient for our purpose and that our machine no longer can turn out the articles that the United Kingdom requires? " He continued:

It is not Governments; it is not Members of Parliament. No, it is that times have changed, and we have got to change with them. The need for legislation is greater. The power of our people to appreciate their deficiencies and their wants, and to suggest remedies for them, has immensely increased. The power to express their needs in powerful language which reaches us here is far more widespread than it was in those earlier days. Parliament must realize it has a different task to accomplish today from that which it had ten, fifteen, or twenty years ago, that it has to bear a heavier burden, that it has to realize it has to meet much greater and more widespread demands. It cannot do that itself, and it must ask for some other means by which this burden can be borne, because borne I believe it must be or you will have discontent, and dissatisfaction among our people, and not only will you discredit parliamentary institutions, but you will do worse than that—you will endanger the very fabric upon which the United Kingdom, and, therefore, the Empire, rests. You must give the people the feeling of confidence that when they come here their just and legitimate demands can be met without undue delay, or you will have them say, as they are beginning to say now, that Parliament is of no use and they have lost their respect for it. Can you do this unless you are prepared to set up subordinate Parliaments, and to devolve some part of your work upon them? I support this general principle, because I believe that the answer to that question must be in the negative. I believe you cannot accomplish this great task unless you are prepared to look facts in the face, and adopt the new plan which is suggested in this Resolution.[1]

[1] *Ibid.*, pp. 1909-1910.

Major Mackenzie Wood favored the resolution from the point of view of Scotland.[1] Mr. Mackinder, another Scottish member, spoke in favor of regional devolution as against National devolution. He suggested that England might be divided into several units. His argument is as follows:

Under the headings 1 and 2 quite clearly it makes nationality the criterion of the amount of devolution and not efficiency in Government. I am amply satisfied with the success of the Amendment in drawing attention to this defect. Almost every honorable Member who has spoken has referred to this Amendment, and the right honorable gentleman on the Front Bench (Mr. Long) and the right honorable gentleman, the Member for Duncairn (Sir E. Carson) emphatically endorsed the point of view I wish to urge. They both urged in connection with the subordinate Legislatures which are proposed to be set up that they should not be set up in respect of nationalities, which they regard as a retrogressive measure, but they should be in regard to regions which have today common interests which may be national but not necessarily so.[2]

Sir Ryland Adkins, an English Member, was in favor of Home Rule for England as a whole, but opposed to its division into units. The chief argument for English Home Rule from the standpoint of England was that her business had been neglected. With regard to the English Government he said:

When I first entered this House thirteen years ago we spent double the time in discussing and passing Estimates which were largely concerned with the internal Government of this country than is given to them today. Take Department after Department. The Local Government Board, now reborn as the Ministry of Health, the Board of Education, the Home Office, the Board of Trade—the greater part of their admin-

---

[1] *Ibid.*, p. 1918.
[2] *Ibid.*, p. 1920.

istrative work is work controlling the government of England, and yet it is only for a few odd hours in each Session, and then only by concerted action on the part of large numbers of Members of the House, that there is any reasoned and continuous investigation as to how that government is carried on and how it is to be linked up with the local government of the country over which it has such great power.[1]

He further deplored the fact that in the last thirty or forty years, the control of the House of Commons over the administrative departments had dwindled year after year. This amounted to a silent revolution in the Government of England. Bureaucracy was rampant. The representatives of the people were no longer able to supervise and guide the administration as they used to do in the past. All this could be remedied by devolution. Thus Mr. Adkins concluded:

Is it not part of our duty to recover for our race that special note and principle and method of Government which has been so successful in the ages that came before us, and that can only be done by the creation of a subordinate legislature for England as a great national unit, just as for Scotland and for Ireland, in recovering for England by means of a subordinate legislature that which would exercise constant and vigilant oversight for the administration of the country, and which would provide that initiative which may be wanting in technical knowledge, which may be wanting in the accomplishments of the expert, but which would have that vitality which only comes when it comes from a popular assembly representing the real tendencies and desires of the people. Therefore I most earnestly support, on the grounds that it is necessary to complete and to vitalize local government in this country, the proposal now before the House, and so far from this leading to undue parochialism, the principle of the Motion of subordinate legis-

[1] *Ibid.*, pp. 1932-1933.

latures would set free this mother of Parliaments for even greater and higher duties.[1]

Sir Robert Thomas spoke for Welsh Home Rule.[2] Another member, Mr. Ronald McNeill, spoke against the Motion. He said there are two propositions involved in the debate: (1) that the congestion of business demands a change, and (2) that devolution is the best and the only way of making that change.[3] Even granted that the first point is true, he did not believe that the second proposition could be maintained. He pointed out that there were two alternative methods of relieving this House, neither of which would he himself advocate, but both of which he thought were better than the one proposed.

The first was the creation of a super-Parliament or Imperial Council (in which all the Dominions would be represented) for the consideration of Imperial matters and foreign affairs. This was indeed a hope but it was the true federal principle. If this was desired, as some of the Members seemed to desire, then this Parliament should retain its present position and its present functions so far as the United Kingdom was concerned, leaving the future Imperial Council to deal with Imperial questions. This was one method of relief.[4]

The second method was to devolve legislative powers to County Councils instead of to national legislatures. You never could work a federal system in Great Britain, if you had a great discrepancy in wealth and population between the several units. Therefore the better way would be to delegate some of the functions of Parliament to the existing

[1] *Ibid.,* pp. 1933-1934.

[2] *Ibid.,* pp. 1948-1950.

[3] *Ibid.,* pp. 2068.

[4] *Ibid.,* pp. 2076-2077.

County Councils which were more nearly equal in every respect than the existing nationalities of Great Britain.[1]

A number of other members spoke in favor of the Motion, such as Captain Ormsby-Gore, Major Warning, Major O'Neil, Sir Donald Maclean, Mr. T. A. Lewis, Mr. F. C. Thomson, Sir T. Whittaker, Mr. Wallace, Mr. Hugh Edwards, Mr. Marriott, and Mr. Clynes. Mr. Kidd spoke against the Motion.

The Motion was carried by a vote of 187 to 34.

Pursuant to the above resolution, a Speaker's Conference was appointed in October of the same year. The conference made a report in the next spring. It agreed on many points but failed to agree on the organization of subordinate Legislatures. The details of the report will be dealt with in the next Chapter. Suffice it to say in this connection that the failure of the conference in reaching a unanimous agreement was no small blow to the immediate success of the proposal.

Since the Speaker's Conference the Government has not taken any action on this subject. But the question is by no means dead. The interests of many private members on this subject are as great as ever. The recent development of the subject in the House of Commons may be briefly stated.

## II. SINCE THE SPEAKERS' CONFERENCE

On February 10, 1922, the Government of Wales Bill " to provide for the better government of Wales; and for other purposes connected therewith," was presented by Sir Robert Thomas; supported by Lieut. Colonel Watts-Morgan, Mr. Hinds, Mr. Haydon Jones, and Mr. Hugh Edwards; to be read a second time upon Friday, 28th April, and to be printed.[2]

[1] *Ibid.*, p. 2077.
[2] Bill 17, *Parliamentary Debates*, 5th ser. (Commons), vol. 150, p. 471.

On the same day, the Government of Scotland Bill, " to provide for the better government of Scotland," was presented by Mr. John Wallace; supported by Mr. Alexander Shaw, Mr. Johnstone, Mr. Hogge, Mr. MacCallum Scott; to be read a second time upon Friday, 26th May, and to be printed.[1]  In moving the second reading of the Government of Wales Bill on April 28, 1922, Sir Robert Thomas said:

This Bill is the outcome of a very strong desire in Wales that that little country should be created a separate entity.  We feel that we are not today in that position that a great though little country ought to be; in fact we feel, according to the law of the land, we are no better situated than an English county. We hope before very long that when legislation comes to be considered, Wales may be considered from her own particular point of view. That can only be done by creating her a separate entity.[2]

Then he alluded to the fact that he had introduced last year the Secretary for Wales Bill which met with little support from the Government.  The Prime Minister advised them to drop that Bill and go in for devolution.  Consequently a Committee of the Welsh Parliamentary Party was brought into existence, the chairman of which was Mr. Herbert Lewis.  The Committee came to the conclusion that the only possible scheme was one based upon the Report of the Speaker's Conference on Devolution, and the Parliamentary Relief Bill of 1921, introduced by Mr. Murray Macdonald and backed up by important Members of all parties.  He said that this Bill was an " agreed Bill ", and that a Committee of the Welsh Parliamentary Party and a Committee of the Scottish Parliamentary party had

[1] Bill 23, *ibid.*, p. 472.
[2] *Parliamentary Debates*, 5th ser. (Commons), vol. 153, p. 929.

agreed upon this Bill as being applicable to both countries with the exception of the Judiciary in the case of Scotland, and when the turn of Scotland came, they would introduce a Bill in the same terms as this Bill.[1]  The Bill may be divided into four parts:

(1) The powers to be granted are legislative and administrative powers in all matters connected with local Government, public health, including housing and national health insurance, liquor licensing, order and good Government, including the administration of the police force, prisons and reformatories, the Poor Law, land and agriculture, including land tenure, commons, and enclosures, the game laws, projects for drainage and improvements, and public education in all its forms.[2]

(2) The powers excluded are the Crown and matters relating thereto; the making of peace or war or matters arising from a state of war; the Navy; the Army; the Air Force; foreign and colonial relations, dignities or titles of honour, treason, felony, alienage, aerial navigation, lighthouse; buoys or beacons; currency; standards of weights and measures; trade marks; designs; merchandise marks; companies including insurance and banking companies, railways and canals; the regulation of trade; banking and commercial law; industrial legislation, and marriage law and divorce.[3]

(3) The financial relations between the Imperial Parliament and the Welsh Legislature are based upon the Report of the committee on financial relations of the Speaker's Conference, presided over by Lord Chalmers.  All that is asked for is executive power in Wales on the basis of the grants Wales obtains from the Imperial Parliament at the present time.[4]

[1] *Ibid.*, pp. 929-930.
[2] *Ibid.*, p. 930.
[3] *Ibid.*, p. 930.
[4] *Ibid.*, p. 930.

(4) With respect to the constitution of the Welsh Legislature, the Bill provides that the Lower Chamber shall consist of two representatives for every Parliamentary constituency in Wales. It will contain 72 members in all, elected upon the existing Parliamentary franchise. The Upper Chamber shall consist of two representatives to be elected by the council of each county and county borough in Wales and two by the University of Wales. The members of the Upper Chamber shall be elected for six years and one-third of their members shall retire every second year.

Mr. Hayden Jones said that there was an apprehension in North Wales that if local government were given on the basis of population or on the basis of assessable value, two counties in Wales—Monmouthshire and Glamorganshire—would swamp the whole of Wales and that industrial Wales would swamp agricultural Wales. The bi-cameral system was designed to allay that misapprehension.[1]

Sir Owen Thomas opposed the Bill, saying that the bulk of the Welsh people were not asking for this measure.[2] He alluded to the fact that a Conference had been held at Shrewsbury about April 1st of this year. It was convened on behalf of the Welsh National Parliamentary Party and invitations were sent out to every county council, borough council, urban district council and rural district council throughout the Principality. Only 40 delegates attended. Glamorganshire, the biggest county, did not send a representative.[3] (Mr. Hugh Edwards said Sir Owen Thomas belonged to no party and spoke only for himself.) [4]

Mr. Hugh Edwards said that the Bill was based on a two-fold ground, first " on the inalienable right of a re-

[1] *Ibid.*, p. 932.

[2] *Ibid.*, p. 933.

[3] *Ibid.*, pp. 933-934.

[4] *Ibid.*, p. 935.

sponsible and free people to manage its own domestic affairs,[1] and second, on the congestion of the House of Commons." [2]   As to the demand for Home Rule in Wales he declared:

In spite of what the honorable member has said I assure the House that most of the Welsh Members are in favor of the principle of the Bill, and so are all the Welsh constituencies. This Bill simply seeks to confer upon Wales the right to manage her own affairs, to develop her own national life upon lines in harmony with her own peculiar genius, to set up on Welsh soil a Parliament which should be the emblem of her unity, the radiating center of her distinctive interests and the pledge of her destiny in the comity of nations which compose this Empire.[3]

There was another Conference at Shrewsbury in June, 1919, when all the county councils were represented and unanimously passed a resolution in favor of the principle of this Bill.[4]

The Government of Scotland Bill was read a second time on 26 May, 1922.   The provisions of the Bill may be briefly summarized.   The Bill represents a further installment of the policy of devolution, initiated by the Government of Ireland Act, 1914.   It provides for a single-Chamber Parliament of 148 members.   The powers of the Scots Parliament include all those conferred on the Irish Parliament in the Government of Ireland Bill, October, 1914, except the control of the Post Office, and the power to vary customs and excise, but with the addition of the administration of Old Age Pensions, National Insurance, and Labour Exchanges.

[1] *Ibid.*, p. 936.
[2] *Ibid.*, p. 937.
[3] *Ibid.*, pp. 937-938.
[4] *Ibid.*, p. 940.

The executive power will continue vested in His Majesty the King, who will be represented by a Lord High Commissioner. The administration will be carried on by the Lord Commissioner advised by an Executive Committee of a Scottish Privy Council.

The power of varying Imperial taxes, excepting customs and excise, is conferred upon the Scots Parliament which will also have power to levy the existing Imperial taxes on inheritable property in Scotland. Provision is made for the payment by the Imperial Exchequer to the Scottish Exchequer out of the proceeds of Scottish taxes, of an annual sum towards defraying the cost of Scottish services. A Government Exchequer Board is established to determine all questions arising under the financial provisions.

The Judicial Committee of the Privy Council is substituted for the House of Lords as the Final Court of Appeal, and all consitutional questions will be determined by that tribunal.[1]

On the debate on the second reading Mr. J. Wallace said: " I can assure the House that behind the Scottish Home Rule movement there is a rising tide of well-informed and resolute Scottish opinion." [2] Then he continued:

What are the governing considerations behind this question? There are two. We demand a Scottish Parliament, firstly, on national grounds and secondly, on the ground of legislative efficiency. I am aware that certain Scottish colleagues of my own are not in favor of the advocacy of nationalism in any form. They believe that the advocacy of nationalism is pernicious and has the worst possible effect from the standpoint of the interests of the nation. But surely that must depend upon the kind of nationalism you advocate, and also upon the sphere in which that nationalism desires to find expression.

[1] 12 Geo. 5, 1922, Memorandum of the Government of Scotland Bill.
[2] *Parliamentary Debates* (Commons), 5th ser., vol. 154, p. 1609.

. . . It is my belief that a healthy nationalism, a healthy competition between nations, develop inherent capacities and adds virility to the races of Mankind. . . . My point is that national point of view still survives, and we claim the right to govern ourselves along the lines of our own history and traditions.[1]

The second ground is legislative efficiency. " We base our claim for this legislative efficiency as being necessary to Scotland on the ground that efficiency under present conditions is absolutely impossible in this House." [2]

Mr. Alexander Shaw seconded the Motion. He spoke in favor of the Bill and interpreted the point of view of the Government as being favorable to its early adoption.

Sir H. Craik spoke against the Bill. He said:

I would ask the House to give a little more consideration to the more serious aspect of the question. You are arousing by artificial, and, as I think, by camouflaged methods a cry in Scotland, which is really not understood, for Home Rule. Have you considered what that is likely to lead to? You will arouse in Scotland some of that dread, pernicious, fatal feeling which Home Rule has aroused in Ireland.[3]

On the other hand, Sir Donald Maclean said: " There is no doubt that the general feeling in Scotland, irrespective of party, is in favor of devolution of parliamentary powers to Scotland, where the work can be done by Scotsmen in the Parliament House of Edinburg." [4]

Lieutenant-Colonel Ward was in favor of the principle of the Bill out not the Nationalism in which it was expressed.[5] Lord Eustace Percy spoke against the Bill. He said that the Bill was an imitation of the Home Rule Bill of

[1] *Ibid.*, pp. 1610-1611.

[2] *Ibid.*, pp. 1612-1613.

[3] *Ibid.*, p. 1618.

[4] *Ibid.*, p. 1631.

[5] *Ibid.*, p. 1636.

1914, as applied to Ireland.[1]  The Bill was a bad one from a constitutional point of view, because it does not clearly provide for the constitutional connection between the Imperial Parliament and the Scottish Parliament.[2]

I confess that, in principle, I am a Home Ruler all round if you can get a practical and possible scheme.  Scotland at the present moment . . . is the touchstone of a workable and efficient scheme, and until the Government get down to a real consideration of what is needed in the way of practical devolution, so long shall we have thrown at us Bills of which kind, which represent no constitutional knowledge and deep thought on the difficulty and the problem of founding a new constitution.[3]

Dr. Murray, in answering to Sir H. Craik, said:

The right honorable gentleman's strongest point against this Bill was that there was not at the back of it any strong public feeling or agitation.  I rather think that one of the reasons why we should pass the Bill is that the atmosphere is so calm.  It is better for the House to pass it now than to be coerced into passing it later on.[4]

Mr. Johnstone also touched upon the same point.  He said:

I know something about public opinion in Scotland.  I am connected with many public bodies in Scotland.  I am afraid the right honorable gentleman the member for the Scottish Universities (Sir H. Craik) for whom I have the utmost admiration, is out of touch with the living forces of Scotland and is not coming into close contact with public life there.  Take the Convention of Burghs in Scotland. . . . The Convention of Burghs has declared in favor of Scottish Home Rule.[5] . . .

---

[1] *Ibid.*, p. 1637.

[2] *Ibid.*, p. 1638.

[3] *Ibid.*, p. 1639.

[4] *Ibid.*, p. 1641.

[5] *Ibid.*, p. 1644.

The right honorable gentleman will find that the ordinary business and public-spirited men in Scotland desire that they should be associated more closely with the administration of Scottish affairs, that Scottish business should be done in Scottish ways, and that the Scottish people should have more control than they have at the present time. If you disregard peaceful methods of that sort and the expression of moderate opinion, you will play into the hands of the extremists, and you will teach people that the only way to get a reform which is agitating the minds of the people of Scotland is to emulate the example of the people of the sister isle.[1]

Mr. Gideon Murray also participated in the debate. He said that he had been a convinced devolutionalist but he could not support this Bill, because of the financial difficulties and of the relationship with the Island across the Channel, Ireland. It would cost perhaps two or three million pounds to set up such a constitution.[2]

On May 8, 1922, a joint Bill " to provide for the better government of Scotland and Wales, and for other matters relating thereto " was presented by Mr. Murray Macdonald. It was orderd to be read a second time on May 22 and to be printed.[3] The second reading did not take place, however.[4] The important provisions of the Bill may be briefly noted.[5]

The Bill provides for a Parliament for Scotland " to be called the Scots Parliament, consisting of His Majesty the King, the Senate of Scotland, and the House of Commons of Scotland; " and a Parliament for Wales " to be called

---

[1] *Ibid.*, p. 1645.

[2] *Ibid.*, p. 1647.

[3] *Parliamentary Debates* (Commons), 5th ser., vol. 153, p. 1808.

[4] *Ibid.*, vol. 154, p. 972.

[5] 12 and 13 Geo. 5, Bills; Public (1) 1922.

the Welsh Parliament, consisting of His Majesty, the Senate of Wales, and the House of Commons of Wales." [1]

It is provided that, " notwithstanding the establishment of the Parliaments as aforesaid, or anything contained in the Act, the supreme authority of the Parliament of the United Kingdom shall remain unaffected and undiminished over all persons, matters, and things in the United Kingdom and every part thereof." [2]

The powers of the Scots and the Welsh Parliaments are confined to making laws for the peace, order, and good government of Scotland and Wales within their respective jurisdictions. They are expressly forbidden to make laws with regard to the following matters: [3] (1) Anything relating to the Crown; (2) anything relationg to peace and war; (3) all matters relating to the Army and Navy and Air forces; (4) Treaties and Foreign affairs; (5) dignities or titles of honour; (6) treason, treason felony, alienage, naturalization, or aliens or domicile; (7) trade without their respective jurisdictions and bounties on exports, quarantine and navigation; (8) Aerial navigation; (9) Postal service under the control of His Majesty's Postmaster-General; (10) Lighthouses, buoys, or beacons; (11) Coinage, legal tender, and negotiable instruments; (12) Trade marks, designs, merchandise marks, copyright or patent rights; (13) Companies, including insurance and banking; (14) Railways and canals; (15) Employer's liability, workmen's Compensation, Friendly Societies, Trade Unions, industrial disputes, or unemployment insurance; (16) Public loans made before the passing of this Act; (17) the charging, levying, and collection of customs duties, excise duties on articles manufactured or produced within their respective

[1] *Ibid.*, sec. i(1).
[2] *Ibid.*, sec. i(2).
[3] *Ibid.*, sec. ii.

jurisdictions, income taxes and super taxes or any other tax of a similar nature; (18) they are also forbidden to pass laws infringing the freedom of religion.[1]  Neither do they have power to repeal or alter any provisions of this Act of any laws passed by the Imperial Parliament.[2]

The Executive power in Scotland and Wales shall continue vested in His Majesty the King except with regard to Scottish or Welsh services.  For the administration of the latter His Majesty may appoint a Secretary of State to represent the Crown in the exercise of all powers delegated to him.  These powers may be exercised through such Departments as may be established in Scotland and Wales.  The Ministers of these Departments shall be appointed by the Secretary of State and they shall constitute an Executive Committee to advise and assist the Secretary of the State.[3]. .

The Secretary of State is given power to summon, prorogue and dissolve the Parliaments of Scotland and Wales. The House of Commons of Scotland and Wales shall be elected for a period of five years unless sooner dissolved.[4]

The Senate of the Scots Parliament shall consist of 36 members to be elected by the members of the House of Commons of the Scots Parliament by ballot and by proportional representation by the method of the single transferrable vote, and of the following ex-officio members, namely, the Lord President and the Lord Justice Clerk of the Court of Session.  The elected members shall serve for nine years, one-third retiring every third year.[5]

The Senate of the Welsh Parliament shall consist of thirty-six members to be elected as follows: two members by

[1] *Ibid.*, sec. iii(1).

[2] *Ibid.*, sec. iv(1 and 2).

[3] *Ibid.*, sec. 5.

[4] *Ibid.*, sec. vi.

[5] *Ibid.*, sec. viii(1).

the Council of each County and County Borough in Wales and two by the Council of the University of Wales. They shall also serve for nine years, one-third retiring every third year.[1]

The House of Commons of the Scots Parliament shall consist of 74 members returned by the Constituencies in Scotland named in the Representation of the People Act, 1918. The House of Commons of Wales shall consist of 72 members returned in the same way. Peers shall not be debarred from voting. After three years the Parliaments of Scotland and Wales shall have power to make modifications in the election laws.[2]

Money Bills shall originate in the House of Commons upon the recommendation from the Secretary of State, and the Senate cannot amend them. After a Bill has been passed in the House of Commons for two successive sessions and failed to pass the Senate, the Secretary of State may convene a joint session of both Houses; and, if passed by a majority in such joint session, the Bill is deemed to have passed both Houses.[3]

With regard to finance, a Scottish Exchequer and Consolidated Fund, and a Welsh Exchequer and Consolidated Fund shall be established. The Scots and Welsh Parliaments shall have power to levy taxes within their respective jurisdictions, except Customs duties, Excise duties on articles manufactured and produced, Income taxes and Capital taxes.[4] Provision is also made for certain Imperial contributions to the Scottish and Welsh Exchequers to be determined by a Joint Board of Exchequer.[5]

---

[1] *Ibid.*, sec. viii(2).

[2] *Ibid.*, secs. 8-9.

[3] *Ibid.*, sec. xii.

[4] *Ibid.*, sec. xiv.

[5] *Ibid.*, sec. xv.

As to the Judiciary, the existing system shall remain unchanged except that in Scotland a judge of the Court of Session shall be appointed by the Secretary of State.[1] An appeal shall lie from the Court of Session in Scotland and from the Court of Appeal in England and Wales to the House of Lords. All constitutional questions shall be determined by the Judicial Committee of the Privy Council.[2]

The most recent development was the Government of Scotland Bill of May 9, 1924. It was introduced by Mr. Buchanan who said that the Bill was representative of Scottish labour opinion in so far as it was represented by Members of Parliament.[3] Mr. Johnston seconded the Motion. Many Members expressed the opinion in favor of a general scheme of devolution but in opposition to the Bill on the ground that it sought to retain Scottish representation in the House of Commons. Sir A. H. Western said:

We cannot uphold as either fair or honest the provision that we Scots are to remove all our Scottish affairs from the cooperation of our English Members, and at the same time we are to retain our full Parliamentary powers in this House and to interfere in every blessed thing with regard to England. That is so grotesquely unfair that it alone condemns the Bill.[4]

The Secretary of State for Scotland, Mr. Adamson, spoke on behalf of the Government. He said that the Government gave the general principle of this Bill their approval. "At the same time they recognize," said Mr. Adamson, " that it raises a large and vital issue which is of importance to this country as well as to Scotland, and what they suggest they are prepared to do is to appoint a Committee to examine this whole question and report to the House. That Com-

[1] *Ibid.*, sec. xix.
[2] *Ibid.*, sec. xx.
[3] *Parliamentary Debates* (Commons), 5th ser., vol. 173, 1924, p. 789.
[4] *Ibid.*, pp. 865-866.

mittee, they suggest, should be arranged through the ordinary channels.  I hope the Bill will get a Second Reading, and in this way will express the feelings of the present Parliament on this important question.  If it gets a Second Reading, I suggest that it should be committed to a Committee of the Whole House, and in conclusion I hope that the overwhelming majority of Members will give it their support." [1]

Mr. Buchanan and several other Members moved the closure, but the Speaker declined to put the question.  It was previously understood that the closure would be put, but the Speaker changed his mind.  As a result a dispute arose between some of the Members and the Speaker.  Grave disorder ensued and the debate was adjourned without question put according to Standing Order No. 21,[2] which provides that " In the case of grave disorder arising in the House, the Speaker may, if he thinks is necessary to do so, adjourn the House without question put, or suspend any sitting for a time to be named by him."

Later on in the same year, on May 14, Mr. Ayles asked the Prime Minister, Mr. J. Ramsay MacDonald, about the appointment of a Committee of Inquiry into the matter of devolution.  Mr. MacDonald replied that the Government were quite prepared to appoint such a Committee, and were causing inquiries to be made through the ordinary channels.[3] Again, on May 21, Mr. Ayles asked him a second time about the question.  Mr. MacDonald said that this matter was being dealt with, but a little time must elapse before the Government were in a position to make a statement.  Thus the matter has stood.  Whether the present Conservative Government will take up the matter or not remains yet uncertain.

[1] *Ibid.*, pp. 869-870.

[2] *Ibid.*, p. 874.

[3] *Ibid.*, p. 1340.

# CHAPTER VI

## The Speaker's Conference on Devolution and the Proposed Schemes [1]

THE conference on devolution, which was created in October of 1919, consisted of thirty-two members chosen from both Houses of Parliament with Speaker Lowther as Chairman.[2] There were two official secretaries, Mr. G. F. M. Campion and Assistant Secretary Captain C. R. P. Diver. Besides these officers, the conference appointed two special committees to deal with specific problems—a financial committee consisting of Lord Chalmers (Chairman), Lord Faringdon, Mr. Murray Macdonald, Mr. Charles Edwards, and Sir Edward Goulding; and a judicial committee consisting of Lord Stuart of Wortley (Chairman), Lord Charnwood, Sir W. Ryland Adkins, Mr. D. Macmaster, and Mr.

[1] This chapter is based entirely upon the Letter from Mr. Speaker to the Prime Minister regarding the Conference on Devolution, House of Commons, 27th April, 1920.

[2] The other members of the conference were: Lord Aberdare, Earl Brassey, Duke of Buccleuch, Lord Inchcape, Lord Charnwood, Lord Denman, Marquis of Dufferin and Ava, Lord Emmott, Lord Faringdon, Viscount Gladstone, Lord Gorell, Viscount Hambleden, Viscount Harcourt, Lord Oranmore and Browne, Lord Southborough, Lord Stuart of Wortley, Sir W. Ryland Adkins, Sir Henry Cowan, Captain C. Craig, Mr. Charles Edwards, Mr. J. Hugh Edwards, Mr. Forestier-Walker, Sir Edward Goulding, Mr. W. Graham, Mr. J. M. Hogge, Mr. Murray Macdonald, Mr. D. Macmaster, Mr. Ronald McNeill, Mr. T. Moles, Mr. Gideon Murray, Mr. Tyson Wilson and Sir Frederick W. Young. Lord Brassey died during the conference and was substituted by Lord Strafford. The conference also lost the service of Lord Inchcape, Lord Hambleden, Lord Harcourt and Lord Dufferin. They were replaced by Lord Chalmers, Lord Elgin and Lord Selborne.

J. Hugh Edwards.    The first meeting of the conference was held on Tuesday, October 23, 1919.    There were altogether thirty-two meetings.

The aim of the conference was not the discussion of general principles, but the consideration of practical schemes of devolution.    The scope of its work, as set forth in the Resolution of June 4, 1919, was to consider and report: (1) upon a measure of Federal Devolution applicable to England, Scotland, and Ireland, defined in its general outlines by existing differences in law and administration between the three countries; (2) upon the extent to which these differences are applicable to Welsh conditions and requirements; and (3) upon the financial aspects and requirements of the measure.    Because of the fact that the Resolution specifically reserved Ireland for separate treatment, and that before the conference met the Government of Ireland Bill was pending in Parliament, the conference did not go into the question of Ireland but restricted the scope of its inquiry to Great Britain only.    However, the conference felt that eventually it might be possible or even necessary to bring Ireland into a general scheme of devolution that might be adopted.

As a guide to the work of the conference, the following terms of reference were adopted to consider and report upon a scheme of Legislative and Administrative Devolution within the United Kingdom having regard to (1) The need of reserving to the Imperial Parliament the exclusive consideration of (a) Foreign and Imperial affairs, and (b) Subjects affecting the United Kingdom as a whole; (2) The allocation of financial powers as between the Imperial Parliament and the subordinate legislatures, special consideration being given to the need of providing for the effective administration of the allocated powers; and (3) The special needs and characteristics of the component portions of the

United Kingdom in which subordinate legislatures are set up.[1]

THE POINTS UPON WHICH THE CONFERENCE AGREED

## A. *The Problem of Areas*

The first problem that engaged the attention of the conference was that of areas. If the object of devolution were purely to relieve Parliament of its congestion of business, the question would be much simpler. In that case the creation of a number of regions of approximately the same wealth and population would have been the best solution of the problem. But the object as set forth in the resolution is not only " to enable the Imperial Parliament to devote more attention to the general interest of the United Kingdom : nd to matters of common Imperial concern," but also to accomplish this through " a measure of Federal Devolution applicable to England, Scotland and Ireland " (without prejudice to any proposals that may be provided therefor) and to Wales as far as conditions permit. Thus the aim of devolution is really two-fold, namely, to relieve Parliament of its congestion and, at the same time, to satisfy the spirit of nationality of the different countries. Consequently, the conference recognized from the outset the three national divisions—England, Scotland, and Wales—as the proper and natural basis of a scheme of devolution. The question of regionalism was not within the authority of the conference either to adopt or to reject, and was, therefore, excluded from discussion.

The adoption of nationality as the basis for devolution is, however, not without its difficulties. It was said both before and in the conference that the preponderance of England in respect to size and population was a serious objection to this scheme. Hence it was suggested by some mem-

[1] *Letter from Mr. Speaker to the Prime Minister*, 1920, p. 3.

bers of the conference that England should be subdivided into two or three units.   However, it was finally agreed upon that such a subdivision of England would present more difficulties than it purported to solve, and so the existing national lines were unanimously recommended as the basis for devolution.

## B. Allocation of Powers

The second problem upon which substantial agreement was reached was the allocation of powers.   As a result of numerous discussions, the conference recommended the allocation of powers according to the following three lists:[1]

### List A

#### POWERS DEVOLVED ON LOCAL LEGISLATURES

1. Regulation of Internal Commercial Undertakings, Professions, and societies:
       Advertisements,
       Amusement Places and Theatres,
       Auctioneers,
       Building Societies and Loan Societies,
       Licensing (liquor),
       Markets and Fairs.
2. Order and Good Government:
       Cruelty to Animals,
       Betting and Gaming,
       Charities and Charitable Trust Acts,
       Inebriates,
       Police (other than Metropolitan police),
     Poor Law and Vagrancy,
       Prisons,
       Reformatories.
3. Ecclesiastical Matters:
       Burial Law,
       Matters affecting Religious Denominations.

[1] *Letter from Mr. Speaker to the Prime Minister*, pp. 16-18, appendix iii.

4. Agriculture and Land:
> Commons and Enclosures,
> Game Laws,
> Land:
>> (a) Drainage,
>> (b) Improvements,
>> (c) Settled Land Acts,
>> (d) Distress and Tenure.

5. Judiciary and Minor Legal Matters:
> Coroners,
> County Courts,
> Criminal Law, Minor Offences (Procedure, definition, and punishment).
> Law of Inheritance,
> Intestates' Estates,
> Conveyancing and Registration of Land,
> Minor Torts,
> Trustees, Guardians, and Wards.

6. Education:
> Primary,
> Secondary,
> University (except Oxford, **Cambridge**, **and** London).

7. Local Government and Municipal Undertakings:
> County Council and Municipal Bills,
> Fire Brigades,
> Local Legislation:
>> (Private Bills, Gas, Water, and Electricity Undertakings).
> Municipal Government:
>> (including Local Franchise).

8. Public Health:
> Public Health Matters:
>> (a) Preventive measures,
>> (b) Contagious diseases,
> Hospitals,

Housing,
National Health Insurance,
Lunacy and Mental Deficiency.

## List B

### POWERS RESERVED FOR THE UNITED KINGDOM PARLIAMENT

1. Crown and Matters relating thereto.
     (a) Succession to the Crown,
     (b) Regency,
     (c) Civil List,
     (d) Crown Properties,
     (e) Treasure Trove.
2. Peace and War.
3. Navy, Army and Air Services.
4. Foreign Affairs and Extradition.
5. Dominions, Colonies and Overseas Possessions.
6. Dignities and Titles.
7. Treason and Alienage.
8. Postal, Telegraph and Telephone Services.
9. Submarine Cables.
10. Wireless Telegraphy.
11. Aerial Navigation (civil).
12. Light Houses, Buoys and Beacons.
13. Currency, Coinage, Legal Tender and Weights and Measures.
14. Trade Marks, Patents and Copyrights.
15. Regulations of Trade, Banking and Commercial Law.
     Law of Agency,
     Banking,
     Census of Production,
     Internal Commerce,
     Company Law,
     Bills of Exchange and Negotiable Instruments,
     Insurance Companies,
     Sale of Poisons,
     Bankruptcy,

Bills of Sale,
Sale of Goods,
Shipping and Pilotage,
Quarantine.

16. Fisheries, Forestry and certain Agricultural Services.
Forestry Commission.
Ordinance Survey,
Import and Diseases of Animals,
Fisheries:
(a) Inland,
(b) Sea.
Wild Birds' Protection.

17. Industrial Legislation:
Employers' Liability and Workmen's Compensation,
Factories and Workshops,
Industrial Disputes,
Regulation of Hours and Wages,
Truck Acts,
Law of Master and Servant,
Unemployment Insurance,
Mines and Quarries,
Trades Unions,
Friendly Societies,
Old-Age Pensions,
Development Commission.

18. Railways and Canals.
19. Registration and Census.
20. Food Regulations.
21. Marriage Law and Divorce.
22. Vivisection.
23. Criminal Law.—Major Offences (procedure, definition and punishment).
24. Civil Torts—Major Torts.
25. Education—University (Oxford, Cambridge and London).
26. Metropolitan Police.

## List C

POWERS TO BE PARTLY EXERCISED BY THE UNITED KINGDOM
PARLIAMENT AND PARTLY BY LOCAL LEGISLATURES

1. Corrupt Practices.
2. Explosives.
3. Harbours.
4. Land.—Acquisition for Public Purposes.
5. Transport.—Roads and Highways.

All other matters not expressly enumerated in the above lists
are reserved to the United Kingdom Parliament.

The principle underlying the division of powers as enumerated above is the same as that of the Dominion of
Canada, and different from that of the United States. Like
the several provinces of Canada, the subordinate legislatures
will have only such powers as have been specifically granted
to them, which are strictly domestic in nature; all other
powers whether enumerated or not, are reserved to the
United Kingdom. The result of this will be federalism in
the broader sense, for the common features of all federal
states is the division of powers; but beyond this, it will not
resemble in any way the strict federalism of the United
States, in which, limited powers of the Federal Government, the rigid written constitution, and judicial supremacy
have been peculiar features. The supremacy of the Imperial Parliament will remain intact although its omnicom-
petence will from now on disappear. By delegating all the
local affairs to the subordinate legislatures, a great portion
of the ordinary business in Parliament, a chief source of
congestion, will certainly be removed. But still the powers
reserved to it, are more than plenty for any Parliament to
exercise effectively and adequately.

## C. The Problem of Finance

The creation of subordinate legislatures and the carrying on of the local governments of the several countries require also a plan for the readjustment of finance. On this subject the conference adopted the recommendations of the Committee on Finance.[1] With regard to supply, the conservative estimates based upon the national figures of the Treasury for the year 1919-1920 of the several nations are: £52,664,500 for England, £9,100,000 for Scotland, and £3,988,000 for Wales.[2] Additional expenses for additional national ministers, national staff, additional election outlays, and possibly new buildings are not included.

With regard to the ways and means, it was recommended that the following sources of revenue be assigned to the local legislatures for a period of five years:

(1) Liquor Licenses (Dealers and Retailers but not Producers),
(2) Establishment Licenses,
(3) Traders Licenses,
(4) Entertainments Duty,
(5) Inhabited House Duty,
(6) Land Values Duties.

together with the equivalent of the net yield of so many pence in the pound of the annual Income Tax (excluding Super Tax) as will, at the outset, balance the account. After the period of five years the whole matter of allocation of funds and taxes shall be reviewed.[1] It was estimated on the revenue figures of 1919-1920, that the total yield from the above sources will be: £42,355,000 for England £5,825,000

---

[1] *Letter from Mr. Speaker to the Prime Minister*, p. 5.

[2] *Ibid.*, p. 19, appendix iv.

[3] *Ibid.*, p. 5.

for Scotland, and £2,474,000 for Wales. There shall be a deficiency of £10,309,500;£3,275,000; and £1,514,000 respective each year. The Committee recommended that these deficiencies might be dealt with by Grants-in-Aid, which apparently was not adopted by the conference.[1]

## D. *The Problem of the Judiciary*

On the question as to how the Judiciary system should be reorganized under a scheme of devolution, the Committee on the Judiciary made a number of recommendations, which were substantially adopted by the conference. With regard to Scotland, the Committee suggested that the present system should be left intact; any change as may hereafter be found necessary should be left to the local legislature to determine. It is necessary to point out the fact that Scotland has always had a separate system of judicature of her own, and a separate system of law based largely upon the Civil Law of Justinian and not upon the Common Law of England. Appeals in criminal cases are finally disposed of by Scotch tribunals. Civil cases are disposed of in the same way, subject, however, to a final recourse to the House of Lords as the supreme appellate court of the United Kingdom. The only changes to be made are: The definition, punishment, and procedure of major crimes (*mala in se*) as usually found in Extradition Treaties should be reserved to the United Kingdom Parliament; secondly, the appointment of certain higher judicial officers hithertofore made by the Crown upon the recommendations of the Prime Minister should in the future be made upon the recommendation of the United Kingdom Prime Minister; and thirdly, other judiciary appointments now made on the advice of the Secretary of Scotland should in the future be made on the advice of the Minister of Scotland. Other judiciary officers and ad-

[1] *Ibid.*, p. 21, appendix iv.

ministrative officers subsidiary thereto should be appointed
in the same way as they now are.[1]

As to Wales, the case is somewhat different. The judiciary system of Wales is substantially the same as that of
England, and practically the same law is administered. Up
to 1830, however, Wales did enjoy a separate Judiciary of
her own under the name of the King's Court of Great
Sessions: an institution which dated from the year 1542.
Wales may, therefore, wish to re-establish under a scheme
of devolution such an independent judiciary as she had before. However, the Committee thought that such a change,
if necessary, should be determined by the Welsh legislature
when it is constituted, and that, meanwhile, no change
should be made, except that Monmouthshire should be taken
out of the Oxford circuit and added to the South Wales
circuit. With regard to England, no change would be
necessary, even though a separate Welsh judiciary be created,
excepting such reduction in the number of English judges
and judiciary officers as might be found expedient.[2]

To sum up, the general effects of the Report of the Committee which was adopted by the conference, may be recapitulated as follows: [3]

(1) That, in the case of England, Scotland, and Wales, the
    definition and punishment and the regulation of pro-
    cedure in the trial of major crimes (*mala in se*) adopting
    for this purpose the list usually found in Extradition
    Treaties, should be reserved to the United Kingdom
    Parliament, and that such changes as may hereafter be
    found necessary in other matters should be left to the
    local legislatures to determine.

(2) That the Scottish judicial system should remain un-

---

[1] *Letter from Mr. Speaker to the Prime Minister*, p. 22, appendix v.

[2] *Ibid.*, pp. 22-24, appendix v.

[3] *Ibid.*, p. 5.

changed, and that any change with regard to Wales should take place only if and when asked for by the Welsh legislature.

(3) That, as to the county of Monmouth, it is suggested that when devolution takes place Monmouthshire should be taken out of the Oxford circuit and added to the South Wales circuit.

### PROPOSED SCHEMES FOR THE ORGANIZATION OF SUBORDINATE LEGISLATURES

On the question of the organization of subordinate legislatures the conference did not reach an unanimous agreement. That was the only question upon which it split. Two separate plans were proposed, one by Mr. Speaker and the other by Mr. Macdonald.

### I. THE SPEAKER'S PLAN

*A. Composition of the Local Legislatures:*

The Speaker's plan was proposed by Mr. Lowther and modified somewhat in the course of discussion in the Conference. It was called a transitional scheme. According to this plan, there shall be established local subordinate legislatures for England, Scotland, and Wales (including Monmouthshire), which shall be composed not of specially elected members, but of persons who are members of the United Kingdom Parliament. They are to be called " Grand Councils " each consisting of two chambers, namely, " the Council of Commons ", and " the Council of Peers ". The members of the first Chamber of the Grand Council for each area shall consist of the same Members returned to the House of Commons for that area. Those of the second Chamber shall consist of the members of the House of Lords equal to half the number of Members of the House of Commons for that area, and chosen for the duration of five years (the

period of each Parliament) by the Committee of Selection
of the House of Lords.

The time and place of the first meeting as well as the date
of its termination shall be fixed by the Home Secretary.
The commencement and termination of each session of each
Grand Council shall be fixed jointly by the Home Secretary
and the Chairman of the Executive Committee of each Grand
Council. It was suggested that the spring and summer
months should be reserved for the ordinary session of Par-
liament and the autumn months for that of the Grand
Councils. The place of permanent session should be decided by each Grand Council either at London or elsewhere.
In case Parliament should be meeting at a time when a
Grand Council is in session, the latter should be suspended.
But in case a Grand Council desires to meet when Parliament is in session, the Home Secretary shall, upon application by the Chairman of the Executive Committee of that
Grand Council, fix a date for the commencement of the
session of the Grand Council, which shall then sit on any
day or at any hour when Parliament is not sitting and may
so continue in session until terminated by the same authority and by the same procedure. Finally, it was suggested
that, when Parliament is not sitting, the Palace of Westminster and the staff thereof shall be at the disposal of the
Grand Councils.

The Council of Commons and the Council of Peers of
each Grand Council shall at their first meeting elect, for the
duration of Parliament, a President and, if desired, a vice-
President to preside over their debates. Each Grand Council shall have control of its internal organization, but they
should adopt the procedure of the House of Commons at
the first meeting with power to change it later on.

*B. Legislative Powers:*

The powers of each Grand Council shall be those de-

volved on Local Subordinate Legislatures as specified in
" List A ".   Further powers may be granted, however, by
Act of Parliament originating either from the request of a
Grand Council or on the initiative of Parliament.   The
powers granted to all Grand Councils shall be the same.
In order to keep the Grand Councils within their powers,
the Home Secretary shall watch all Bills of a Grand Council
and must satisfy himself that they are not *ultra vires*.   In
case of doubt, he may refer the Bill at any stage to the
Judicial Committee of the Privy Council for decision.
Furthermore, the Crown may, upon advice of the United
Kingdom Parliament, withhold its assent to the legislation
of a Grand Council pending such inquiry.   These provisions
do not affect private rights; individuals may still question
their validity in a court of law if such has not been previously determined by the Judicial Committee of the Privy
Council.   Finally, it is provided that the United Kingdom
Parliament shall not be debarred from legislation on any
devolved subjects and may override any act of a Grand
Council.   The Royal assent may be withheld from a Grand
Council act, upon advice of the United Kingdom Parlia-
met, not only on the ground of *ultra vires* but also on that
of policy.

*C. Legislative Procedure:*

All the bills of the Grand Councils shall be known as
" Grand Council Bills (and Acts) " as distinguished from
Parliamentary Bills (and Acts).   The Council of Commons
shall have the privileges with respect to finance possessed by
the House of Commons.   In case of doubt, the Speaker of
the House of Commons shall, after consultation with the
President of the Council of Commons and of the Council
of Peers, decide whether a Grand Council bill is or is not
a money bill as defined in the Parliament Act, and shall give
his certificate in the manner thereby prescribed.   With re-

gard to other bills, disagreement between the two councils shall be referred to a joint conference, or, if not settled in this way, to a joint session of both councils where members may sit, vote, and debate together.

With regard to Private Bill Legislation, the principles of the Scottish Private Bill Procedure shall be extended to England and Wales. The date of the preliminary deposit of such bills shall be changed so as to suit the time of the Grand Council. Private business left over from a previous session may be carried over to the next.

### D. Organization of the Executive of a Grand Council:

Each Grand Council shall exercise the powers and discharge the duties devolved upon it through the departments transferred, or the parts of departments transferred. There shall be an Executive Committee for each Grand Council, responsible to it. The said Committee shall consist of a Chairman appointed by the Grand Council and of heads of departments appointed by the Chairman as his colleagues. No member shall be on the Executive Committee for more than six months without being a member of the Grand Council. The existing practice regarding the vacation of seats shall not apply to members of the Executive Committee. At least one member of the Executive Committee must be a member of the Council of Peers. The communications between the Executive Committee and the Imperial Government shall be conducted through the Home Secretary.

With regard to civil servants, the interest of transferred civil servants shall be protected (on the model of Clause 52 in the Government of Ireland Bill of 1920). Appointments of civil servants shall be made according to the existing practice regulating appointments in the Home civil service.

### E. Financial Powers:

During the first five years the following sources of revenue shall be handed over to the Grand Councils in order to enable them to carry on the transferred services together with the net yield of so many pence in the pound of the annual Income Tax (excluding Super Tax) to balance the account:

1. Liquor Licences (Dealers and Retailers but not Producers),
2. Establishment Licences,
3. Traders' Licences,
4. Entertainments Duty,
5. Inhabited House Duty,
6. Land Values Duties.

In conformity with general practice, all money bills shall originate in the Council of Commons and must receive the recommendation of the Crown, which shall be signified through the Home Secretary upon application by the financial member of the Executive Committee. In order to provide for the current expenditure of the departments during the period of the ensuing financial year, it is recommended that the Grand Council shall meet before the end of March so as to pass a vote on account. The taxes imposed by the Grand Councils shall be assessed and collected through the existing United Kingdom machinery, so far as this is practicable. It is also provided that the Grand Councils shall have power to borrow money upon their own credits under similar conditions to those observed by the United Kingdom Parliament. The auditing of the accounts of the local administrations shall be referred to the Comptroller and Auditor General, who shall report to the Grand Councils separately.

*F. Provisions for Transitional Period:*

Three transitional periods are provided in this scheme. They look towards a final plan to be devised after these periods. The first period consists of three years in which

this scheme shall be put into operation; a second period of
two years is provided during which each Grand Council
shall consider its future consitution; and, lastly, there is a
final period of one year during which such schemes as may
be devised by the Grand Councils, shall be submitted to Parliament.   The schemes that may be then worked out shall
give effect to the following conclusions:

(a)  To substitute for itself a separately elected legislature of one or two chambers, or

(b)  To continue as at the time constituted, or

(c)  To revert to the *status quo ante,* or

(d)  To continue as at the time constituted for a further
limited period, or

(e)  To make any other proposals it may choose, dealing exclusively with the composition and organization of the body or bodies to which it proposes to
entrust the functions then discharged by itself.

Schemes submitted in the future shall deal only with the
constitution of the Grand Council, and not with the devolution of further powers.   Such schemes need not be uniform
with one another.   In case such schemes are submitted to
Parliament in the form of a Bill through the Home Secretary, they may be accepted or rejected by Parliament without any amendment.   But, if no adverse action is taken by
Parliament within one year after their submission, the bill
shall be deemed to have been passed by both Houses and
shall be submitted for the Royal assent.

The above scheme was indorsed and signed by thirteen
members of the Conference including the Speaker.[1]   Five
others [2] also signed but they based their approval of the

[1] James W. Lowther (Chairman); Chalmers; C. Craig; Elgin and
Kincardine; Faringdon; J. M. Hogge; D. Macmaster; R. McNeill;
T. Moles; Oranmore and Browne; Southborough; Strafford and Stuart
of Wortley.

[2] Aberdare; Henry Cowan; Charles Edwards; J. Hugh Edwards and
W. Tyson Wilson.

scheme on the ground that it provides an immediate prospect of securing a considerable measure of devolution on national lines, and at the same time paves the way for a larger scheme of devolution in the near future.[1]

II. MR. MURRAY MACDONALD'S PLAN

The plan recommended by Mr. Macdonald is designed to secure four objectives, namely, (a) effective relief of the present Parliamentary congestion; (b) the strengthening of the control of electors over their representatives; (c) effective control of the representative bodies over their executives; and (d) the avoidance of that hopeless confusion of political issues and responsibilities inseparable from a scheme which charges the same representatives, acting in separate and independent legislatures, with the control and management both of local and central interests.[2]   The whole scheme is divided into four parts and thirty-two clauses. The following is a general summary of the important points, especially those points on which this plan differs from that of Mr. Speaker.

*A. Constitution of the Subordinate Legislatures:*

The subordinate legislatures to be established for England Scotland, and Wales are to be true legislatures, subordinate but separate from the Parliament of the United Kingdom. They may be either unicameral or bicameral as the Government itself may determine according to the prevailing opinion of the particular country.   Each subordinate legislature shall have a directly elected Chamber consisting of the same number of members as now represent England, Scotland, and Wales (including Monmouthshire) in the United Kingdom Parliament.   The members of each Chamber shall be

[1] *Letter from Speaker to Prime Minister*, pp. 9-12, appendix i.
[2] *Ibid.*, p. 13, appendix ii.

elected for the same constituencies and by the same electors
in the different countries as now return members to the
United Kingdom Parliament.   Whether subordinate legislatures are to be unicameral or bicameral, peers shall not be
disqualified for election to the popularly elected chambers.
All the subordinate legislatures shall sit for five years unless sooner dissolved.   They shall determine the question
of the payment of their members.

## B. *Legislative Powers:*

With regard to legislative powers, this scheme is in substantial agreement with the Speaker's scheme.   Subordinate
legislatures may exercise only such powers as are specified
in " List A."   Any further devolution of powers must be
obtained by an Act of Parliament, originating either in a
request from a subordinate legislature or on the initiative
of Parliament.   It is expressly provided that the inherent
and supreme rights and powers of the Parliament of the
United Kingdom shall remain absolutely unimpaired.   Consequently, the latter shall not be debarred from legislating
on any of the devolved subjects and may pass an act over-
riding any act of a subordinate legislature.   Furthermore,
Royal assent may be withheld upon the advice of the United
Kingdom Parliament on the ground not only of *ultra vires*
but of policy.   The Secretary of State shall watch all bills
of a subordinate legislature to satisfy himself as to whether
they are *ultra vires*.   He may also refer a bill at any stage
to the judicial committee of the Privy Council which shall
decide upon its validity.   The Crown, on the advice of the
United Kingdom Cabinet, may withhold its assent pending
such inquiry.   In case the validity of a bill has not been so
decided, the right of an individual to question its validity
in a court of law shall remain unaffected.

*C. Organization of the Executive of a Subordinate Legislature.*

This part of the scheme is also in substantial accord with that of the Speaker. The only differences are: first, that, so far as necessary, separate administrative departments are to be established in England, Scotland, and Wales; and, secondly, that each subordinate legislature shall have an Executive Committee responsible to it, and this Committee shall be appointed by His Majesty the King in accordance with the existing constitutional practice.

*D. Financial Powers.*

This part of the scheme is in entire agreement with the Speaker's scheme. If the subordinate legislatures are to be bicameral, all Money Bills must originate in the popularly elected Chamber. The Secretary of State shall, on application of the Finance minister of a subordinate legislature, signify the recommendation of the Crown to proposals for creating charges upon the public. The other provisions are exactly the same as in the other scheme.

This scheme was also indorsed and signed by thirteen members of the Conference.[1] Five others [2] signified their approval of the general principles of this scheme; but, if the scheme of national legislatures should prove impracticable at an earlier date, they would accept the Speaker's tentative proposal. Thus each scheme was supported by thirteen members, while five others approved of both.[3]

The two proposed schemes for the organization of sub-

[1] J. A. Murray Macdonald, W. Ryland Adkins, Charnwood, Denman, Emmott, Leolin Forestier-Walker, Gladstone, Gorell, Edward Goulding, William Graham, Gideon Murray, Selborne and Frederick Young.

[2] Aberdare, Henry Cowan, Charles Edwards, J. Hugh Edwards and W. Tyson Wilson.

[3] *Letter from Mr. Speaker to the Prime Minister,* pp. 13-15, appendix ii.

ordinate legislatures differ in some very important particulars, which may be briefly recapitulated as follows:

1. The Speaker's scheme is designed to be transitory, while that of Mr. Macdonald is to be permanent.

2. In the one scheme, the subordinate legislatures are to be called " Grand Councils ", while, in the other, they are to be truly national legislatures.

3. The " Grand Councils " are to be composed of the same members as are now returned to the United Kingdom Parliament from the three different countries, while the national legislatures are to be composed of members separately elected.

4. The " Grand Councils " are to be bicameral, while the national legislatures are to be either bicameral or unicameral.

5. In the Speaker's plan, the communication between the Imperial Government and the Executive Committees of " Grand Councils " shall be through the Home Secretary, while in Mr. Macdonald's plan, all powers vested in the Crown, so far as they affect the powers of the subordinate legislatures, shall be exercised through a Secretary of State, who shall act on instructions issued to him by His Majesty the King in Council.

6. In the Speaker's scheme, the Executive Committee of a " Grand Council " shall consist of a Chairman appointed by the Grand Council and heads of departments appointed by the Chairman as his colleagues, while in the other scheme, the members of each Executive Committee shall be appointed by His Majesty the King in accordance with the existing constitutional practice.

7. Finally, in the Speaker's scheme, each Grand Council shall exercise the powers and discharge the duties so transferred through departments transferred, or the parts of departments transferred, while in the other scheme, separate administrative departments are to be established in England, Scotland, and Wales, so far as is necessary.

CRITICISMS AND COMMENTS ON THE PROPOSED SCHEMES

## 1. Mr. Speaker's Scheme

The Memorandum by Lord Southborough attached to
the Letter to the Prime Minister mentions several advantages of the scheme proposed by Mr. Speaker.[1]  In the first
place, " it is of an experimental and transitory character."
It can be adopted immediately without delay and at the same
time it provides a period of time " for further experience,
consultation, and consideration before finally committing the
country to a violent change in its constitution."   Secondly,
" it makes the least possible change in our present constitutional arrangements compatible with any system of Devolution."   In fact it is said to be " the extension of the standing committee system and its adaptation to the new demands."   Thirdly, " it utilizes the abilities and character
of the Peers and Members of Parliament who are now serving their country, and have acquired great stores of administrative and parliamentary experience, and enables parliamentary traditions to be continued unbroken."   Fourthly,
" it avoids the expenditure of vast sums of money in installa-
tion, by utilizing the existing facilities supplied by the Palace
of Westminster."   Fifthly, " it retains the new legislative
bodies in a strictly subordinate position."   Sixthly, " it will
not occupy more parliamentary time than at present."   According to the analysis made by Mr. Diver an average
about 80 days are now devoted to central, and about 40
days to local, business.  Under this scheme Parliament
would sit from, say, 10th February to 10 August, about 117
Parliamentary days; and the Grand Councils would sit from,
say, 5th October to 21st December, about 50 Parliamentary
days.  Lastly, it affords a certain relief to members because the Grand Councils would sit simultaneously to con-

[1] *Letter from Mr. Speaker to the Prime Minister*, p. 27.

sider the business of the three countries and because each
country would deal with its own business without the interference from the rest.

The above scheme was, however, severely criticised in a
Memorandum by Mr. Macdonald.[1]  In the first place, it
was said " that the Scheme would not be an effective remedy
for the existing congestion in the House of Commons."
The chief objection is that the Grand Councils would be
manned by the same individuals who are Members of the
two Houses of Parliament.  They would be Parliament but
acting in a different capacity.  Under that plan the same
members would have to sit for at least nine months of the
year, but the amount of debate and routine work would
probably be increased, even assuming that the work devolved
would not be greater than it is in the House of Commons—
which assumption is not tenable because the local legislatures are supposed to be able to do more for the localities
than does the House of Commons.   " It was, therefore, held
that, so far as the House of Commons itself would be relieved, it would be by the imposition of increased duties and
responsibilities on its Members; and that the net result would
be a great and dangerous addition to the existing strain on
their time and strength." [2]

Secondly, it was pointed out " that it would aggravate in
the House of Commons and at General Elections the present
evils arising from the confusion of local and central issues."
Under that scheme although the local and central issues
would be seemingly separated, they would still be imposed
upon the same set of persons in the House of Commons and
consequently they would not be able to devote their energy
entirely to the one or the other set of issues.   Furthermore,
as the same set of members are to be returned at the General

[1] *Letter from Mr. Speaker to the Prime Minister*, pp. 31-35.
[2] *Ibid.*, p. 31.

Elections for both Parliament and the Grand Councils, the confusion of issues at election time, which is one of the reasons for devolution, would be actually worse. The Memorandum says: " Every candidate would have to play a double role. He might try to ride two horses at once or the one of his special choice. Whatever, in the exigencies of the situation, the candidate might decide to do, the elector, who in two capacities would have only one vote to cast, confused as he often is now by the mere multiplicity of questions, would under the Scheme have the impossible task imposed upon him of endeavoring to decide which candidate would best serve in which capacity. It must end in the elector's being forced to vote for local interests to the absolute exclusion of central, or vice versa." [1]

Thirdly, the scheme is objectionable from a purely constitutional standpoint. The Grand Councils would be in substance the House of Commons but appear in a novel form. They could not be dissolved by the Sovereign, nor would they be responsible to the House of Commons. The chief Minister of each Council would be elected by the Council and not appointed by the Crown. This would be a great departure from an important constitutional principle. " Under the Scheme," says the Memorandum, " the Councils were to have full legislative power to change the whole system of local government; to control education; to determine whether or not religion was to be taught in the schools; to decide the question of church establishment, and to regulate and control the ownership of land. The refusal to the Local Executive Governments of the hallmark of the sovereign sanction would be derogatory to the authoritative discharge of duties so important. The refusal, moreover, was all the more remarkable and inexplicable because it did not extend to the legislative measures of the Councils, the

[1] *Letter from Mr. Speaker to the Prime Minister,* p. 32.

Royal assent being necessary to constitute them legal enactments." [1]

Fourthly, the plan is productive of grave difficulties. In the first place, there would be great difficulties in selecting the Ministers of the Councils. Conceivably the supporters of the central Government would have the majority in the English Council, and that majority would appoint and control the Ministers of the English Council. " This would cut at the very root of devolution, which, ex hypothesi, was to give to each component part of the United Kingdom the rights and the powers to manage its assigned local affairs free from the trammels of the Honse of Commons returned to deal with issues which, by general agreement, should be kept separate and distinct." [2] Furthermore, it would be very difficult under the scheme to keep the Executive Ministry of each Council stable. The power and stability of the Prime Minister of the United Kingdom, as we know, depends upon his ability to dissolve Parliament in the event of a deadlock. But the Chief Minister of a Grand Council will not have this power. The dissolution of the Grand Councils would depend upon the dissolution of Parliament. " Their Ministries would, therefore, be at the mercy of chance majorities in the Councils. Frequent and capricious changes of Administration and deadlocks might occur." [3] The Ministry of a Council could never dissolve the Council in the event of a deadlock, but, on the other hand, it might be suddenly dissolved against its will upon the dissolution of the House of Commons brought about by an issue totally unconnected with its work.

Fifthly, the scheme would exclude certain classes of persons who would be best qualified to deal with local business.

[1] *Letter from Mr. Speaker to the Prime Minister*, p. 33.

[2] *Ibid.*

[3] *Ibid.*

It would exclude all Peers except those selected as members of the Council of Peers; all defeated candidates at General Elections; and the large class of capable men and women who have not the means or the money to enable them to serve in Parliament.

Sixthly, it was pointed out that the time allotted to the Grand Councils would not be sufficient for the work assigned to them. " The first-class Bills on social reform, such as Licensing and Education Bills, have occupied from 30 to 50 sittings of the House of Commons, and they would certainly not occupy a less number of sittings of the Grand Councils. Even, therefore, if the Councils met early in September, the time allotted to them would not be sufficient." [1]

Finally, that part of the scheme with regard to the transitional period is held to be unworkable. Under the scheme, it was provided that during the second period of two years the Grand Councils were to sit as Constituent Councils charged with the duty of devising a new scheme of devolution or to continue as they were. For the performance of this function they would not be responsible to anybody but themselves. They could adopt any scheme they liked and the House of Commons could only say " aye " or " no " to whatever they chose to propose.

### 2. *Mr. Macdonald's Scheme*

The second scheme is claimed by Mr. Macdonald as the only possible scheme of devolution which would secure the following results: [2]

    (a) effective relief of the present parliamentary congestion;
    (b) the strengthening of the control of electors over their representatives;

[1] *Letter from Mr. Speaker to the Prime Minister*, p. 34.
[2] *Ibid.*, p. 13.

(c) effective control of the representative bodies over their executives; and

(d) the avoidance of that hopeless confusion of political issues and responsibilities inseparable from a scheme which charges the same representatives, acting in separate and independent legislatures, with the control and management both of local and central interests.

Several objections, however, were raised against the scheme by the supporters of the Speaker's scheme.[1] In the first place, it was pointed out that at the present time there is no desire on the part of England for a separate English Parliament. If England declines to accept it, the adoption of the scheme would be very difficult. Secondly, even if England accepts it, the cost of such a scheme would be very great. "Such a Parliament would require an important site in London, a large and dignified House of Parliament commensurate with its importance, a considerable annual expenditure for its upkeep and maintenance and a large staff of officials of all grades to work the organization, and salaries for some 500 members whose sittings would, after all, only occupy a quarter, or at most, a third, of the year." Thirdly, and this is perhaps the most serious objection, "there seems to be a considerable danger that a large and important legislative and administrative body, independently elected, might easily be brought into collision with the existing Parliament, and if feeling ran high the friction between the two Governments and the two Parliaments might develop into an extremely dangerous situation." This seems to be the general feeling of those members of the Conference, who indorsed the Speaker's scheme. In the Memorandum by Mr. Ronald McNeill which was signed by two other members, Mr. C. C. Craig and Mr. T. Moles, the following observation appears:

[1] *Memorandum by Lord Southborough, ibid.*, pp. 26-27.

We do not share Mr. Murray Macdonald's optimistic view that the Constitution of a Parliament for England with 500 Members, sitting in London, with legislative and administrative functions in all matters of domestic concern to Englishmen, would be in no danger of becoming a serious rival to the authority and prestige of the Imperial Parliament. Friction between subordinate and central legislatures is by no means an unknown feature in the history of federal institutions. Although the preponderance of a single federal unit has not caused difficulty in the United States, it was difference of opinion between the central Government and a group of federal units as to the proper limits of State rights that led to the American Civil War. Yet the safeguards in which Mr. Macdonald places confidence were fully operative in America, the "ultimate controlling factor" there as here being the electorate which had to return members to Congress as well as to State legislatures. It is not, however, grave conflict on the American precedent so much as rivalry of a less serious, but still of an embarassing nature, between an English Parliament and the Imperial Parliament that is to be feared. It must be remembered that the majority in one of these Assemblies might well be of a different party from that in the other. If such a state of affairs were to exist at a moment of National crisis, such as that of August, 1914, the effect might be more than inconvenient. It is true that the English Parliament would have no concern directly with issues of peace or war. But it requires no great effort of imagination to picture the paralysis of National effort which would in such circumstances arise from the existence of a National Assembly within a mile of Westminster in which a majority representing the constituencies of England were hostile to the policy of His Majesty's Government. Constitutionally they would be debarred from influencing that policy; but they would have no difficulty in effectually impeding its execution.

Apart from the dangers that might thus arise on occasions of National emergency, a considerable decline of public interest in the proceedings of the Imperial Parliament would occur in

normal unexciting times. The powers proposed to be en-
trusted to the subordinate National legislatures constitute something far beyond " gas and water Home Rule." To meet this
objection, Mr. Macdonald maintains that proper interest in
" licensing and ecclesiastical measures " would be insufficient to
bring this about. The contrary is surely the truth. In the
decade before the War, the most intense and bitter controversy
raged round measures for dealing with the liquor traffic, for
disestablishing a church, and for reforming the Education Law.
In comparison with these subjects, those which will be reserved
for the Imperial Parliament, such as Army and Navy Estimates,
the Indian Budget, or matters affecting the Crown Colonies,
arouse no interest at all. The Imperial Parliament would, for
the most part, become the home of dignified dullness, to whose
proceedings, with rare exceptions, the Press would pay but little
attention; while the Parliament of England, engaged it may be
in discussing the disestablishment of the Church of England,
Nationalisation of the land, or the total prohibition of alcohol,
would day by day fill the public eye. The election of its members, who would be responsible for most of the legislation that
intimately touches the daily lives of the people, would excite
far more interest than elections to the Imperial Parliament,
with the probable result that the best candidates would be
attracted to the former in preference to the latter.[1]

To the above argument it was answered by Mr. Macdonald that " this was equally valid against an English
Grand Council, for that legislature was to possess the same
power, and might acquire the same prestige as a separately
elected legislature. But the conclusive answer was that the
House of Commons remained the sovereign authority with
undiminished control of the main resources of the country,
and of all the great matters vital to the United Kingdom
itself, and to the Empire at large. It was pointed out, also,
that experience in the United States showed that in the com-

[1] *Memorandum by Mr. Ronald McNeill, ibid.,* p. 37.

ponent parts of a great federal system no menace to the supreme federal authority arose from mere numbers in particular States.   It was true that in population and wealth England in a marked sense was the ' predominant partner '. But the ultimate controlling factor was the electorate, which would have to elect members of the House of Commons and of the subordinate legislatures.   The common sense of the country would not tolerate any aspirations of the subordinate legislatures which conflicted with the supreme authority of the House of Commons." [1]

But there are other objections to the scheme.   The fourth objection is that it would greatly increase the cost of elections and add to the warfare between the parties.   The scheme requires every constituency to return two members, one to the Imperial Parliament and the other to the National legislature.   Most likely elections of members to these various Parliaments would not take place at the same time. Hence the taxpayers would have to contribute more and the various parties would have to do more than at present.

Fifthly, there would be difficulty in finding, in Scotland, a sufficient number of candidates suitably qualified to represent the 74 Scottish constituencies.   Furthermore, under the scheme the number of members to be returned to the United Kingdom Parliament would eventually have to be considerably reduced.   The latter would involve a redistribution of seats and a recombination of existing constituencies.   It would be undesirable to reopen all these complicated questions, so soon after the enactment of the Representation of the People Act, 1918.

Sixthly, it was said that Mr. Macdonald's scheme leaves the question of second chambers in the local legislatures entirely unsolved.   It was pointed out that the solution pro-

---

[1] *Memorandum by Macdonald, ibid.,* p. 34.

posed in Lord Bryce's Report is not applicable to any but the existing Second Chamber, i. e., the House of Lords.[1]

Finally, by way of rebuttal, it was said that although the confusion of issues at present makes the choice by an elector rather difficult, " a combination of these issues tends to keep them in their relative importance in the eyes of the electorate, and the presentment of the really important national problems has a beneficially educative effect upon voters who might, under Mr. Murray Macdonald's scheme, sacrifice issues of imperial importance to those of merely local interest." Secondly, as to the overpressure on Members, it was pointed out that it is not true of all Members. While there is nothing in Mr. Macdonald's scheme that would distribute this burden more evenly, Mr. Speaker's scheme affords " opportunities to members who do not desire to play an active part in the wider matters of the Empire to take their share in the direction of purely domestic affairs." [2]

Having presented most of the important arguments pro and con with regard to the two schemes, we are in a position to make a few comments. It seems that on the whole Mr Macdonald's scheme is the better of the two, so far as the principles of devolution are concerned. If devolution is necessary, that is the only way to attain it. Mr. Speaker's scheme is in substance not devolution to national legislatures such as has been advocated in the House of Commons for the last twenty-five or thirty years, but rather an extension of the Standing Committee system applied to nationalities. In other words, it amounts to the same thing as the National Committees that were proposed by some members in the Select Committee on Procedure, 1914, with the exception

---

[1] The Bryce report is reprinted in McBain and Rogers, *The New Constitutions of Europe*, pp. 573-601, appendix v.

[2] *Op. cit.*, pp. 26-29.

that the Grand Councils would have the power to recommend a new scheme of devolution after five years.

The chief arguments for the Speaker's scheme are three: first, it is tentative; second, it is costless; and third, it calls for the least possible change in the existing system. The trouble with the scheme is that it does not attempt to go to the root of the evils that devolution is supposed to remedy. On the contrary, it ignores those evils such as the congestion of business in the House of Commons and the confusion of local, national, and Imperial issues. The real reason for the scheme seems to be that those who supported the scheme felt that the Conference was not in a position to adopt such a far-reaching plan as proposed by Mr. Macdonald, and that much more thorough investigation of the whole subject will have to be made before committing the country to such a great constitutional change.

The principles of devolution are two-fold: first to relieve the congestion of business in the House of Commons, and secondly, to meet the demand of Home Rule that has been made by Scotland and Wales for a number of years. Mr. Macdonald's scheme would be able to satisfy both, while Mr. Speaker's plan would not satisfy either. The arguments against Mr. Macdonald's scheme are not very convincing. All the arguments can be reduced to one, namely, the undesirability of dividing the authority of the House of Commons. Those who have power are loath to share it with other bodies. Dangers such as the possible conflict between the English Parliament and the Imperial Parliament, and the possible decline of the interest that the people have in the House of Commons are all imaginary. The existence of local legislatures in other countries certainly does not have these effects. In the management of their assigned duties, it is not conceivable that the subordinate Legislatures can ever come into conflict with the Imperial

Parliament. The argument we have quoted at some length admitted that constitutionally they would have no right to interfere with the policy of the Imperial Parliament, but it ends by saying that " they would have no difficulty in effectually impeding its execution." No reason was given for the latter assumption.

After all, the House of Commons is only a representative organ of the people, in which the people's will is supposed to control. Even without the establishment of local legislatures, the policy of Parliament may be frustrated by the people themselves. Nowadays under a democratic franchise the electorate is the ultimate controlling factor. The prestige of the House of Commons has already declined in recent years. Powerful organizations such as Trade Unions are doing more for the labouring class than can Parliament. The danger, as one sees it, does not lie in the setting up of subordinate legislatures, but in the development of extra-parliamentary power groups, which may eventually impose a more drastic change upon the Constitution than devolution to subordinate National Legislatures.

# CHAPTER VII

## THE CASE AGAINST DEVOLUTION

### CONSTITUTIONAL AND PRACTICAL OBJECTIONS

THUS far we have been dealing with the case for devolution. We have seen that there is an imperative demand for devolution as the only effective remedy for relieving the congestion of business in the House of Commons. The next question is: Will devolution bring with it any difficulties or dangers which may be more undesirable than the evil that it is intended to remedy? In other words, are there serious objections against the proposed reform? Various objections have been urged against it. They may be divided into two classes, namely, constitutional objections and practical objections. It is the purpose of this chapter to state and answer these objections.

## I. CONSTITUTIONAL OBJECTIONS

From a constitutional point of view two objections have been urged against devolution. The first objection is that devolution means federation of the United Kingdom or Great Britain, which means in turn the impairment of parliamentary sovereignty and the enfeeblement of the English Government both at home and abroad. The second objection is that devolution is a retrogressive step, which is contrary to the policy of the Union and to the spirit of the Constitution. Let us examine these two objections in their order.

1. As to the first objection. Most of the opponents to devolution have invariably mistaken devolution for strict

federalism.  Even Viscount Bryce argues in this fashion.
In the debate on a Motion for devolution on March 5, 1919,
he said in the House of Lords:

> What we are asked to do is to turn the United Kingdom into
> a Federation—a very unusual process in history.  Nearly all
> Federations have been formed by taking States formerly loosely
> connected, or unconnected, and grouping them into a Feder-
> ation.  The contrary process has been a rare one, and is in
> some respects more difficult.[1]

By thus identifying devolution with federalism, the opponents proceed to deduce a number of subordinate objections all based upon the federal premise.  They are as
follows:

(1) Federalism by its very nature means the division of
political powers between the Federal Government and the
Government of every state belonging to the Federation, and
such division would, from the nature of things, be a source
of weakness to the country.[2]

(2) Federalism in Great Britain will of necessity destroy
the sovereignty of the Imperial Parliament, and thus all
English constitutional arrangements would be dislocated.[3]

(3) Federalism as carried on by Englishmen, or under
the influence of Englishmen, has meant the supremacy of
the judiciary, which inevitably becomes the arbiter of all
constitutional questions.  Such a practice is absolutely foreign to the constitutional theory of England.[4]

(4) Federalism inevitably, and from its very nature,
creates divided allegiance.[5]

[1] *Parliamentary Debates* (Lords), 5th ser., vol. 33, p. 534.

[2] Dicey, *A Fool's Paradise*, p. 18.

[3] Dicey, *England's Case Against Home Rule*, p. 186.

[4] Dicey, *A Fool's Paradise*, p. 18.

[5] *Ibid.*, p. 19.

(5) The Federal Constitution is conservative as compared with the Unitary Constitution.[1]

(6) Federalism, whenever successful, is and must be a step towards national unity, which is the aim of all constitutions.[2]

The simple answer to the main objection is that devolution does not mean federalism. The reasons for this have been stated in a previous chapter at some length. There we have seen that the purpose of devolution is not to create a strict federal system in the United Kingdom, but simply to delegate to the several countries in the United Kingdom, or Great Britain, the management of their strictly domestic affairs and nothing else. In this sense it is nothing revolutionary, but, as Sir Sidney Low aptly points out, the natural development of the system of local government which England has gradually built up through the municipal corporations and the County Councils.[3] No matter what powers may be assigned to the subordinate legislatures, the supremacy of the Imperial Parliament will be maintained absolutely intact and unimpaired. If that is the case, then devolution cannot possibly mean the federation of the United Kingdom in the strict sense of the word. This will suffice to dispose of the objection of federalism.

However, it may be argued that everything depends upon what you mean by the maintenance of the supremacy of the Imperial Parliament. There are two possible meanings of the word supremacy; it may be theoretical supremacy or actual supremacy. It sounds very well to preserve the supremacy of Parliament in theory, but in actual practice the result may prove quite the opposite. Devolution may virtually result in federalism although in theory the supremacy of

[1] Dicey, *Law of the Constitution*, Introduction, p. lxxx (8th ed.).

[2] Dicey, *A Fool's Paradise*, p. 19.

[3] *The Governance of England*, p. 294.

Parliament will be reserved. " Never does any Home Ruler, or radical," says Professor Dicey, " propose, as he well might do, devolution of Parliamentary powers to bodies undoubtedly subordinate (such as County Councils, or conceivably Councils including several counties) which neither would nor could defy the supremacy of Parliament. It is a suspicious circumstance that the devolution favored by our Home Rulers is invariably devolution to some authority, such as a new Irish Parliament or a revived Parliament of Scotland, which by its very name and traditions will be tempted into conflict with the Imperial Parliament." [1]  Two underlying assumptions are implicit in this line of reasoning; first, that devolution will inevitably arouse the spirit of local nationalism as against the nationalism of England, and second, that devolution in this sense will virtually amount to federalism.   Neither assumption is justifiable.

The local legislatures to be set up in England, Scotland, and Wales are by definition strictly subordinate bodies just like the County Councils at the present time. There is nothing suspicious in the fact that nationality is used as the basis of devolution. Indeed, devolution may strengthen local nationalism or nationality, whatever you choose to call it, but such local nationalism is not necessarily incompatible with the wider nationalism of Great Britain. The word nationalism has two possible meanings: it may mean local prejudice and antagonism towards other peoples outside the locality, or simply local patriotism and local attachment. The former nationalism is of course undesirable, but the latter is quite natural and wholesome. Nationalism in the former sense might, no doubt, have existed prior to the Union between England and Scotland and between England and Wales. But conditions have changed. The Union between these counties has been admittedly successful and

---

[1] Dicey, *A Fool's Paradise*, pp. 16-17.

nobody in these countries has desired to go back on it.  So far as Ireland was concerned, however, the Union was not a success and it did not of itself create that sentiment ot common patriotism which exists among the other countries in the United Kingdom.  The Union between Great Britain and Ireland did not create a common nationalism which did not and could not naturally exist because of the geographical and racial divergences between these two countries, and devolution is not likely to destroy that common nationalism in Great Britain which has already fully developed.

As to local nationalism in the proper sense, it is there with or without devolution.  It is admittedly good and devolution has nothing to do with it.  It arises from the natural differences that exist among the several countries of Great Britain.  Take Scotland for example.  She has a different historical background, different traditions, and different religious and educational institutions from those of England.  The Union of 1707 did not obliterate these differences but purposely left them undisturbed.  Scotland has always had its local nationalism based upon these differences.  What is the nature of this local nationalism? It is best described by Professor Dicey in the following words:

It means the love of a special country by the inhabitants thereof as their homeland.  They love this home, be it England, Scotland, or Wales, its religion, its institutions, its laws, its traditions, its history, its heroes, and above all its spirit, with a love resembling the affection which a man feels for his family, for his father, for his mother, for his brothers and sisters. The love, it is true, may originate in various causes, in community of race, of language, of religion, or of history, but whatever its origin, this attachment of a man to his own country is itself a matter of moral value.  It is at once the cause and the result of patriotism.  If two nations really wish to unite into one State they will desire, if they understand the nature of man, that they shall each preserve as much of the noble spirit and traditions of their separate nationality as may be compatible with the wider sense and the extended patriotism which ought to bind together all the citizens of the one politically united country.[1]

Nationalism in this sense is natural and highly desirable, and it is in this sense that the word nationalism is used sometimes as an additional reason for devolution. If devolution should help strengthen it, there ought to be no objection at all, and as such it will not lead to any conflict between the local government and the central government.

We have so far made it clear that devolution does not mean and would not lead to strict federalism. This is enough to answer the main objection. But for the sake of argument we may go further. Suppose that devolution means federalism or will result in federalism. Will the subordinate objections necessarily follow? Are they universally true? It is perhaps not altogether superfluous to answer these questions with regard to each of the objections we have mentioned.

The first objection is that Federalism implies division of powers, which, from the nature of things, is a source of weakness. In other words it has been said that the federal system is a weak form of government as compared with a unitary one. This is not always true. A federal government may indeed be weak as any other democratic government is weak, in the sense that the Government cannot do anything against the will of the majority of the people. The strength of any government does not depend so much upon the form of government as upon the ability of the government to secure the consent of the people to any policy that it wishes to carry out, and upon the support the people are

[1] Dicey and Rait, *Thoughts on the Union between England and Scotland*, p. 326.

able to give to it.   Sometimes it is said that a federal government must needs be weak in that prompt actions cannot
be taken on important national questions, especially in matters connected with war and peace and foreign affairs.   This
argument is wholly erroneous.   In every federal system such
matters as war and peace and foreign affairs and any other
matter concerning the interest of the whole nation are invariably reserved to the central government.   The powers
of the state with regard to these matters are and should
never be divided.   Therefore, so far as these powers are
concerned there is no division whatsoever.   The details
of every federal constitution may vary; the provisions for
the distribution of powers may not be perfect; and as a
result the central government may find itself unable to do
many things that it ought to do.   But that is the defect of
some particular constitution and cannot be used generally
as an objection against all federal constitutions.

The second objection is that federalism will of necessity
destroy the sovereignty of the Imperial Parliament.   This
may be true, but what of it?   The idea back of this objection seems to be that parliamentary sovereignty is something really vital and important, the impairment of which
will entail serious practical consequences.   " Under all the
formality, the antiquarianism, the shams of the British Constitution," says Professor Dicey, " there lies latent an element of power which has been the true source of its life
and growth.   This secret source of strength is the absolute
omnipotence, the sovereignty of Parliament." [1]   Following
out this line of reasoning one may suppose that if parliamentary sovereignty is impaired or destroyed, the English
Government will be at an end or will stop growing.   A
sceptic may, however, doubt whether such a result would
follow.   Parliamentary sovereignty is after all but a theory,

[1] Dicey, *England's Case against Home Rule*, p. 168.

and as such it has not that absolute truth which has been
attributed to it.   The theory is entirely transitory and artificial.   It is transitory because it was not known in the Middle Ages.   It was simply a description and a justification of
the results of parliamentary activities during the sixteenth
and seventeenth centuries.   In the first place, it was used
by Parliament primarily as a weapon for the struggle against
the King.   Secondly, it was in the nature of a justification
of the revolution, which resulted in the abdication of the
powers of the King and in the supremacy of Parliament.
It was more an apology for a cause than an expression of a
disinterested truth.   " It was a generalisation," says Sir
Frederick Pollock, " from the omnipotence of the British
Parliament, an attribute which has been the offspring of our
peculiar history, and may possibly suffer some considerable
change within times not far distant." [1]

In the second place, the theory is artificial, because it is,
in the last analysis, nothing but a legal fiction predicated
upon a peculiar theory of law and legislation of the English
orthodox school of jurisprudence.   Austin defines law as
a command obliging a person or a class of persons to act or
to forbear.[2]   It implies a superior to command and an
inferior to obey.   The one who gives commands is the
sovereign, and the one who obeys such commands is the
subject.   " If a determinate human superior, not in the
habit of obedience to a like superior, receives habitual obedience from the bulk of a given society, that determinate
superior is sovereign of that society, and the society (including the superior) is a society political and independent."
According to this notion of Austin's both law and sover-

[1] *First Book of Jurisprudence*, p. 261.   Quoted, McIlwain, *The High
Court of Parliament and Its Supremacy*, p. 355.

[2] Austin, *Lectures of Jurisprudence* (1896), p. 96.

[3] *Ibid.*, p. 227.

eignty must be essentially personal in character; law pre-supposes a law-giver, and sovereignty must needs reside in some determinate person or body of persons.   Since sovereignty is based upon the idea of positive law which by definition is the command of the sovereign, it naturally cannot be limited.   Therefore the sovereign is omnipotent.   The sovereign power of England resides in Parliament which means the King, the House of Commons, and the House of Lords acting together; therefore Parliament is omnipotent.

This, in short, is the theoretical or legal basis of the theory of parliamentary sovereignty.   The fallacy of the theory is two-fold: in the first place, it is reasoning in a circle.   Austin defines law in terms of sovereign commands, and then defines sovereignty again in terms of law to the effect that it cannot be limited.   Secondly, the definition of law, which is the major premise of the theory, is too narrow and arbitrary.   Law need not be commands of any determinate person or body of persons.   As a matter of fact, the chief source of law of every country is founded upon the customs of the people.   The so-called law-makers or law-givers do no more than declare the law already in existence. Even the most elaborate codes of modern times are not complete statements of the law.   A great many of the fundamental principles are necessarily left unwritten.   " The truth of legal history is," as pointed out by Mr. Bliss, " that the common law of every country, the great body of the law, if generally obeyed, is founded upon usage, upon the moral sense, upon consent, and not upon command." [1]   Therefore, the theory of sovereignty based upon the English orthodox theory of law cannot be accepted as absolute truth.

From this brief criticism of the theory of parliamentary sovereignty, we have seen that it has not that practical importance which has been attributed to it.   One cannot justly

---

[1] Bliss, *On Sovereignty*, p. 52.

claim it to be the source of the life and growth of the Constitution. On the contrary, it is itself the product of the life and growth of the Constitution. The real strength of the Constitution lies, it seeems, in its elasticity, in its ability to adapt itself to new conditions and requirements. The English Constitution is a growing constitution, and as new conditions arise, many of its rules must needs be changed. Every one would admit that the development of the Cabinet system and the expansion of parliamentary functions have considerably modified the Constitution of the eighteenth century. And as the Consitution continues to grow, one would naturally expect that the time-honoured theory of parliamentary sovereignty of the past may suffer some change in order to harmonise theory with practice. Therefore, even if it should be impaired as a result of devolution, it would not be such an impairment as would be productive of serious practical consequences, and hence may be regarded as not an impairment at all.

The third objection is that federalism will of necessity mean the dominance of the Law Courts. This may or may not be true. It is true that in the United States or in Canada the Supreme Court has the power to pass upon all constitutional questions that come before it, and to declare the laws of the legislature unconstitutional, when the latter are rejugnant to the Constitution. Such a practice is, however, not absolutely essential to all federal constitutions. The true cause of judicial supremacy in the United States is found not so much in its federal form of government as in the principle of the separation of powers between the three departments of the state. Under the latter theory, it is the exclusive province of the judiciary to say what the law is, and if the laws of Congress should contravene the provisions of the Constitution, the Supreme Court is duty bound to uphold the Constitution as against the laws of Congress.

In other countries like England where the theory of the separation of powers does not obtain such a result would not follow. Furthermore, under the federal constitutions on the Continent, the courts as a rule have no power to review legislation. This is true in Germany and Switzerland. Take Switzerland for example. " It is worthy of note," says Mr. Haines, " that Switzerland with a federal form of government and a written constitution deliberately rejected the main feature of the American plan of judicial review after a careful study and report on the plan by a group of experts." [1] There the legislature is the final interpreter of the Constitution, subject to a referendum by which such a decision may be changed. But in order to make the federal system effective and to adjust the relations between the central government and the cantons, the Courts were given the powers to review the Acts of Cantonal legislatures. This is quite different from judicial review in the United States. Under a system of devolution, there is obviously no need for such a practice. Devolution is itself an act of Parliament and Parliament alone will have the power to interpret it. If it is necessary, Parliament may conceivably authorize the courts to review the Acts of subordinate legislatures, subject to an appeal to Parliament. But it is inconceivable that, while all the powers are united in Parliament, the Courts can ever dominate the Legislature either under the present system or under devolution.

The fourth objection is that federalism, inevitably and from the nature of things, creates divided allegiance. To support this objection the example of the United States is sometimes cited. During the Civil War the allegiance of the people was divided between the North and the South. Such an example is hardly appropriate, since the North and the South were clearly two sections and not two states of the

[1] Haines, C. G., *The Nation*, May 14, 1924, p. 554.

Union; the divided allegiance was not because of but in spite of the Federal Constitution. Conditions in Great Britain are quite different and there is no reason to suppose that devolution will create divided allegiance. Allegiance in the sense of local patriotism is there already; it is by no means incompatible with allegiance to the whole country. Professor Dicey himself fully recognizes that the perfect self-government of the Dominions does not necessarily interfere with the allegiance to the British Empire. This was amply demonstrated during the War. Thus, if the objection of divided allegiance cannot be applied to self-government in the Dominions, it is certainly less applicable to devolution in Great Britain.

The fifth objection is that the federal constitution, because of the rigidity of its character, is necessarily conservative as compared with the unitary constitution. This observation is not wholly sound. " One who comes to America from Europe," says Professor Laski, " may well crave leave to doubt whether, fundamentally, there is truth in the judgment that federalism is conservative. The form, it is true, may be preserved, may even seem to be revered as sacred things, but the spirit glows with a life that is ever new and abundant. The one thing that must strike the modern observer of any federal Constitution is the growing impatience with its rigid encasement, the ever insistent demand that the form shall be made equally elastic with the spirit. And in the variety of its group life, the wide distribution of its sovereign powers, he may not unjustly see the surest guarantee of its perennial youth." [1] But even granted that a rigid constitution is conducive to conservatism, the objection does not apply to devolution, because there will be no rigid constitution in England. Parliament is a legislative as well as a constituent Assembly, and whatever it does today

[1] Laski, H. J., *The Problem of Sovereignty*, p. 275.

it may change tomorrow, provided the change is necessary
and desired by a majority of the electors.

The last, though not the least, objection is that federalism,
whenever successful, is a stage towards unity. In other
words, there is a natural and inevitable tendency for federalism to pass into nationalism. There is no doubt a tendency
towards federal centralization in some of the federal countries in recent years, but it would be a hasty conclusion to
say that federalism is going to disappear from the face of
the earth. The phenomenon of federal centralization is due
to a variety of causes. One of them is the development of
industry and commerce which renders the division of powers
made two centuries ago, as in the United States, inappro
priate. Another reason is that the people are looking more
and more to the federal government for legislation which
they cannot obtain in the states. But this tendency obviously
has a limit; there is a point beyond which centralization in
any government cannot safely go. The recent extension of
the federal power in the United States regarding police
regulations such as Prohibition and Child Labor has been
viewed by many students of government as unwise. "There
are inherent limitations," says a recent writer, "as well as
constitutional restrictions to federal centralization. Limitations which inhere in human nature and established society,
though frequently ignored by students of government, are
obviously more important than are the artificial restrictions
imposed by constitutional provisions."[1] There are two
inherent limitations of centralization, namely, first, the divergence of local interests and local needs, and secondly, the
congestion of business in the central government. "Centralization in government, as well as in business organization, has its limitations beyond which it cannot be carried
without a sacrifice of efficiency and without being conducive

[1] Thompson, W., *Federal Centralization*, p. 348.

to resentment or indifference in local areas."[1]   " Entire
national unity is obviously impossible, and, regardless of
how mature a nation is, there will always remain distinct
local as well as general national interests."[2]   The supposed
unity of the state even in a unitary system is never a complete unity but only a partial unity.   Local life and group
life are no less important than national life.   While many a
pluralist is apt to see only the trees, the monist on the other
hand is apt to see only the forest.   Either sees but half of
reality.   Therefore it is an idle dream to suppose that federalism is a stage towards final unity.   " It is the fashion to
regard federalism," says Professor Laski, " as the merest
*pis aller* and to hope piously for the time when a more adequate centralization will render it unnecessary.   This seems
to me to neglect certain obvious lessons to be drawn from
other experience.   In education, for example, we have learned
that the more pupils per teacher, the less efficient, on the
whole, is the instruction.   Commercially, Mr. Brandeis has
shown that certain business units may become so large as
to be physically incapable of successful administration.   I
would urge that a similar law of diminishing returns applies
also to the sphere of government."[3]   This is already true
of the government of England, and it is precisely for that
reason that devolution is necessary.

From the criticisms we have offered to the objections
against federalism, we have seen that even if devolution
should result in federalism as its opponents would suppose,
these objections do not apply.   After all, federalism is not
so bad as the Unionists believe.   Furthermore, although
there may be valid criticisms of federalism as found in other
countries, the unitary form of government in England is
not free from objections either.   Indeed, several objections

---

[1] Thompson, *op. cit.*, p. 370.         [2] *Ibid.*, p. 358.
[3] Laski, *op. cit.*, pp. 283-284.

may be urged against it.   First of all, it is unfavorable to freedom in the sense of " continuous intiative."   When all the powers are concentrated in one government, local affairs are inevitably neglected to some extent, and the citizens are apt to lose interest in local affairs.   The central government, especially in a great community like England, has neither the time nor the requisite knowledge to legislate adequately for the ever growing needs of its citizens.   Baffled by parliamentary inactivity, they are liable to and do resort to extrapolitical means to protect or to promote their interests. Secondly, the unitary system encourages bureaucracy, despotism, and discontent.   We have touched upon this point in a previous connection.   Lastly, and this is perhaps the most serious objection, it invariably results in the congestion of business at the center.   We have seen that the latter is the main reason for the proposal of devolution.

2. Now the second main objection from a constitutional point of view is that devolution is a retrogressive step, which runs counter to the policy of the Union and to the spirit of the Constitution.   In other words, it has been said that the tendency of devolution is towards separation and disruption of the Union.   " I know of only one objection," says Mr. Murray Macdonald, " which has been seriously urged against it.   It is that there has been a movement, both in our life and in the life of all the great States of the world, towards an ever deepening and extending union, and that the interests of a peaceful and progressive life are everywhere bound up with the furtherance of this movement and that the proposal we are considering is opposed to it and goes in the direction of separation." [1]   This is perhaps the most cogent statement of this objection.

In answering this objection, let us look at the facts of the case; let us, first of all, look at the facts in the United King-

[1] *Parliamentary Debates*, 5th ser. (Commons), vol. 116, pp. 1887-1888.

dom.  The Union was the result of three separate Acts, namely, the Union between England and Wales under Henry VIII, the Union between England and Scotland in 1707, and the Union between Great Britain and Ireland in 1800. The Union with Wales was the most complete for it was both a legislative and executive union.  The Union with Scotland was not a complete union, it was only a legislative and never an executive union.  This was also, to a great extent, true of the Union with Ireland.  Ireland is now out of the Union.  And leaving the case of Wales on one side, let us consider for a moment the Union with Scotland. What has been the result of that Union?  For a short while after 1707 there was a separate Scottish Secretary for Scotland, which was later abolished.  Then Scottish affairs were carried on more or less under the supervision of the Home Office.  Some thirty years ago the Secretaryship of Scotland was reestablished and, since that time, Scotland has had her separate administration.  In the field of legislation, also, the separate interests of Scotland have been recognized. She has her own educational system, which is, in some respects, different from, and superior to, the English system. For that reason she has always had separate Educational Acts.  Again in a great many other matters she has been treated differently from the rest.  Many of the Public Acts annually passed by Parliament have been Acts with special application to Scotland.  Since the institution of the Procedure on Scottish Private Bill legislation, all the Private Bills for Scotland have been dealt with in Scotland subject to confirmation by Parliament.  With regard to all Bills concerning Scotland that come before the House of Commons a Grand Committee for Scotland has been set up to deal with them.  These being the facts, what difference will devolution make?

The difference comes down to this: that all Scottish af-

fairs, instead of being dealt with in Parliament by separate
Acts, separate Committees, and a separate procedure as at
present, will be dealt with by a Scottish Legislature in Scotland.   This is after all not so radical a change as it at first
seems.   But there is a great difference between these two
methods of handling Scottish business.   Under the present
system the same set of men are required to do two things at
the same time.   They are doing Imperial business and, at the
same time, are required to transact the separate business
of Scotland.   What devolution aims to accomplish is to
have another set of men take care of these local matters and
save the time of Parliament for more important matters.

Is such a change contrary to the policy of the Union and
to the spirit of the Constitution?   Assuredly not.   The
people who urge this objection mean by Union something
quite different from what it actually is.   The policy of the
Union and the spirit of the Constitution have never aimed at
the obliteration of local differences and have not had this
effect.   The following quotations will serve to elucidate this
point:

" The Union between the three Kingdoms (including Ireland)," says Mr. Murray Macdonald, " is concerned with
four spheres of interest, and it has not operated in the same
way in all four.   In respect of the domestic interests common to the three peoples, and in respect of their relations
with the other peoples of the Empire and of the world outside the Empire it has been a complete integrating Union.
In these three respects the three peoples have been as one.
If we attempted to impose the English system on the peoples
of Scotland so that there would be one administration common to both countries, we know that the attempt would
break the Union.   The attempt has not been made in the
case of the Dominions, and the Union between us and them
is due to the fact that it has not been made.   It was made in

the case of the American Colonies, and we lost them. It has been made in the case of Ireland, and Ireland remains today the one outstanding failure in the government of the peoples of the Empire. To give to peoples the right to control the conditions of their domestic life is not to pave the way for separation. It is to recognise one essential condition of a real and abiding union between them." [1]

Again, Sir Edward Carson says:

One thing which has been said today I agree with entirely, and that is that I do not believe devolution is a step towards separation. Indeed, I am not sure that devolution, if properly carried out, may not lead to closer Union, because when all have agreed as to the local contribution to Imperial taxation and to the maintenance in the Imperial Parliament of certain rights, you will find when you have set them up that you cannot touch any of these Parliaments, no matter what their demands may be, without touching the whole fabric of the Constitution. [2]

To conclude the answer to this objection, we may quote another important opinion as to the nature of the Union and the spirit of the Constitution. " If you consult the regular textbooks on these questions," says Sir John Marriott, " you find that the Constitution of the United Kingdom is invariably described—and perfectly accurately described—as a Unitary Constitution. But look at the matter from the point of view, not of constitutional theory, but of political practice, . . . there is a very great deal more of what is loosely called federalism in the working of the United Kingdom than is commonly supposed. Take the judicial system. England, Scotland, Ireland, already each has its own separate judicial system, its separate staff of judges, and, for the most part, its separate law officers. The only link be-

[1] *Parliamentary Debates*, 5th ser. (Commons), vol. 116, p. 1888.
[2] *Ibid.*, pp. 1898-1899.

tween the several parts of the United Kingdom in respect
of judicature is the Supreme Appellate jurisdiction of the
House of Lords.  Then, leaving the Judicature on one side,
take the Legislature.  It will be said that that, at any rate,
is a unitary body.  If the Legislature itself is a unitary body,
the resulting legislation is not.  I take the first ten years of
the present century.  During those ten years there were 458
public Acts passed in this House.  Of those 458 public
Acts, only 252 were uniformly applicable to all parts of the
United Kingdom.  The Legislature may be unitary; the
resulting legislation is not.

" Then as to the Eexecutive.  The Cabinet system is, I
suppose, no longer in existence, although I hear it is to be
reconstituted.  But before the War we had a Cabinet.  Of
that Cabinet of some twenty members, there were fifteen
members dealing with home affairs, leaving the Foreign
Secretary and Colonial Secretary on one side, and of those
fifteen members, only four exercised their administrative
powers uniformly in each of the three parts of the United
Kingdom.  Those four were the Prime Minister, the Chancellor of the Exchequer, the President of the Board of
Trade and the Post Master-General, and, of those four,
only one—the Post Master-General—included in the ambit
of his jurisdiction the Channel Islands and the Isle of Man.
Of the rest, the Local Government Board is, of course, exclusively English, and also the Education Board and the
Chancellor of the Duchy of Lancaster.  The Board of Agriculture is exclusively an English Board in regard to everything except the diseases of animals.  Diseased Animals
appear to be common to all parts of the United Kingdom,
but that is only part of the jurisdiction of the Board of Agriculture.  Then take the Home Secretary: he is in a curiously
anomalous position.  In regard to the judicial side of his
functions, his prisons, and so on, he is exclusively an

English officer.   In regard to the industrial side of his functions, aliens, and so on, he is an officer of the United Kingdom.   Well, then, can it be said, in view of these facts, which will not, I think, be controverted—they cannot be—that our present system is really and essentially a unitary system? " [1]

If the English Constitution is in fact not a completely unitary Constitution, and if its policy is not to create such a constitution, then clearly it cannot be maintained that devolution runs counter to the policy of the Union and to the spirit of the Constitution.   With regard to that part of the objection concerning the tendency towards unity in other countries, the argument is entirely misleading.   In addition to what has already been said in connection with federal centralization, we may quote a few very illuminating remarks on this particular point from the Members of Parliament. In introducing the Home Rule Bill of 1912, Mr. Asquith declared in the House of Commons :

The Dominions started with separate states, which needed to be combined and centralized for matters of common concern. We start with a congested center, which needs, if it is to do efficiently that which is common to the whole, to be relieved of everything else and to delegate local interests to local management.   In a word, the great Dominions and ourselves, starting out from opposite poles, animated by the same purpose, are going to meet at the same goal. [2]

Sir Whittaker remarked in the House of Commons on June 4, 1919:

I have heard it suggested that the tendency of the world is towards unity, and that to devolve your power is to go back. I suggest that it is nothing of the kind.   The tendency is to-

[1] *Parliamentary Debates* (Commons), 5th ser., vol. 116, pp. 2103-2104.

[2] *Parliamentary Debates* (Commons), 5th ser., vol. 36, pp. 1406-1407.

wards unity, but nowhere is the tendency towards unity in one Parliament. . . . The tendency of the times is obviously towards a supreme Parliament with subordinate provincial legislatures to deal with subordinate matters. Other countries have reached this stage by federation; we shall reach it by devolution. The aim of both is the same, only our condition is different.[1]

## II. PRACTICAL OBJECTIONS

So much then for the constitutional objections. We have seen that they are on the whole unsound. There are, however, a number of practical objections which should now be considered. They are no less than six in number: first, the difficulty of the distribution of powers; secondly, the difficulty of the allocation of finance; thirdly, the divergence and the conflict of laws; fourthly, the multiplicity of executives; fifthly, the preponderance of England; and lastly, the lack of public opinion. Let us consider these objections one by one.

First, as to the difficulty of the distribution of powers. " It is easy to say," argues Viscount Bryce, ". . . . that all questions dealing with one particular part of the country should belong to its local Legislature, and all questions which do not belong to any particular part but concern the United Kingdom as a whole should be left to what is generally called the Imperial, but what I will call, the United Kingdom, Parliament. That is a much too simple presentation of the question.

" There is a large number of topics of which you cannot say, . . . that they are distinctly British or distinctly Scottish, or Welsh, or English. Take, for instance, such questions as those relating to labour, to strikes and to public health. Can you say that they are fit for special treatment in England, in Scotland, and in Wales? Is there any reason

---

[1] *Ibid.*. vol. 116, pp. 2113-2114.

why they should not be treated by the Parliament of the United Kingdom upon uniform and similar lines? Surely it would be a great deal better to have similar legislation in labour matters, for instance, in England and in Scotland. Here I may remind your Lordships of what no doubt is familiar to you, that in the Australian Commonwealth the tendency has been entirely the other way. There the tendency is not to assign labour questions and matters of that kind more to the State Legislatures and less to the Commonwealth Legislature, but, on the contrary, to enlarge the powers of the Commonwealth Legislature and to diminish the powers of the State Legislatures. Therefore, these are questions which, according to Australia's experience—and the same thing, I think, is generally true of Canada—are better dealt with in the Central Legislature on lines which are similar for the whole country.

" There is a different class of subjects which are left indefinite by the Canadian Constitution, upon which it is hard to say from the terms of the Constitution whether they ought to be dealt with by the Dominion Government or by the Provincial Governments. That includes such questions as bankruptcy, the law of corporations, criminal law and procedure, local works and undertakings. Now, local works and undertakings would appear to be specially matters for local legislatures, and, of course, everyone who has discussed these questions from the point of view of our own country has suggested that local Bills should all go to Local English or Scottish or Welsh Legislatures. That has been already done very largely as regards Scotland. A special system of procedure for Scottish Bills was set up, I think, some fourteen years ago, and it has worked with very reasonable success. There really would be no great relief to Parliament from taking local Bills away altogether. It would save a little time for Members in the middle of the

day, but a great deal more time might be saved in this House
and in the other House if you had Joint Committees instead
of having Bills dealt with by two Committees, one here and
one there.

"The relief afforded in that way would not be appreciable
relief, but I have no doubt it ought to be done, and I agree
that if we were to set up a proper tribunal for dealing with
private Bills—gas, water, municipal, and railway Bills (of
which there will be very few in future), we should relieve
a great deal of the work and should probably have the work
as well done.   But there remains a very large number indeed
of Bills about which it would be doubtful whether they belonged to the sphere of the United Kingdom or Central
Parliament or to the spheres of the local Parliaments for
England, Scotland, Ireland, and Wales.   As was observed
by the noble and learned Lord, and as I had the honour to
observe to your Lordships some months ago, it would be
quite necessary to have a legal line of demarcation between
the powers of the United Kingdom Parliament and the
powers of the local Parliaments.   If there were to be a legal
line of demarcation the law laying it down would require to
be interpreted; that interpretation would require to be carried
out by the Law Courts, and the Law Courts would find a
great deal of occupation in doing this work.

"I may remind your Lordships that in the United States
they began litigating upon the question of what had been
assigned to Congress, the National Legislature, and what
to the State Legislatures—in spite of the carefully drawn
terms of their Constitution they began litigating 130 years
ago, and they have not got through yet.   There are fresh
questions continually coming up in the United States Courts
as to whether a matter belongs to the Federal Government
or to a State Government, so that after all those years
these questions have not been finally disposed of.   The

same thing is true of Canada. . . . That is in the nature of things. You cannot exhaust these questions. New cases will arise and will require to be dealt with afresh. . . . So much for the difficulty of discriminating between the powers of Legislatures." [1]

The gist of Viscount Bryce's remarks, which are about the best statement of this objection, is two-fold: first, there is a certain class of topics such as labour and health, which cannot very well be distributed. If they are not distributed, as Viscount Bryce thinks they should not be, then you will not have your relief. Secondly, if they are distributed, you must draw a legal line of demarcation, which means litigation and work for the Courts.[2] There is, of course, some difficulty in effecting a proper distribution of powers, and this is indeed the crux of the whole problem of devolution, but the difficulty is by no means insurmountable. No hard and fast line can be drawn or needs to be drawn between the national interests and the local interests. The general principle would be to effect such a distribution of powers, that both the central authority and the local authorities may be enabled to discharge those functions that each is best qualified to discharge under the present circumstances.[3] Experience has shown that certain functions are obviously national in character, such as national communication, foreign affairs, defence, navigation, customs, currency, etc. Experience has also shown that certain functions are

[1] *Parliamentary Debates* (Lords), vol. 33, pp. 535-537.

[2] Professor H. J. Laski makes the same criticism in his recent book, *A Grammar of Politics*, pp. 309-311.

[3] An illuminating statement of the principle is that of James Wilson as follows: "Whatever object of government is confined in its operation and effect within the bounds of a particular state, should be considered as belonging to the government of that state; whatever object of government extends in its operation or effects beyond the bounds of a particular State, should be considered as belonging to the Government of the United States." Quoted, Thompson, *op. cit.*, p. 381.

obviously local in character, such as local government, local education, police power, local commerce and industry, etc. The difficulty lies in the middle zone between these two classes of subjects. Here nothing but constant experimentation can bring about the most satisfactory arrangement. Government, like an organism, is a growing thing and it cannot be put into a strait-jacket which will be good forever. With regard to the United Kingdom, there is already some guidance in this matter in the various Home Rule Bills, and in the annual statutes which are applicable to particular parts of the country. After all, the question is not so difficult as it looks. In general the powers to be retained by Parliament would be questions affecting the Crown, questions of coinage, weights and measures, the control of harbours, of naval or military importance, light houses, questions concerning the Army, the Navy, and Foreign Affairs. The powers to be devolved would include questions connected with local government, agriculture, education, licensing, and so on. With regard to labor and factory legislation Earl Brassey has suggested that the several countries need not be treated the same. In short, whatever method of distribution is adopted for the time being, it cannot but result in a considerable saving of the time of Parliament. As we have seen all the local and private legislation occupies at present, a great part of parliamentary time which undoubtedly can be saved by devolution.

The second objection is the difficulty of the allocation of finance. This is perhaps the most difficult question of all. At the present time a uniform system of finance runs through England, Scotland and Wales. The subordinate Governments must somehow be assigned certain independent sources of revenue if the system of devolution is to work effectively. This means that the financial system of Great Britain has to be broken up. On the side of supply it is perhaps not very hard to determine how much each subordinate Government will require at the outset; but on the side of revenue it is not easy to decide as to what sources should be assigned. The National Exchequer may give a lump-sum to each subordinate Legislature in the form of a Grant-in-Aid, or it may allot to it certain definite sources of revenue. In no case should the resources of the Imperial Exchequer be impaired. The problem is a technical one, but is by no means too difficult to solve. In this respect again, there has already been much guidance in the various Home Rule Bills in the past. A scheme of allocation, as we have seen, has been suggested by the Speaker's Conference on Devolution, which scheme seems to be very satisfactory.

The third objection is the divergence and conflict of laws. If the several countries are given power to make laws over certain subjects assigned to them, there is bound to be some divergence of laws on the same subject matter in the different parts of the United Kingdom, which will give rise to a conflict of laws between them. This would be a very undesirable thing especially when such matters as labour and health are divided. Even in the field of private law uniformity is highly desirable. This is the substance of the objection. Granted that the objection is sound, it is hard to see how it can be avoided. Under the present system there have already been in existence among the peoples of Great Britain two different systems of law: the Scottish law which is founded upon the Roman Law, and the English law. As to matters where uniform treatment is indispensable, they need not be divided at all. On the whole it may be admitted that devolution may create some divergence and conflict of laws, but it is not such a great evil as to overbalance the benefits to be obtained.

The fourth objection is the multiplicity of executives. " Now every Legislature," says Viscount Bryce, " implies an Executive. If the Scottish Legislature or the English Legislature is to legislate for Scotland or for England, clearly that legislation must be carried out by an Executive which is responsible to the Scottish Parliament or the English Parliament. If that is so, you will have a new set of Executives. Besides the present Executive, which will remain as the United Kingdom Executive, you will have four others. . . . Therefore you will have to establish four new Executive staffs, besides the Executive staff we have at present, and you will have to distribute the work which is done by our present Executive between it and the several Executives of the several countries. If any of your Lordships will be at the pains of taking up a summary account of the work done now by the Home Office or by the Board of Trade and will consider what part of that work ought to be left to belong to the National or United Kingdom Executive and how much ought to be assigned to the Irish, Scottish, Welsh, and English Executives, you will find how great the difficulty will be and how very troublesome it may be to take one of our great Departments like the Board of Trade and make mincemeat of it by assigning its functions, some to these different new Executives and some to the old Executive which will continue." [1]

The answer to this objection is that to a great extent those Executives exist at the present time. We have seen

---

[1] *Parliamentary Debates* (Lords), vol. 33, pp. 537-538. Sidney Webb makes the same criticism from another point of view. His arguments may be summarized as follows: first, it is highly inconvenient to split up "the administration of a country so nearly homogeneous as Great Britain has become"; and secondly, even if this could be done, Parliament would still remain impotent because of the heterogeneity of political and economic issues with which it has to deal. Therefore he thinks that not devolution but the spitting up of the work of Parliament into two coordinated Legislatures has become necessary in Great Britain. (*A Constitution for the Socialist Commonwealth of Great Britain*, pp. 122, 132, 133-134.)

that the Board of Education, the Local Government Board (now the Minister of Health), the Board of Agriculture (excluding diseases of animals) are all purely English Boards. "In fact, the whole province of education;" says Lord Charnwood, "the whole province of poor law and charity; the whole province of the administration of justice; the whole subject of private law, or what I may briefly call the lawyer's law, with some slight qualifications; pretty nearly the whole of what one may class as land policy; matters coming under the jurisdiction of the Board of Agriculture; questions of land tenure, the development of small holdings, and the like, the whole of sanitation, and various other matters which escape my mind at this moment—pretty nearly the whole of those subjects are treated at the present moment by separate Executive Departments. In regard to these there would be no necessity to set up separate Executives so far as England, Scotland, and Ireland are concerned, as separate Executive machinery already exists." [1]

The fifth objection is the preponderance of England. This has been a much mooted problem in the whole subject of devolution. It has been said that the successful operation of a federal arrangement or of devolution depends upon the approximate equality of the different units in wealth and population. England is said to be more than three times as populous and much more than three times as wealthy as Scotland, Ireland, and Wales put together. A federation with such a predominant partner as England would be a queer kind of a federation, and would be difficult to work. This is another of Viscount Bryce's objections. It has been suggested that England might be divided into several units in order to avoid the preponderance. There are, however, difficulties in that too. So it is going to be difficult to break up England on the one hand, and it is also going to be diffi-

---

[1] *Parliamentary Debates*, 5th ser. (Lords), vol. 33, p. 546.

cult to work a federation in which England remains not broken up. The danger of having an unbroken England is described by Mr. Mackinder:

Think of what England will be, and think of the English Parliament. The Parliament which will be set up . . . would be one representing 36,000,000 people, and your Imperial Parliament would represent 45,000,000 people. The Premier for England will be a very big man alongside the Premier for the United Kingdom. Supposing there was a difference of opinion as to the delimitation of powers between the superior and the subordinate Parliaments, is it going to be an easy thing to keep in order that great giant in the Federal system? Let me assume that it is an acute difference rousing passion. Your scrap of paper will be in very great danger of being torn up, human beings being human beings. Even if we put ourselves as a nation into the strait-waistcoat of a supreme court of judicature for the purpose of interpreting the Constitution and Supreme Act of Parliament, I venture to say that the Court itself will find the need of all the support it can get if one of the suitors before it is this suitor representing the 36,000,000 out of 45,000,000 people in this country. How in practice do you keep the Parliaments which are nominally subordinate in a truly subordinate position? Simply by letting no one be predominant, so that the supreme Parliament may always be sure that if there is a difference between it and one of these other Parliaments it will at once have the assistance of the remaining subordinate Parliaments who become jealous of the ambition of that one Parliament.[1]

The above argument is plausible but unreal. The whole purpose of devolution is simply to delegate local affairs to local management and not to create rivalry either between the subordinate Legislatures and the Imperial Parliament, or between themselves. In the management of their separate

[1] *Parliamentary Debates*, 5th ser. (Commons), vol. 116, p. 1922.

interests there will be no occasion for friction whatsoever. What does it matter if one country happens to be less populous and less wealthy than the rest, or more populous and more wealthy than the rest? Take the United States for example. You have a state like New York or Illinois which is several times as populous and wealthy as a little state like Rhode Island. So long as constitutionally they receive equal treatment in matters concerning them all, there has never been any friction or rivalry between them. Each state, whether big or small, minds its own business and, so far as its internal affairs are concerned, no state can interfere with another. If this is true of a strict federal system, it ought to be even truer of devolution, where the local legislatures have but delegated powers. As to the influence that England might possess over the Imperial Parliament, it is there already. It is in the Imperial Parliament under the present system that the preponderance should be deplored, because it is when the domestic affairs of the several countries are controlled by one Parliament at Westminster that England can make her preponderance effective. Devolution, instead of aggravating, will remove that predominance.

The last objection is that there is no sufficient public opinion in favour of the proposed change. It has been said over and over again that the public is not interested in this question and that during the recent elections devolution has not been put before the public. Whether there is sufficient public opinion in favour of the proposal or not will be dealt with in a later connection. Undoubtedly there has been considerable agitation about it for a number of years by prominent citizens both in and out of Parliament. After all devolution is rather a technical subject, a subject which cannot be readily understood by the man in the street and in which the ordinary citizens have no immediate interest. If by public opinion is meant popular opinion, then the objection is clearly misleading. " If nothing were ever done," says Lord Charnwood, " which was not thoroughly understood and of which the importance was not appreciated by the ' man in the street ', a great many of the most important measures in history would never have taken effect. Amongst other things, there certainly never would have been the Union of the United States if it had been left to the public opinion of the ordinary man in the ordinary State to insist that in their situation it was necessary that some sort of Union should be formed. I rather protest against taking that line in regard to this question. The people will not, of course, become interested in this subject till they see those to whom they look for guidance in such matters, those with experience of government and Parliamentary life, take it seriously." [1]    Therefore this objection does not seem to be very important.

We have pretty nearly exhausted all the objections that have been raised against devolution. So far as the constitutional objections are concerned, they are theoretically very weighty but we have seen that none of them is really sound. Some of the practical objections such as the divergence of laws and the difficulties of the distribution of powers, and of financial arrangement do contain an element of truth, but such objections are by no means fatal to the proposed reform. On the whole the question is one of balancing the advantages and disadvantages on both sides. In conclusion it may be safely said that the balance is on the side for devolution and not on the side against it.

[1] *Parliamentary Debates*, 5th ser. (Lords), vol. 33, pp. 548-549.

# CHAPTER VIII

## Public Opinion on Devolution

In the previous chapters we have seen that ever since 1874 there has been a growing movement for devolution or Home Rule All Round in the House of Commons. The effort has been confined chiefly to private members who have now and then voiced their opinions through resolutions and private members' Bills. The Governments have thus far done nothing to put the proposal on the Statute Book aside from the enactment of the Government of Ireland Act, 1920, which has endowed Ulster, at any rate, with a local Parliament. Every Home Rule statesman, however, has professed that he was also a devolutionist and regarded Home Rule for Ireland as only the first installment of a general scheme of Home Rule All Round. The case for devolution, nevertheless, stands quite apart from the question of Irish Home Rule. Although there has been a continuous demand for Home Rule on the part of Scotland and Wales, their demand has not been anything like that of Ireland, and no party has, therefore, thought it necessary or expedient to make devolution a part of its political programme. The case for devolution is nevertheless an impregnable one and rests upon the congestion of the House of Commons, which is admitted by all observers of Parliament. They differ only as to the remedy. Those who do not think that devolution is the proper remedy assert, among other objections, that there has been no public opinion on the subject. Such is, however, not the case. It is true that there has not been any strong public opinion in favor of it, because it is only those who know anything about the work of Parliament that appreciate the problem, but it would be erroneous to suppose that no public opinion exists at all and that such public opinion as does exist is necessarily opposed to it. The purpose of this chapter is, therefore, to present, in a general way, the state of public opinion on devolution from the expressions made by the leaders of the movement outside Parliament, from the comments of the press and from the resolutions passed by various political, civic and labour organizations.

As early as 1886, Mr. Chamberlain approved devolution not only as the best way of approaching the Irish question but also as a means of enabling the other countries in the United Kingdom to have a greater degree of control over their separate domestic affairs. In a Manifesto addressed to his constituents after the first Home Rule Bill he declared:

It will be expedient to establish a complete system of popular local government alike in its main features for England, Scotland, Ireland and Wales. But apart and beyond a purely municipal organization of the kind, I believe that a larger arrangement will be found safe and desirable under which, subject to the concurrent and supreme authority of the Imperial Parliament, the various portions of the United Kingdom shall be enabled to exercise greater influence over administration and over legislation for their specific needs.[1]

In the year 1890 a series of articles appeared in the *Westminster Review* under the section entitled " The New Round Table " dealing with the subject of devolution and with Home Rule for Scotland and Wales. Mr. John Leng, a Member of Parliament, wrote an article on " Home Rule All Round " in which he made several very remarkable suggestions: first, to consider the Members for each division

---

[1] Quoted, *Parliamentary Debates* (Lords), vol. xiii, p. 486.

of the Kingdom as an Assembly of Representatives, Council, or House of Parliament, for dealing with the specific and exclusive affairs of that country.   Secondly, to hand over to the Representative Parliament of each part of the Kingdom as nearly as possible the same legislative and executive powers that are committed to the state legislatures of the United States.   Thirdly, to reserve to the Imperial Parliament all the powers now reserved to the United States Congress.   Fourthly, that the National Parliaments should meet in the months of October and November in each year to transact the business of each country.   And lastly, that the same Members of Parliament should meet collectively as the Imperial Parliament in the month of February each year for the discussion and transaction of Imperial business.[1]

The above scheme embodies, as the author pointed out, what was long ago suggested by Mr. Bright, namely, the scheme of a Grand Committee of Members for each country.[2] It is remarkable how closely the scheme suggested above resembles the plan of Mr. Speaker Lowther.   And with Mr. Leng, as with all the modern advocates of devolution, the chief purpose of such a scheme was to relieve the business of Parliament.   Mr. Leng said:

With me, the practical argument is the strongest.   The so-called Imperial Parliament is weighted and hampered and clogged by the necessity of dealing, or attempting to deal, with innumerable local details which should be dealt with by local representative assemblies.   The great majority of the questions put to the Ministers of the Crown every day in the House of Commons relate exclusively to local affairs.   The great majority of the Bills brought before the Imperial Parliament are not Imperial, but Local or National Bills.   Besides 237 Private Bills now before the House of Commons, there are sixty-nine

[1] *The Westminster Review*, 1890, vol. 133, N. S. 77, p. 573.
[2] There is now a Grand Committee for Scottish Bills.

which may be considered Imperial, that is, applying to the whole of the United Kingdom, or our foreign possessions; ninety to England alone, thirty-one to Ireland alone, thirty to Scotland alone; and five to Wales alone. It is obvious that Parliament, as now constituted, is quite unable to deal satisfactorily with this mass of legislative proposals, and I therefore advocate the extension of the system of devolution, and the constitution of representative assemblies—consisting wholly or mainly of the Parliamentary representatives of each division of the country—to deal with the specific and exclusive affairs of England, Ireland, Scotland, and Wales, respectively.[1]

There was undoubtedly a general feeling on the part of many Scotchmen that their national affairs had been neglected in Parliament and that Home Rule for Scotland was necessary on that ground. A writer in 1890 said: " The desire of Home Rule for Scotland is partly the outcome of national sentiment, but mainly practical and utilitarian." [2] The same writer thought that there was an unfavorable influence of England over Scottish affairs. ". . . . of the seventy-two Members Scotland sends up to Parliament, twelve are Tories and sixty are Liberals. Yet the twelve Tories govern Scotland, because England wills it so. In every relation in life the same influence is brought to bear adversely upon the interests of Scotland." [3]

Certain writers went even further in their demand for Scottish Home Rule. Their demand was based not on practical grounds alone, but preeminently on the ground of nationality. Thus another writer said:

But underneath these grievances, aggravating them all, is the wrong done . . . to Scotland's life and honour and progress as a nation. England seems scarcely to know that Scotland

---

[1] *The Westminster Review*, vol. 133 (N. S. 77), pp. 577-578.

[2] *Ibid.*, p. 65.

[3] *Ibid.*, p. 67.

remains a nation. Only now, indeed, for the first time since the Union, is England beginning to hear the real voice of Scotland. What she has hitherto heard and taken for the voice of Scotland is the voice of a denationalized and Anglicized class of Scotchmen who, educated in England and growing up with English ideas, have ceased to understand or truly represent their country. . . .

There is a strength in nationality which an Empire like ours, instead of seeking to destroy, should seek to develop and utilize. For as honour and self-respect in the individual man make him a better and more valuable citizen, so, in a nation, honour and self-respect make it a worthier, stronger, and more valuable member in a Union of nations. . . .

What Britain needs, and what I believe Scotland is setting herself to seek, is Home Rule for England, Scotland, Ireland, and Wales, with an Imperial Parliament in which all parts of the United Kingdom shall be represented (as the United States are in Congress), and which shall confine itself to Imperial affairs.[1]

Home Rule for Wales stood on a little different footing from that for Scotland. Wales is not so different from England as Scotland is, nor is it as big as Scotland. Yet her case is by no means a weak one. Thus Professor Jones wrote in 1890:

All the elements of the Irish argument can be used for Wales under two limitations: Wales is smaller, and its social disorganization is not so great—we neither shoot each other nor hate England, as yet. But these differences are only of degree and can be made use of in two ways. For if it be urged on the one hand that the smallness of Wales brings it beneath the " limit of self-sufficiency ", or makes it a matter of indifference to the Empire whether or not the Principality is allowed to regulate its own life, the concession of self-government could, on the other hand, be made without running any serious im-

[1] *Ibid.*, pp. 68-69.

perial risks, and while the absence of social disorder and hatred of England does not point to the absolute failure of the English Parliament to govern Wales on its present method, this also diminishes the probability that Wales would make a violent use of powers granted to it.[1]

Professor Jones also pointed out that Wales was bound together by a consciousness of organic life and animated by national aspirations and that the necessities of land and ecclesiastical legislation in Wales demanded some sort of a Home Rule.[2]

On January 18, 1895, Lord Rosebery made a speech in which he said:

The more I see of our political system, the more I am convinced of this: that, in a large measure of devolution, subject to Imperial control, lies the secret of the future working of our Empire. Daily, also, in my opinion, that devolution comes nearer and nearer. . . . It has been by such a system of devolution that we have been able to found, outside these kingdoms, the greatest Empire that the world has ever seen; and we shall find, in the same principle, the solution of many, if not most, of our difficulties inside. In that respect, the cause of Ireland stands first, but not last. The liberal party, in my opinion, will never find its full strength until it has enlisted all the power and sympathy and freedom which it would gain in every part of the United Kinglom by the systematised devolution of local business to the localities themselves.[3]

In the same year another great liberal leader, Sir Henry Campbell-Bannerman declared himself in favor of devolution. In an address to the electors of the Stirling Burghs he said:

[1] *The Westminster Review*, vol. 133 (N. S. 77), p. 401.

[2] *Ibid.*, pp. 402-403.

[3] Quoted, *The Liberal Magazine*, vol. xx, 1912, p. 295.

The excessive burden of work now imposed upon Parliament can only be relieved by a large system of devolution. It is for this reason, as well as from a sense of right and justice to the nationalities concerned, that I regard as urgently necessary the creation for the three kingdoms of subordinate legislative assemblies dealing with the distinctive affairs of each.[1]

But the most outstanding figure in the movement was Viscount Hythe who was a strong imperialist well acquainted with the political systems of the several dominions. In 1901 he published an article in the *Nineteenth Century* advocating federal government for the United Kingdom and the Empire.[2] By federal government he meant devolution. Devolution, besides being the best scheme under which " the difficulties which have been pointed out in devising a satisfactory measure of Home Rule for Ireland only disappear ", would greatly relieve the congestion of Parliament. He said:

The House of Commons is the responsible guardian of the interests of the greatest Empire the world has ever seen. It has to deal with questions affecting the United Kingdom as a whole; and it also legislates for the special interests of the several countries of the United Kingdom. The diversity of business is extraordinary, the quantity enormous; and it is not to be wondered at that the House of Commons is unequal to the task now imposed on it. In no other country of the civilized world is such a task attempted. The conclusion is inevitable, that parliamentary government is breaking down because the needs of the Empire, of the United Kingdom as a whole, and of its several parts, have outgrown the existing means for dealing with them. The remedy lies in the recognition of the distinction between the different classes of business which we either attempt to deal with, often very ineffectually, or do not attempt to deal with at all, in the House of Commons, and of

[1] Quoted, Viscount Hythe, *Problems of Empire*, pp. 60-61.
[2] Reprinted in *Problems of Empire*, new edition, 1913, pp. 56-78.

the necessity of allocating what may here be roughly described as Imperial business and domestic business to different legislative assemblies.[1]

Twelve years later, on January 21, 1913, he delivered an address at Hythe on the subject, " The Breakdown of Parliamentary Government, and the Remedy ",[2] in which he again advocated the policy of devolution.  He said that even from an English Conservative's point of view devolution would be highly desirable.  For " why should socialistic legislation be imposed on England by the votes of men who are certainly not Socialists?", asked Earl Brassey, " Why should the Church in Wales be disestablished by the votes of Irishmen and Scotchmen, who have no concern in the matter at all?  Why should the Church of England in England be disestablished by Irish Roman Catholics, Scotch Presbyterians, and Welsh Nonconformists?  It is a question which concerns us Englishmen, and by the votes of our representatives alone should such a question be decided.  I think that if English Conservatives would reflect on the consequences of maintaining the present system of government, they would arrive at the same conclusion as I have, viz., that it is time we Englishmen managed our own affairs without the interference of Irishmen or Scotchmen, and that Home Rule is needed for England quite as much as for Ireland." [3]  After speaking from the Imperial point of view and after criticising the Home Rule Bill, he concluded by saying:

The present situation is intolerable.  A way out must be found.  Parliamentary government must be restored.  The Home Rule question, which has been the bane of British politics

[1] Viscount Hythe, *ibid.*, p. 61.
[2] Reprinted in *Problems of Empire*, pp. 181-198.
[3] *Ibid.*, pp. 187-188.

for so many years, must be settled. A measure of Federal Home Rule, which will relieve the congestion of business in Parliament, which will put an end to the Irish controversy, and which will incidentally go far to solve the House of Lords questions, is the obvious and, in my belief, the only remedy.[1]

Earl Brassey was not a mere preacher. For many years he was an ardent promotor of devolution. From 1901 to 1903 he tried to unite all the liberals under a devolution policy through the Federal Union Committee, in which were, among others, Murray Macdonald and Professor Henry Jones. A large number of meetings were held in the great towns of England and Scotland. At Liverpool, for instance, a large public meeting attended by no less than 900 persons was addressed by Earl Brassey. A resolution in favor of devolution was unanimously passed.[2] In his campaign in 1902 in Devonport he also made devolution a chief topic of his Address. In the Winter Session of the Royal Colonial Institute in the same year, he presented a paper on " Steps to Imperial Federation ", in which he urged the establishment of a federal form of government for the United Kingdom as an essential preliminary step towards Imperial Federation.[3] Again, in the same year a resolution was adopted by the Birkenhead Liberal Association, which was moved by Mr. James Moon and seconded by Earl Brassey.[4] The Resolution reads:

That this Committee, regarding the congestion of business in the House of Commons as a fatal obstacle to progress in social and domestic legislation, is of the opinion that this obstacle can best be overcome by the establishment of local legislatures in

[1] *Ibid.*, pp. 197-198.
[2] Partridge, *T. A. B. 2nd Earl Brassey,* p. 144.
[3] *Ibid.*, p. 145.
[4] *The Liberal Magazine,* 1902, p. 92.

the several countries of the United Kingdom, each having
power to deal with its own internal affairs, leaving to the
existing Imperial Parliament the management of those matters
which affect the United Kingdom as a whole, and of all Imperial
business.

On the whole it may be safely said that most of the Liberals have been in favour of devolution, while most of the
Unionists and Conservatives have been opposed to it.   But
apart from party reasons some of the latter did recognize
the merits of devolution quite as frankly as the Liberals.
During the Constitutional Conference, 1910, Mr. F. S.
Oliver, a Unionist member, wrote a series of letters on devolution in the London *Times* with a view to influencing his
party brothers.   They appeared under the pseudonym of
" Pacificus " and were reprinted in 1911 under the title of
" Federalism and Home Rule ".   By federalism was meant
devolution.   The following passages are worth quoting:

The Proposal for Federal Home Rule, as I understand it,
leaves the principle of sovereignty untouched.   It merely proposes that various functions, which this Imperial Parliament
performs not too successfully in regard to the local legislation
and administration of the various countries and provinces which
together make up the United Kingdom, should be delegated
to a certain number of national and provincial parliaments of
a subordinate character.   It is contended that it will be a great
advantage if our overloaded Parliament at Westminster (which
now finds it necessary to sit all the year round in order to get
through its work), and also an overloaded Cabinet, could pass
over a portion of their local duties into the hands of people
who understand the local conditions a great deal better than
they are understood in London.   It is hoped by this arrangement not merely to appease the Irish, or to divert their un-
tiring dialectics against Britain into another channel, but to
secure two very considerable benefits.

The first of these anticipated benefits is that the Imperial

Parliament will then be relieved of a great burden of pressing local considerations, and by this means will be left free to attend to those greater problems which concern the United Kingdom as a whole and the Empire as a whole.

The second benefit is that the local customs and traditions, the national and racial habits of life and thought, will be better understood by these subordinate parliaments, and that the measures which are desirable in the interests of each locality will be more promptly undertaken than is the case at present.[1]

Mr. Oliver further pointed out that federalism in this sense does not run counter to the Union.

The aim, therefore, of Federalism is not to break up or weaken the sovereignty of the Union, but to confirm and strengthen this sovereignty by mitigating the evils and discontents which have arisen owing to the centralization of many matters which only concern localities, and not the interests of the United Kingdom as a whole. Federalism is for giving to certain units (whether national or provincial is a matter for future consileration) the fullest possible control of their own local affairs. It is not proposed that there should be any absolute or irrevocable disposition. The Imperial Parliament will retain its full rights, and as it gave, so it can alter or extend the powers of its subordinates. It is possible that, upon investigation, the Federalist idea may turn out to be impracticable, but the grounds on which it may be discarded will assuredly not be that it tends to impair the unity either of the United Kingdom or of the Empire.[2]

The writer also discussed the question of units for the subordinate legislatures. On this point, it was said, the Federalists were not in complete agreement among themselves. Three distinct proposals were current; first, there was the extreme view that there should be only two Parlia-

---

[1] Pacificus, *Federalism and Home Rule*, Introduction, pp. lv-lvi.
[2] *Ibid.*, pp. lvii-lviii.

ments—a national Parliament for Great Britain and another for Ireland. Another extreme view was that the units should be based upon population of more or less equal size. Neither of them, as the writer pointed out, was regarded favorably by the majority of the Federalists. Then there was the third proposal of establishing four parliaments upon the existing basis of nationality of England, Scotland, Ireland and Wales. " And they urge us to accept this arrangement," says the writer, " not so much as a compromise between the two extremes, as because the division suggested corresponds with certain historical ideas of national life. They contend that the success of the Federal idea depends not at all upon equality of numbers, but upon a spiritual force, upon the intimate association of men possessing a common tradition. They admit frankly that they set sentiment above any purely practical considerations. They claim that the result under their plan will be more dignified and vital than any artificial combination into groups of counties; and that it will be a thing much safer, much less liable to schism, than a division into two. . . ." [1]

Again, in the Spring of 1918 many Unionist members joined in a letter to the *Times* urging the immediate solution of the Irish problem on federal lines. But that is not all. " Apart altogether from the urgency of Ireland," the writers declared, " we are deeply impressed by the need of a far-reaching system of Federal Devolution for the United Kingdom. We cannot see how otherwise the problems which are awaiting solution after the War can possibly be dealt with, or how, without it, we can escape from the most dangerous congestion." It also suggested that a Speaker's Conference on devolution be appointed and a Government of Ireland Bill be immediately introduced.[2] The same view

[1] *Ibid.*, pp. 56-57.
[2] *London Times*, April 16, 1918, p. 7c.

was expressed by other Unionist members. Mr. F. S. Oliver said that the wisest constitutional check in a democracy was the federal principle.[1] Mr. L. S. Amery thought that the federal solution was the only one which would reconcile the passionate and insistent demand of the Nationalists, the just and indefeasible claims of Ulster, and the legitimate rights of the United Kingdom. However, he did not favor the introduction of the Irish Bill. What was needed was a United Kingdom Bill for the setting up of national governments.[2]

From the above account of the opinions of some of the Unionist members, it would seem that there have been a considerable number in the rank and file of the party who are in favor of the policy of devolution, although the leaders of the party have, on the whole, been against it.

Now let us turn to another angle of the survey. Probably it is true that the general public has not shown much interest in the problem one way or the other; that is the case with many important and urgent problems. But there is, nevertheless, some public interest. In June, 1914, a debate took place in Oxford on the question of devolution. It was attended by many prominent members of the University. The following resolution was unanimously adopted.

That this meeting regards it of urgent importance that a commission representative of all the parties should be at once appointed to consider the possibility of solving the present constitutional crisis by a scheme of devolution applicable to the United Kingdom as a whole.[3]

On October 23, 1917, a deputation of the Scottish Trade Union Congress interviewed Mr. Lloyd George on Scottish

[1] *London Times*, April 18, 1918, p. 8c.
[2] *Ibid.*
[3] *Ibid.*, May 2, p. 4f.

Home Rule.    Mr. Lloyd George expressed himself as in complete agreement with the princible of devolution as desirable politically, and as a business proposition.    His fear, however, was that the English Parliament might prove to be a rival to the Imperial Parliament.[1]

In general, public opinion in Scotland and Wales was strongly in favor of devolution.    Various resolutions were passed from time to time by different civic and political organizations.    To give a few instances, the Scottish National Committee, consisting of Liberals and Labour members, which was responsible for the Scottish Home Rule Bill in 1913, held its first meeting during the War on May 7, 1918.    It was decided to ask the Government to frame an Irish Bill " with a view to the immediate extension of a similar measure of self-government to Scotland and the consequent establishment of a complete Federal system for the United Kingdom."    The general body of the Scottish Liberals also reaffirmed the principle of Home Rule for Scotland and asked the Government to appoint a committee to report on the problem.[2]    Again, on May 21, a Welsh conference consisting mostly of Liberals was held at Llandrindod for the purpose of opening a campaign for self-government for Wales and Monmouth.    A resolution was moved by J. E. Powell and supported by H. M. Hughes, calling for a comprehensive measure of self-government on federal lines for Wales and asking the Welsh members in Parliament to do their utmost to secure the realization of this object.    After a lengthy discussion the resolution was carried with only one dissenting vote.[3]

The Labour Party has also declared itself in favor of devolution.    Early in 1918 a draft report of reconstruc-

[1] *The Liberal Magazine,* 1917, p. 494.

[2] *London Times,* May 8, 1918, p. 7c.

[3] *Ibid.,* May 22, p. 3c.

tion policy, prepared by the sub-committee of the Executive, was circulated among the constituent organizations of the party in the form of a pamphlet, entitled " Labour and the New Social Order ". At the annual conference on June 26, 1918, the Executive issued for discussion a series of resolutions based upon that report. The resolutions favored among other matters a wide and generous measure of Home Rule for Scotland, Wales, and " even England ". They proposed that the Westminster Parliament should be a Federal Assembly for the United Kingdom; and that there should be a Federal Government for the British Commonwealth. All these were adopted by the Conference on June 28.[1] Again, on July 27, the South Wales Labour Federation held a special conference at Cardiff. There were present about 124 delegates representing 174,211 members. Resolutions were unanimously carried recognizing Ireland's claim to immediate Home Rule, and declaring that it should be an advance installment of Federal Home Rule for England, Scotland, and Wales as well as Ireland.[2]

More recently, on January 5, 1924, the annual Scottish Divisional Conference of the Independent Labour Party was held at Edinburg. A resolution was unanimously passed, calling upon the Government to summon a National convention, representative of political, civic and industrial Scotland, in order to frame a scheme of self-government suited to the people's needs.[3]

The ex-Premier, Mr. J. Ramsay MacDonald, has also declared himself in favor of devolution. He says:

As a method of increasing Parliamentary efficiency I put more and more value upon devolution. The case for an Irish

[1] *Ibid.*, May 9, 1918, p. 7d.

[2] *Ibid.*, July 29, 1918.

[3] *Glasgow Herald,* Jan. 7, 1924, quoted Gleanings and Memoranda, vol 59, 1924.

Parliament is complete. The matter does not end there, however. The overwhelming influence of England on Scottish and Welsh affairs is destroying the native political instincts of these nations. It is a profound calamity that our "predominant partner" possesses political instincts and educational equipment of a much lower order than those of the two nations joined to it. Their capacities are thus lost, are slowly being crushed out and stifled, and the Imperial Parliament comes nearer to the political intelligence of Sussex and Surrey, Rutland and Kent, than to the constituencies of the smaller nationalities where people are accustomed to think independently and where political affairs are followed with keen intelligence. Moreover, Parliamentary action is deprived of the support which would be given to it by the vigorous examples of legislation and administration which would come from beyond the Tweed and Severn.[1]

Lastly let us see what the attitude of the press has been on this question. In general it may be said that devolution has not excited very much interest in the press, but still a great deal of comment has appeared in some of the leading papers. The opinion is divided. Some papers are clearly in favor of devolution, while others are opposed to it. To give a few examples, let us quote some interesting comments as follows:

Commenting upon the debate on devolution in the House of Commons on June 3 and 4, 1919, the *Outlook* made this statement:

Whether the Government has any serious thought of plunging into the appalling task of remodelling the legislative and administrative framework of the kingdom, we do not know. But the time is certainly over-ripe for the appointment of a Parliamentary Commission to explore the whole problem. If we take forty years as the average period that elapses between the first clear perception of the need of a reform and its embodi-

---

[1] *Parliament and Revolution*, pp. 97-98.

ment in legislation, then the devolution movement ought to be nearing its moment of triumph. The nation, we are very confident, will face this possibility with an equal mind. It has no genuine appetite for Constitutional discussion; it dislikes tinkering with the machinery of government; it would far rather go on as it is, performing the daily miracle—and never realizing what a miracle it is—of obtaining results from a Parliamentary and administrative plant that would probably disable the political engineers of any other nationality. We have always as a people been much better at working a bad system than at devising a good one. But if the country is assured that the bad system has become so bad that it has ceased to function, and if the required interval of forty years for rumination has been duly observed, then the advocates of a revolutionary change may stand a chance of writing their views on the Statute Book.[1]

In the opinion of the editor the time has come for such a revolutionary change. The paper continued:

They certainly have, both in theory and in fact, a strong case. They can show that Parliament becomes less and less capable every year of meeting the demands made upon it by the ever-growing complexity of national and Imperial problems. . . . The machine works—let that always be remembered and acknowledged. But it works with gathering friction and difficulty, at a considerable and definite loss to the nation, and at a cost to itself which must in the long run be fatal to its efficiency as an independent and deliberative organ of government. The loss to the nation consists partly in the failure of the law-making body to keep pace with the varied needs of an extraordinarily complex society, and partly in the enforced neglect of local and specialised interests. For example, several of the laws which the executive Departments have to administer in relation to public health have hardly been altered for forty years and are ludicrously obsolete. Again, great ques-

---

[1] *The Outlook,* June 7, 1919, vol. 122, p. 557.

tions like the reform of local taxation, of the poor law and of
land registration get shelved from session to session and Parliament to Parliament because there is no great force of party
enthusiasm behind them, and because Ministers dare not risk
the loss of Parliamentary time involved in straying beyond
their electioneering programme. For the same reason it is a
matter of the utmost difficulty to amend a contentious measure
that has once become law, even though the amendments concern only a defect in administration and raise no controversial
issues. And, finally, the peculiar needs of distinctive parts of
the kingdom like Wales and Ireland and Scotland receive, and
under the present system inevitably must receive, scrappy and
ill-informed treatment.

But Parliament is itself the chief victim of the defective
conditions under which it has to work. Every year finds it
more and more of a chamber whose principal function is to
ratify the decrees of an autocratic Cabinet. It has almost lost
all power of moulding legislation. Much of its former authority has been taken over by the executive Departments and
still more by the unescapable encroachments of the Government.
It has tried many times to reform its procedure, but no reform
of that kind, no limitation of debates, or closure system, or
abolition of the opportunities of private members, enables it to
make headway against the cataract of public business. The
latest device of expanding the powers of Grand Committees is
already proved to have shifted the very center of Parliamentary
existence. Legislation is speeded up, but the House of Commons is losing interest even in itself.

The devolutionists, therefore, have no difficulty in making out
a case, and a case that stands quite apart from the Irish question.
The plain truth is that our machinery for making laws and ad-
ministering them is congested to a point where the confidence of
the nation in its institutions might well be shaken. That has not
happened yet; we are a patient people. But the War has un-
leashed many forces, some of them turbulent, all of them rest-
less and hungering; and if they can find neither satisfaction
nor self-expression in Parliament they will seek it elsewhere.

We are entering a phase when decentralization, besides being a legislative and administrative convenience, may prove a social and political safety-valve of genuine value.[1]

The attitude of this paper is decidedly in favor of devolution. A more persuasive case cannot be stated than what we have just quoted. But the editor was quite disappointed over the report of the Speaker's Conference. The paper declared:

Most people are agreed as to the desirability of shifting on to local legislatures part of the excessive burden which is now imposed on the Imperial Parliament. . . . The result, embodied in the Report published this week, cannot be called satisfying. It states more difficulties than it solves.[2]

Commenting upon the Speaker's scheme, the editorial continued:

It is curious to note how so many men, presumably of so many opinions, have been hypnotised by precedent. The Parliament they know has two houses, and they seem unable to think of a Parliament without two houses. Yet there are not two Houses in a County Council or in a Water Board, or in many other bodies intended for the dispatch of public business. The object of devotion is assumed to be getting things done; the provision of two Houses seems an admirable device to prevent them being done. In the Imperial Parliament the bicameral system is no doubt justified; the House of Lords serves as a check where a check is really needed, and it has a peculiar value in a Commonwealth like ours, in that a great number of its members have an Imperial outlook and a diplomatic, administrative, or military experience less likely to be found in a popularly elected Assembly. But we doubt whether any statesman would claim that the system includes among its considerable advantages that of saving time. It is notoriously other-

[1] *The Outlook,* June 7, 1919, p. 557.

[2] *Ibid.,* May 15, 1920, p. 521.

wise.  Disputes between the two Houses have contrbuted as
much as anything to the delay of the nation's business.  It
seems to us that if the local legislature is to be of any practical
use it should much more resemble a glorified county council
than a watered-down Westminster.  Moreover, the very point
of a Scottish legislature is surely that it should meet in Edin-
burgh, and of a Welsh legislature that it should meet at—, but
who shall decide between the glory of the Welsh cities?  To
bring these more or less august bodies to Westminster is surely
to insult rather than to placate Home Rule feeling.[1]

Furthermore, the editor doubted whether a legislature for
England was necessary.  It was contended that an English
legislature would be too big for the oversight of local and
provincial matters.  The truth is that England is neither
local nor provincial, and that most of the so-called English
affairs really concern the nation as a whole.  Consequently
a devolution of greater powers to the existing County Councils and Borough Councils might just as well serve the same
purpose of a local legislature.

On the other hand, the *Spectator* was strongly opposed to
devolution.  Concerning the debate in the House of Commons the paper said:

The large majority was doubtless influenced by the general
feeling that Parliament is overworked and should devolve some
of its burdens upon lesser bodies.  We sympathize with that
view, and we see no reason why the County Councils and the
large Municipalities should not enjoy larger powers.  But the
so-called Federalists, who would break up the United Kingdom
in order to reunite it on a Federal basis, have yet to produce a
workable scheme, and, above all, to show how such a Government would be financed. . . . Let us decentralize our administration as far as possible.  But to reverse the historic process
by breaking up the United Kingdom would be suicide.[2]

[1] *Ibid.,* p. 521.

[2] *The Spectator,* June 7, 1919, no. 122, p. 719.

The *New Statesman* was also opposed to devolution. Speaking of the same debate the paper said:

We confess that in spite of the unanimity shown in the debate we remain very sceptical both as to the practicability and as to the real value of Devolution. In so far as the scheme is intended to apply to Ireland—and we suspect that a good deal of the support which it received in some quarters was due to a vague idea that it might help to shelve the Irish question—it is manifestly worthless, since it could not even go so far towards Irish self-government as did the Home Rule Act, which every one, excepting its die-hard opponents, is now agreed did not go far enough. Ireland therefore cannot come in under these proposals at all, and there seems to be a strong consensus of opinion against splitting England up into Provinces for general legislative purposes; so that we shall be left with only an English Parliament and a Scotch Parliament, and possibly a Welsh one thrown in. Assuming that these parliaments are to have wide powers—and if they do not what will be the use of them?—the English Parliament, which will be overwhelmingly the greatest of the " subordinate " legislatures, will possess an authority so nearly equal to that of the Imperial Parliament as to make more or less serious friction almost inevitable. Alternatively the powers of the subordinate legislatures will be so small that they will not attract the public spirited ability necessary for efficient administration. . . . [1]

Devolution on territorial lines is apt to mean duplication rather than simplification of work. In any case such division in itself is no gain. If Parliament is indeed overworked, why not set up a second chamber for the whole country and allot to it certain definite spheres of legislative and administrative authority? A better plan probably, would be to create authorities of a new type altogether to deal with certain branches of work throughout the Kingdom. But the question is too large to enter upon here. All we wish to suggest at the moment is

---

[1] *The New Statesman*, June 7, 1919, vol. 13, p. 226.

that if devolution of some sort is necessary it might be worth while to consider the merits of devolution by subjects rather than devolution by areas.[1]

In other words the editor favored functional devolution to " subject groups ".[2]  His main contention was that devolution to the constituent geographical provinces would be extremely uneconomical as well as inconvenient, in that, so far as Great Britain was concerned, the amount of legislative work, of administrative and of financial responsibility which could be devolved upon these provinces would be very small.[3]

Without multiplying other opinions we may safely make the following conclusions: first, there has been a considerable amount of public opinion on the subject as evidenced by the attitude of the various political parties, by popular resolutions, and by the comments of the press.  Secondly, such public opinion as exists is about as divergent as is the opinion in the House of Commons.  Thirdly, it is practically admitted on all hands that the House of Commons is over-worked and that some sort of relief is imperative.  Fourthly, the question is narrowed down to a comparison of the different methods of devolution.  Those who do not favor devolution to national areas have invariably put up some counter proposal such as devolution to Grand Committees, devolution to existing municipal and local authorities, or devolution to functional groups.  And lastly, the considerations that weigh most heavily against devolution to national areas are two, namely, the preponderance of England and the question of cost.  The former might make devolution unworkable while the latter would render it expensive.

[1] *Ibid.*, p. 226.
[2] *Ibid.*, Nov. 22, 1919, vol. 14, p. 212.
[3] *Ibid.*, Nov. 15, 1919, vol. 14, p. 183.

# CHAPTER IX

## Conclusions and Comparisons

Throughout this study our aim has been to determine whether devolution is really necessary in Great Britain. The determination of this question depends, as we pointed out in the introductory chapter, upon the following considerations: first, whether there is an imperative demand for the proposed change; secondly, whether the change can effectively meet that demand; thirdly, whether devolution will bring with it any dangers or difficulties of a graver character than the evils it is intended to remove; and, lastly, whether it is practicable. It is the purpose of this final chapter to summarize our inquiry by giving an answer to each of the above questions.

A demand for devolution undoubtedly exists. Such a demand is justifiable from two separate points of view. In the first place, it is justifiable from the standpoint of Parliament, because under the present conditions of the congestion of business, the House of Commons is no longer capable of effectively performing those functions which it ought to perform. That the congestion exists cannot be disputed. That the evil must be in some way remedied is admitted by all. From what has been said by people who know the work of Parliament, and, more than that, from the statistical facts we have gathered it has been proved beyond doubt that the evil is really serious. It has been a natural and inevitable result of the highly centralized system of a single Legislature which has been called upon to cope with all the legislative and administrative problems of the British

Empire. If Parliament is to do its work effectively and efficiently, this evil must be eliminated.

In the second place, the demand is justifiable from the standpoint of the localities, because local business has been neglected, and because the people have no control of their local affairs, such as in a democratic country they ought to have. Parliament has hitherto attempted to legislate for the varying needs of all parts of the United Kingdom, but the attempt has not been successful. In the nature of things, such a task is impossible. A single legislature with all the powers gathered in itself would, perhaps, be the best system, if the functions of government had been confined to a few problems of peace, order, defence and justice. Centralization is desirable if the needs of the people are uniform and if the same laws can be applied throughout the country. Such is not the case in Great Britain. In spite of the Union with Wales and the Union with Scotland which resulted in a single Parliament for the three countries, the interests of the three peoples have, to a considerable extent, remained separate and distinct. Furthermore, in the actual legislation of Parliament the separate interests of the several countries have been recognized. Such being the case, there is no reason why the local affairs should not be delegated to the several countries themselves. Effective legislation requires intimate knowledge of the conditions of the particular locality over which it is to operate, and such knowledge is only possible through actual contact with the life of the locality concerned. It is impossible for a single legislature at Westminster to acquire such knowledge. Even if it could have the proper knowledge, it would still be unable to put out the amount of legislation required by the peoples of the several countries because the time at its disposal is limited.

Certainly in Great Britain there is a demand for devolution, but, as we have seen there is a great divergence of opinion as to whether this is the best and the only remedy for the unsatisfactory situation that exists. Those who oppose devolution have argued that either the creation of National Committees, or the enlargement of the powers of existing local governments, or the creation of certain more or less uniform regions, or delegation to functional groups would bring about a better result than devolution. Changes in Parliamentary procedure as a substitute for devolution may be dismissed at once. Devolution to existing local governments would mean very little so far as relieving the work of Parliament is concerned. The areas of the existing local governments are too small for the exercise of large powers. The question is then narrowed down to a choice between devolution on the one hand and regionalism or functional decentralization on the other.

There is much to be said for both, of the latter proposals. They may be desirable on their own account, but cannot be substitutes for devolution. Both of them ignore the existence of a national spirit in Scotland and Wales, and the demand for Home Rule in these countries. Besides, both would present more difficulties than devolution. The creation of three regions in England, as has been suggested, two or three regions in Scotland and possibly two regions in Wales would certainly entail a far greater burden and result in a greater multiplicity of governmental machinery than the setting up of three national legislatures. So far as functional decentralization is concerned, it cannot be a panacea for all the evils under the present system, and, besides, it would produce an even greater revolution in the constitution of England than devolution. Furthermore, even under a system of functional devolution, the territorial principle cannot be entirely abolished. Aside from the so-called economic and social interests that are capable of division, there

will always remain distinct general interests concerning the
nation as a whole, and distinct local interests concerning the
various localities. These national and local interests will
still have to be dealt with by a general authority of the
nation or the locality.

At the same time devolution would accomplish two purposes that no other scheme of decentralization could effect.
It would relieve the congestion of business in the House of
Commons and also satisfy the demand for Home Rule in
Scotland and Wales. From the calculations recently made
by Mesrs. Henderson and Laski based upon the division of
powers proposed by the Speaker's Conference, devolution
would save one-quarter of parliamentary time.[1] The result
of the investigation may be tabulated in percentages as
follows:[2]

| Year | Debates excluding questions | | Motions, Adjourn-ments, Supply, Finance and Legislation | | Average | |
|---|---|---|---|---|---|---|
| | Central | Local | Central | Local | Central | Local |
| 1910............ | 86% | 14% | 85.9% | 14.1% | 85.95% | 14.05% |
| 1911............ | 64% | 36% | 63.8% | 36.2% | 63.9% | 36.1% |
| 1914...... ..... | 77% | 23% | 76.5% | 23.5% | 76.75% | 23.25% |
| 1919............ | 77% | 23% | 77.4% | 22.6% | 77.2% | 22.8% |
| 1922–23......... | 74% | 26% | 74.1% | 25.9% | 74.05% | 25.95% |
| Average..... | ........ | ........ | .......... | .......... | 75.57% | 24.43% |

It was said that most of the subjects devolved to local
legislatures as specified in the report of the Speaker's Conference are not of great importance,[3] and that the twenty-

[1] *Economica*, March, 1925, p. 91.

[2] *Ibid.*, pp. 91-93.

[3] Laski, *A Grammar of Politics*, pp. 309-311.

five per cent of parliamentary time thus saved would seem quite inappreciable.  Indeed, it was predicted that even this small amount of saving might prove only nominal, because it might be neutralized by the time required for the adjustment of financial matters, with the result that there would be no real saving at all.

We are, however, unable to agree with this conclusion. It should be remembered, first of all, that what was said refers exclusively to the report of the Speaker's Conference and has little bearing on the principles of devolution discussed above.  If Parliament wills to get rid of its congestion it can do so.  If the scheme of the allocation of powers provided by the Speaker's Conference is inadequate, a better scheme can be proposed.  As to the question of finance, there is no reason to suppose that a fairly satisfactory adjustment cannot be made and that Parliament must continue to bother with every conceivable question of local finance after it has devolved other local powers.

In the second place, even if the scheme proposed by the Speaker's Conference be adopted, we are still unable to agree with Professor Laski's criticism.  The effectiveness of devolution does not depend upon the importance of the matters devolved.  The purpose of devolution is to relieve Parliament of its local matters and local matters only, which, in the nature of things, must be of a less important character than those reserved to Parliament.  In our opinion, the twenty-five per cent of parliamentary time thus saved would be fairly adequate for relieving the congestion of business in Parliament.  The question, it seems, is not how much time can be saved in gross, but how much time should be saved, which would be sufficient, under the present circumstances, to accomplish this purpose.

We have pointed out in this study [1] that according to the

---

[1] *Supra*, pp. 114-115.

investigations made by the Round Table, the Government carried through on the average only 50 per cent of its important measures each year as listed in the Speech from the Throne (taking the measures actually introduced, however, the percentage would be little higher, about 68 per cent), and only 63 per cent of other Government measures. Our own investigations show that even including the War years, when Government business monopolized all the time of Parliament, the average percentage of all Government measures passed each year was only 76 per cent, and the total of all public measures passed, only 61 per cent. Thus, making a rather liberal estimate, the Government completes under the present system about from 65 to 70 per cent of its public business. A third or a quarter of public measures fail to pass, principally because of the lack of time, and this is roughly the amount of congestion in the House of Commons, in a purely quantitative sense. If the Government had twenty-five per cent more time at its disposal, probably most, if not all, of the measures introduced would have passed, and there would have been little or no congestion. It cannot, therefore, be maintained that the saving of twenty-five per cent of parliamentary time is inappreciable.

Briefly our conclusion is this: that Parliament is now congested, because it has to spend at least a minimum of twenty-five per cent of its time on local matters to the exclusion of other more important matters concerning the nation as a whole. If this amount of time can be saved, Parliament will be able to deal with an additional twenty-five per cent of general public business, which is roughly the amount of congestion at the present time. Thus devolution even under the scheme proposed by the Speaker's Conference would reasonably relieve the congestion of Parliament, and, so far as Parliament is concerned, this is all that devolution aims at.

This is, however, not all. It is admitted on all hands that local affairs have not been given adequate consideration in Parliament. This is the case for various reasons we need not here repeat. Devolution, besides saving at least twenty-five per cent of the time of Parliament, would give each of the local legislatures a hundred per cent of time to deal with its local matters. Furthermore, under a system of devolution, the quality of legislation (aside from quantity) of the localities and perhaps of Parliament, would be greatly improved. This point seems to have been ignored by some critics of devolution.

Would devolution bring with it any dangers and difficulties greater than the evils at present? The possible dangers and difficulties as have been alleged are the preponderance of England and the cost of setting up such a scheme. They are, however, more apparent than real. The financial side should not prevent a reform that is badly needed. According to the estimates of the conference on devolution probably an annual deficit of £10,309,500 for England, £3,275,-000 for Scotland, and £1,514,000 for Wales (making a total of £15,098,500) would be incurred during the first few years. This does not seem to be an appalling sum. It can be made up either by grants-in-aid as is done in the case of local governments at present, or by assigning new sources of revenue to the different countries, or in some other suitable way, that a future conference may be able to work out.

As to the practicability of devolution at present, it is pretty hard to say. The Speaker's Conference failed to reach an agreement as to the best scheme to be adopted. In 1924 there was an attempt to set up another Committee for the investigation of the problem. The first Report has been considered by many as unsatisfactory. With the results of the first effort, a second Committee will be able to tackle the problem more thoroughly and more courageously. Without making any prophecy about the future, we may, however, safely predict that when a Liberal or Labour Government comes into power again, devolution will be surely reconsidered. Judging from the past election, the strength of the Liberal Party has suffered very greatly. Whether it will ever recover its former power, no one can tell. The Labor Party headed by Mr. Ramsay MacDonald has committed itself in favor of the proposed change. Mr. MacDonald, while he was Prime Minister, promised in 1924 to call another conference on devolution. It is therefore not too much to hope that when the Labour Party comes into office again, this effort will be renewed. As to what the present Conservative Government will do about devolution there is perhaps little doubt. For the past thirty-five years or more they have fought Home Rule and devolution tooth and nail. Home Rule for Ireland has finally succeeded in spite of their continuous opposition. They will probably continue to fight as a party—for many of the members are devolutionists—against devolution which is but the same principle of Home Rule applied to Great Britain. Even if they should be inclined to take a more lenient attitude toward it in the future, as a result of the bitter lessons in the past, it is fairly certain that devolution will not be sponsored in their political programme.

Devolution is one phase of a general movement towards legislative and administrative decentralization which is not confined to Great Britain alone. Even in a small country like the Netherlands where there are already three divisions of government with three sets of legislatures, the national, the provincial, and the communal, the need of decentralization is felt keenly by many of its noted citizens. Professor Hugo Krabbe is of the opinion that the legislatures are proving more and more unequal to the work required. This is especially true of the national Parliament which each year falls more and more in arrears. " The barrenness of the legislature," says Krabbe, " is not the fault of any particular system of Government, least of all of so-called Parliament Government. Our parliaments do the best they can. Service in the representative assembly demands the whole time and attention of the Member and in most cases this is actually given. The Ministers labour at a problem which calls for a head of iron and the health of a professional athlete. And yet in spite of all this labour law-making is in arrears." [1] The remedy that Professor Krabbe proposes for his country is the addition of new legislative organs based upon organized interests. In other words he is in favour of functional decentralization of legislation.

In France the demand for administrative decentralization which would also include the decentralization of legislation has been a much discussed question in the last twenty years or more. The French system is still more centralized than the English system both in name and in fact. While the Union of Great Britain left the traditions and interests of the several countries more or less undisturbed, although the legislatures of Wales and Scotland were abolished, the Revolution of 1789 swept away all the provinces that had existed and created in their place the artificial circumscriptions of the Departments, the Arrondissements, the Cantons, and the Communes. The system was further centralized by Napoleon who gathered all the administrative powers under his control. During the nineteenth century the Communal and Departmental Councils became elective, but the people still had no control either of administration or of legislation. The French system is not only centralized but also " concentralised "; that is to say, not only are the legislative powers of the local councils very much restricted , but the powers

---

[1] *The Modern Idea of the State*, p. 172.

of the local officers of the central Government are under the
direct control and supervision of the central Government.
Such a system has been the target of constant attack by the
French people.   The evils under the system are two, namely,
first, that the central Government is overburdened, and second, that local affairs are neglected and delayed much more
than is the case in England.

Thus the same system of overcentralization in different
degrees, of course, which caused the movement for devolution in England has also caused a parallel movement for
decentralization in France, principally in the form of regionalism.   Decentralization in France is, however, a much
wider problem than devolution in England.   The demand
in France has been for both decentralization and deconcen-
tralization.   In late years the local agents of the central
Government have been given more initiative and independence than before, and the local councils have enjoyed a little
more freedom of action at the same time.   Decentralization may take the form of delegating to the existing local
councils of the departments still greater powers than they
have at present.   The chief proposal for decentralization is
the so-called " Regionalist movement."   It aims at the creation of a certain number of regions, which would be much
larger in area than the Departments and which would be
more in accordance with the historical traditions and the
social life of the people as well as with the geographical and
economic divisions of the country.   The arguments for this
proposal are briefly three in number: first, that the Departments are mere artificial circumscriptions without logical
basis and devoid of historical traditions and local spirit;
secondly, that the substitution of larger circumscriptions
formed with more regard to historical, geographical, and
economic interests would revive and strengthen the local
life; and lastly, that regionalism would relieve the excessive

burden of the central Government and result in economy by
the abolition of a large number of useless offices.[1]

It is interesting to note that the movement for regionalism
in France has occupied about the same period of time as the
devolution movement in England. The question was discussed even before 1900. M. Marlot's proposal in 1902
and M. Beauquier's proposal in 1907 all provided for 25
regions in the place of 89 Departments with a legislative
council for each.[2]   In 1910, it was a very important question in the country and M. Briand declared himself in favor
of the proposed reform.  Since then four other proposals
have been made.  On April 29, 1915, M. Jean Hennessy
submitted a proposition in Parliament " proposing for the
decentralization of the administration and the representation
of economic interests by the abolition of Departments and
the creation of regions with elected regional assemblies." [3]
The object of the proposal was three-fold: first, the division
of France into regions; secondly, the representation of economic interests; and thirdly, the administration of regional
affairs by regional assemblies.  On October 24, 1916, M.
Etienne Rognon also submitted a proposition of a similar
nature.[4]  Again, on November 13, 1916, M. Ed. Barthe
submitted another proposal.[5]  And on July 12, 1917, a resolution was presented by MM. Victor Peytral and Henri
Roy proposing the immediate creation of regions, regional
councils, and regional prefects.[6]  The most important proposal was that of the Parliamentary Commission on Admin-

---

[1] Garner, J. W., " Administrative Reform in France ", *The American
Political Science Review*, Feb., 1919, pp. 32-33.

[2] *Ibid.*, p. 34.

[3] Hennessy, J., " Commission Report ", *Revue Général D'Administration*, May-Aug., 1919, pp. 20-26.

[4] *Ibid.*, pp. 32-33.

[5] *Ibid.*, p. 34.

[6] *Ibid.*, pp. 36-37.

istrative Decentralization in 1919. The important points of
the proposal may be briefly stated.

The Commission suggests the establishment of 17 regions
in France.[1]  In each region there shall be established a regional Council, sitting in the region. The regional Council
shall elect among themselves a regional Commission. The
Prefect of the chief Department of the region shall be the
representative of the executive power of the region. The
regions shall be established by a decree of the Council of the
Cabinet with the advice of the Council of the State (Conseil
D'Etat). Two months after said decree the electors of
an Arrondissement may be petition protest against the incorporation of the Arrondissement in one region and may
demand its incorporation in another. The members of the
regional council shall be elected for six years by the members
of all the Cantonal Councils in the region. The functions
of the regional Councils are (1) The establishment of and
subsidy to, educational institutions for artistic, professional,
scientific, and technical purposes. (2) Works of charity,
sanitation, and other social works. (3) All the routes in
the region, and all the means of transportation, automobile
and electric within the region. (4) Canals and ports in the
region. The finance of the region would be derived from
contributions by the State out of indirect taxes, contributions by communes and departments in the region; from
borrowing; from gifts and bequests, from investments and
rents, and from other accidental sources.[2]

The above scheme is different from devolution in several
important respects. In the first place, while both devolution and regionalism seek to establish local legislatures in
conformity to historical traditions and local spirit, the historical traditions of the prospective regions are no longer a

[1] *Ibid.,* pp. 161-162.
[2] *Ibid.,* pp. 186-192.

vital reality, whereas in the several countries of Great Britain, with the possible exception of England, the national spirit is still present in a large degree. Secondly, the creation of regions without the abolition of the departments as contemplated by several proposals of regionalism would probably result in a duplication rather than in a simplification of the administrative machinery, whereas the creation of three separate legislatures in Great Britain would not have this effect. Another argument has been urged against regionalism, which has also been urged against devolution, and that is that both schemes would tend to encourage local spirit to the detriment of the nation as a whole. This argument has little foundation in either case. It is probably true, as Professor Garner has pointed out, that the arguments against regionalism in France have the better side of the case. With regard to devolution the contrary is certainly the truth.

# BIBLIOGRAPHY

## I. PRIMARY SOURCES

1. *Parliamentary Debates,* Commons, 3rd Ser., vols. 220 (1874), 335 (1889); 4th Ser., vols. 22 (1894), 32 (1895), 54 (1898), 189 (1908). 5th Ser., vols. 29 (1911), 34 (1912), 36 (1912), 40 (1912), 53 (1913), 112 (1919), 116 (1919), 150 (1922), 153 (1922), 154 (1922), and 173 (1924).
2. *Parliamentary Debates,* Lords, vols. 13 (1913) and 33 (1919).
3. *Parliamentary Papers,* Accounts and Papers, vols. 21 (1900), 23 (1901), 28 (1902), 19 (1903), 30 (1904), 19 (1905), 30 (1906), 20 (1907), 26 (1908), 21 (1909), 15 (1910), 17 (1911), 19 (1912-13), 11 (1913), 16 (1914), 15 (1914-16), 6 (1916), 7 (1917-18), 5 (1918), 9 (1919), 12 (1920), 10 (1921), 1 (1922) and 7 (1923).
4. *Parliamentary Papers,* Bills, Public, vol. i, 1922.
5. *Parliamentary Papers,* Report of the Select Committee on Procedure, 1914.
6. *Law Reports,* Statutes, from 1884-1923.

## II. SECONDARY SOURCES

### 1. *Books*

Adams, G. B., *Constitutional History of England* (1921).
Anson, William, *Law a d Custom of the Constitution* (5th edition, 1922), (ii vols.).
Austin, J., *Lectures on Jurisprudence* (1893).
Blackstone, William, *Commentaries* (London, 16th edition, 1825), vol. i, book i.
Bliss, P., *Of Sovereignty* (1885).
Carr, C. T., *Delegated Legislation* (1921).
Clifford, F. A., *A History of Private Bill Legislation* (ii vols.), (1885).
Cole, G. D. H., *The Future of Local Government* (1921).
——, *Social Theory* (1920).
——, *Guild Socialism Restated* (1920).
Davenport, E. H., *Parliament and the Taxpayer* (1918).
Dicey, A. V., *Introduction to the Study of the Law of the Constitution* (8th ed., 1915).
——, *England's Case against Home Rule* (1886).
——, *A Fool's Paradise* (1913).

——, *Law and Public Opinion in England during the Nineteenth Century* (1914).
Dicey and Rait, *Thoughts on the Union between England and Scotland* (1920).
Duguit, L., *Law in the Modern State*, translated by H. J. Laski (1919).
Freeman, E. A., *History of Federal Government* (2nd edition, 1893), vol. i.
Higgs, H., *The Financial System of the United Kingdom* (1914).
——, *Financial Reform* (1924).
Hythe, T., *Problems of Empire* (1913).
Ilbert, C., *Legislative Methods and Forms* (1901).
——, *Parliament* (1911).
Krabbe, H., *The Modern Idea of the State,* translated by G. H. Sabine and W. J. Shepard (1919).
Laski, H. J., *The Problem of Sovereignty* (1917).
——, *Foundations of Sovereignty* (1921).
——, *Authority in the Modern State* (1919).
——, *A Grammar of Politics* (1925).
Low, Sidney, *The Governance of England* (1920).
Lowell, A. L., *The Government of England* (new ed., ii vols.), (1917).
Masterman, C. F. G., *How England is Governed* (1922).
McBain, H. L. and Rogers, L., *The New Constitutions of Europe* (1922).
MacDonagh, M., *The Pageant of Parliament* (ii vols.), (1921).
MacDonald, J. R., *Parliament and Revolution* (1920).
McIlwain, C. H., *The High Court of Parliament and its Supremacy* (1910).
Newton, A. P., *Federal and Unified Constitutions* (1923).
Ogg, F. A., *The Governments of Europe* (2nd edition, 1922).
Pacificus, *Federalism and Home Rule* (1911).
Partridge, F., *T. A. B., 2nd Earl Brassey* (1924).
Pim, F. W., *Home Rule through Federal Devolution* (1919).
Pollard, A. F., *The Evolution of Parliament* (1920).
Ponsonby, A., *Democracy and Diplomacy* (1915).
Porritt, E., *The Unreformed House of Commons* (ii vols.), (1909).
Redlich, J., *The Procedure of the House of Commons* (iii vols.), (1908).
Sait, E. M., *Government and Politics of France* (1921).
Spencer, F. H., *Municipal Origins* (1911).
Stubbs, W., *The Constitutional History of England in its Origin and Development* (iii vols.), (1896-97).
Thompson, W., *Federal Centralization* (1923).
Webb, Sidney and Beatrice, *A Constitution for the Socialist Commonwealth of Great Britain* (1920).
Willoughby, W. W. and Rogers, L., *The Problem of Government* (1921).

## 2. *Magazines and Newspapers*

*The Liberal Magazine,* from 1894 to 1920.
*Gleanings and Memoranda,* from 1920 to 1924.
*The Round Table,* vols. ii and viii (1911-1912 and 1918).
*The Outlook, London,* 1919 and 1920.
*The New Statesman,* 1919 and 1920.
*The Spectator,* 1919 and 1920.
*The London Times,* 1914 to 1920.

## 3. *Articles*

Allen, C. K., "Bureaucracy Triumphant", *The Quarterly Review,* 1923.
Adkins, W. P. D., "Home Rule for England", *The Contemporary Review,* 1919.
Dicey, A. V., "Thoughts on the Parliament of Scotland", *The Quarterly Review,* April, 1916.
Garner, J. W., "Administrative Reforms in France", *The American Political Science Review,* February, 1919.
Henderson, J. S., and Laski, H. J., "A Note on Parliamentary Time and the Problem of Devolution", *Economica,* March, 1925.
Haines, C. G., *The Nation,* New York, May 14, 1924.
Hennessy, M. J., "Réorganization Administrative de la France", *Révue Général D'Administration,* May to August, 1919.
Hurst, G. B., "Federal Devolution", *The Contemporary Review,* 1918.
Lees-Smith, H. B., "The Time Table of the House of Commons", *Economica,* June, 1924.
Macdonald, J. A. Murray, "Devolution or Destruction", *The Contemporary Review,* August, 1918.
"The New Round Table", *The Westminster Review,* 1890.
Rogers, L., "Parliamentary Commissions in France", *The Political Science Quarterly,* December, 1923.

# INDEX

(the following numbers refer to pages)